Python for Data Science

A. Lakshmi Muddana · Sandhya Vinayakam

Python for Data Science

Ane Books
Pvt. Ltd.

 Springer

A. Lakshmi Muddana
Department of Computer Science
and Engineering
Gandhi Institute of Technology
and Management (GITAM)
Hyderabad, India

Sandhya Vinayakam
Department of Computer Science
and Engineering
Gandhi Institute of Technology
and Management (GITAM)
Hyderabad, India

ISBN 978-3-031-52472-1   ISBN 978-3-031-52473-8   (eBook)
https://doi.org/10.1007/978-3-031-52473-8

Jointly published with Ane Books Pvt. Ltd.
In addition to this printed edition, there is a local printed edition of this work available via Ane Books in
South Asia (India, Pakistan, Sri Lanka, Bangladesh, Nepal and Bhutan) and Africa (all countries in the
African subcontinent).
ISBN of the Co-Publisher's edition: 978-93-94883-30-7

This Springer imprint is published by the registered company Springer Nature Switzerland AG
The registered company address is: Gewerbestrasse 11, 6330 Cham, Switzerland

Paper in this product is recyclable.

We dedicate the book to our parents for their inspiration and support

*Shantha RatnaKumari and Venkateswarlu
Mallika and Vinayakam*

Preface

Python is a general-purpose programming language that is used to solve a variety of problems in different domains. It is widely used in Artificial Intelligence, Data Science, Web Development, Internet of Things, etc. Python uses English-like syntax, easy to read and write code. Its vast library support, improved productivity, strong community base, portability, and availability as a free and open source make it very popular among all types of users.

The book covers basic and advanced concepts. The basic concepts like its unique features, data types, operators, and developing simple programs using selection and loop statements. As functions are the core of any programming, a detailed illustration of defining and invoking functions, recursive functions, and lambda functions is covered. Built-in data structures of Python are popularly used in data science and model building. Strings, Lists, Tuples, Sets, and Dictionary data structures are discussed in detail with example programming problems.

File handling is an important task when handling large data. Data access and manipulation from standard file formats such as CSV, Excel, and JSON files are included in the book. Python is widely used in data analytics and model building. Data manipulations using Pandas and Data visualizations using Matplotlib and Seaborn packages are illustrated with examples and case studies. Regular expressions being an important concept in Natural Language Processing, text manipulation functions are discussed, and a case study is presented with public text data. SQLite3 libraries are discussed for creating and manipulating data in the database.

Advanced concepts of building Machine Learning and Deep Learning models and multi-tasking concepts are explained with examples and case studies. The machine learning chapter discusses concepts of supervised and unsupervised learning and model evaluation algorithms using the SciKit-Learn package. The case studies are presented for different learning algorithms using built-in and public datasets. Deep Learning is a sub-field of Machine Learning that mimics the human brain. Concepts of artificial neural networks for both structured and unstructured data are discussed in detail using the Keras library for deep learning. Case studies are presented for standard neural networks, convolutional neural networks, and recurrent neural networks using Keras libraries,

The book also includes a chapter on multi-threading and multi-processing in Python for improving execution time and effective utilization of system resources.

Every chapter includes illustrations with examples, worked-out problems, multiple-choice questions for knowledge testing, and exercise problems for practice. Case studies are presented on advanced concepts. The book is supported by a solution manual for multiple-choice questions and exercise problems. The aim and scope of the book are to provide the required knowledge and skill in coding and data analysis. The book serves as the basis for data analysis and model building using Python packages. The reader requires basic maths and logical thinking and no other prerequisites.

The book is intended to serve as a textbook for the Problem Solving and Data Science courses of Engineering, Science, and Commerce programs at the undergraduate and postgraduate levels.

The key features of the book include:

- Basic and advanced programming concepts.
- Data manipulation and analysis using Pandas, data visualization, and manipulating text using regular expressions.
- File handling and database creation and manipulation concepts.
- Machine Learning and Deep Learning models and multi-tasking.
- Concepts explained with illustrations and examples.
- Case study for an in-depth understanding of concepts on advanced topics using public datasets.
- Review questions and exercise problems at the end of chapters.

Hyderabad, India   A. Lakshmi Muddana
                                                                          Sandhya Vinayakam

Acknowledgments

We are grateful to Dr. N. Siva Prasad, Retd. Professor IIT Madras, for the motivation in initiating this project. We sincerely acknowledge his constant guidance and support in completing the book. We express our gratitude to Dr. Ghanta Subba Rao, Former Chairman A.P. Skill Development Corporation, for his suggestions and feedback in structuring and writing the book.

We sincerely thank our institution authorities, family members, friends, and colleagues for their direct and indirect support.

Contents

About the Authors

A. Lakshmi Muddana received a Ph.D. in Computer Science and Engineering from Osmania University, Hyderabad. She is currently a professor in the Department of Computer Science and Engineering at GITAM Deemed to be University, Hyderabad, India. She has been in academics, teaching undergraduate and postgraduate students and guiding research scholars in the areas of Deep Learning and Security.

Sandhya Vinayakam received a Ph.D. in Computer Science and Engineering from Osmania University, Hyderabad. She is currently in the Department of Computer Science and Engineering at GITAM Deemed to be University, Hyderabad, India. She has been in academics and doing research in the areas of Image Processing and Deep Learning.

Chapter 1
Basic Python

1.1 Introduction

Python is a simple and easy-to-learn high-level programming language suitable for first-time programmers or experienced with other programming languages. Python was created by Guido Van Rossum and released in 1991, which is a successor to the ABC programming language. Its simple syntax makes the program more readable, easy to understand, and debug the code.

Python's popularity is due to its powerful features and applicability in data science and artificial intelligence. It offers basic built-in data structures like lists, dictionaries, sets, tuples, and strings for elegant data organization and manipulation. Unlike other programming languages like C, C++, and Java, Python does not require variables to be declared. It is a dynamically typed language where data types of variables can change dynamically during the program execution. The language has a rich set of standard library functions and community-contributed modules for application development. All these features make Python programs shorter and attractive for rapid application development.

Python is an interpreted language that does not require a compilation step. This makes testing, debugging, and prototyping process faster. Being an interpreted language, programs run slower than C++ and Java but take less time for program development.

Python's modules and packages encourage modularity and code reusability. The language is extensively used in data science, machine learning, web and API development, etc. It can be connected to database systems, can read and write into files, and can also handle big data. Python runs on different operating systems and platforms like Windows, Mac, Linux, and Raspberry Pi. Python is under an open-source license that makes it freely usable and distributable.

Python is a multiparadigm programming language that supports structured, object-oriented, and functional programming. Indentation is based on white spaces to define the scope of statements, loops, functions, and classes, unlike other programming languages like C++ and Java that use curl braces.

© The Author(s) 2024
A. L. Muddana and S. Vinayakam, *Python for Data Science*,
https://doi.org/10.1007/978-3-031-52473-8_1

Sample Python code

```
print("This is Python code")
x = 10
print("x is a variable with value ", x)
```

Output

```
This is Python code
x is a variable with value 10
```

Comments in Python

Comments in the program provide readability to the code. Python supports the following formats for comments:

(i) **Single line comments:** Comments start with # followed by text. It can be specified on a separate line or in the code line.

Example

```
# This is a single-line comment
print("This is Python code")     # code line comment
# Following statement assign Value 10 to the variable X
x = 10
# print() function display the data
print("x is a variable with value ", x)
```

(ii) **Multiline comments:** Comments can run into multiple lines. Multiline comments are enclosed in triple single quotes or triple double quotes.

Using triple double quotes

Example

```
"""
This is
Multiline comment
in Python
"""
x = 10
print(x)
```

Output

```
10
```

Using triple single quotes

Example

```
'''
This is
Multiline comment
in Python
'''
x = 10
print(x)
```

Output

```
10
```

1.2   Variables

Variable is the name of the memory location that can store a value. The value can be numeric or text or Boolean type.

Example

```
# variable x
x = 10
```

With the above code, the value 10 is stored in the variable named x.

How to Name a Variable?

A variable name is a sequence of characters with the following rules:

- Name can contain alphabets, digits, and underscore (_).
- The first character cannot be a digit.
- Name cannot be a Python keyword.
- Name is case sensitive (variable name *Total* is different from variable *total*).
- By convention, variable names are in all lowercase with underscore separating words. For example, max_value.

Python Keywords are reserved words used for specific purposes and cannot be used for general purposes by the user. The following table shows the keywords used in Python (Table 1.1).

Table 1.1 Python keywords

and	as	assert	async	await	break	class
continue	def	del	else	elif	except	False
finally	for	from	global	if	import	in
is	lambda	None	nonlocal	not	or	pass
raise	return	True	try	while	with	yield

Variable names are case sensitive.

Example

```
count=10     # count is variable with value 10
Count=20     # Count is variable with value 20
print(count,Count)
```

Output

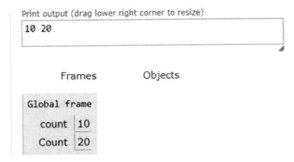

In the above example, *count* and *Count* are two different variables and allocated memory separately as shown in the above figure.

1.3 Data Types

A variable can hold different types of data. Python supports the following **basic data types** (Fig. 1.1).

(i) Numerical data types can hold integer value represented as **int** or real value represented as **float** or complex values represented as **complex**.
(ii) Boolean data type is represented as **bool**.
(iii) Text data type is represented as **str**(string).

Python Feature 1: Variables are Not Declared
Unlike other high-level programming languages, Python variables are not declared. The data type of a variable is determined by the value it holds. The data type of the variable can be determined using the *type()* function.

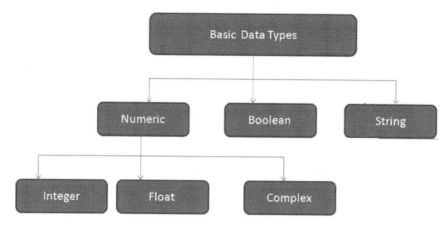

Fig. 1.1 Data types

Example

```
x = 10.5      # Here x is a float variable as it is having decimal value
print(x)      # display x value
print(type(x))      # display data type of x
```

Output

```
10.5
<class 'float'>
```

Python Feature 2: Python is an object-oriented language. It implements data types as classes like class int, class float, class bool, etc.

(i) Integer data as *class int*

Example

```
i = 10      # i is a integer variable
print(type(i))      # display data type of i
```

Output

```
<class 'int'>
```

(ii) Real values as *class float*

Example

```
pi = 3.14      # pi is a float variable
print(type(pi))      # display data type of pi
```

Output

```
<class 'float'>
```

(iii) Complex values as *class complex*. Python uses *j* to indicate the imaginary part.

Example

```
c = 10 + 5j        # Here 10 is real part & 5 imaginary part
print(type(c))      # Display data type of the variable c
print(c)        # Display value of c
```

Output

```
<class 'complex'>
(10+5j)
```

(iv) Boolean data as *class bool*. Boolean variables can have either True or False values.

Example

```
b1 = True
b2 = False
print(type(b1), b1)
print(type(b2), b2)
```

Output

```
<class 'bool'> True
<class 'bool'> False
```

(v) Text data as *class str*. A string is a sequence of characters enclosed in single or double quotes.

Example

```
s1 = "Hello everyone"     # text enclosed in double quotes
s2 = 'Good morning'      # text enclosed in single quotes
print(type(s1), type(s2))
print(s1)
print(s2)
```

Output

```
<class 'str'> <class 'str'>
Hello everyone
Good morning
```

Python supports **user-defined classes**. Instances of that class can be created called as objects.

Example

```
# user defined class
class circle:
    def __init__(self, r):
        self.radius = r
```

```
      def area(self):
        return self.radius * self.radius * 3.14
    c1 = circle(5)      # c1 is object of the class circle
    print(type(c1))
```

Output

```
<class '__main__.circle'>
```

Python Feature 3: Python is a dynamically typed language, i.e., the data type of the variable can change during program execution.

Example

```
num = 2.89      # here the variable num is float data type
print(type(num), num)
num= False      # now num variable is boolean data type
print(type(num), num)
```

Output

```
<class 'float'> 2.89
<class 'bool'> False
```

Python Feature 4: Python is an interpreted language where the code is executed line by line and there is no compilation step. When there is an error in the code, the execution stops at that line and error is reported.

Example

```
a=10
print('Value of a is ', a)
s= "Value of a = " + a
print(s)
```

Output

Value of a is 10

```
TypeError      Traceback (most recent call last)
<ipython-input-9-cd4ee1e21723> in <module>()
    1 a=10
    2 print('Value of a is ', a)
—-> 3 s= "Value of a = " + a
    4 print(s)
```

TypeError: can only concatenate str (not "int") to str

As error occurred at line 3, execution stops and error is reported. But the previous statements are executed as you can see the value of the variable, **a**, in the display.

1.4 Operators

Operators perform operations on the operand values. Python supports the following categories of operators (Fig. 1.2).

   Arithmetic, Relational, Logical, Assignment, Identity, Bitwise, and Membership operators.

   Some operators require two operands called **binary** operators.

E.g.: +, −, &&, < etc.

Whereas some operators take only one operand, called **unary** operators.

E.g.: unary minus −, ! etc.

1.4.1 Arithmetic Operators

Arithmetic operators are used to perform arithmetic operations like addition, subtraction, multiplication, division, modulus, and exponentiation. Symbols for these operations are

   $+, -, *, **, /, //$

(a) The **addition operator, +,** is used with both numeric values and strings.

   (i) Addition on numeric values

   Example

```
x, y = 10,20.6
print(x+y)
```

   Output

   30.6

   (ii) + operator on strings acts as a concatenation operation. The operation returns a new string by appending the second operand to the first operand. Both the operand values are not changed.

   Example

```
s1, s2 = "Hello", " good morning"
s3 = s1+s2
print(s3)
```

   Output

   Hello good morning

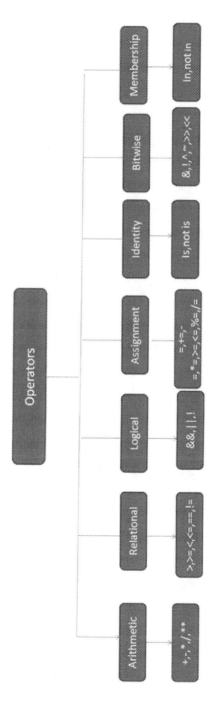

Fig. 1.2 Operators

(b) ** operator performs **exponentiation** operation.

Example

    a,b= 5, 3
    print(a**b)

Output

    125

(c) Python supports two **division operators /, //** for real and integer division, respectively.

Example

    x , y = 20 , 3
    print(x / y)   # / for real division
    print(x // y)   # // for integer division

Output

    6.666666666666667
    6

(d) % operator returns **remainder after division.**

Example

    x , y = 20 , 3
    print(x % y)

Output

    2

When the operands of % operator are negative, sign of the output is sign of divisor and output is determined as follows:

op1 % op2 = op1 - floor(op1 / op2) * op2

Example

    -10 % 3 = (-10) - (floor(-3.33) * 3)
            = -10 - (-4 *3)
            = -10 +12 = 2

Example

    10 % -3 = (10) - (floor(-3.33) * -3)
            = 10 - (-4 *-3)
            = 10 - 12 = - 2

1.4.2 Relational Operators

Relational operators compare the values of the operands. Hence these operators are also called comparison operators. The symbols are

$$<, \; <=, \; >, \; >=, \; ==, \; != $$

These operators form conditional expression and the result of the operation is a Boolean value—**True** or **False**.

Example

```
print('10 < 20 is ',10< 20)
print('-50 > 20 is ', -50 > 20)
print('10 <= 20 is ',10 <= 20)
print('-50>= 20 is ', -50 >= 20)
print('20 == 20 is ',20 == 20)
print('10 != 20 is ',10 != 20)
```

Output

```
10 < 20 is True
-50 > 20 is False
10 <= 20 is True
-50>= 20 is False
20 == 20 is True
10 != 20 is True
```

1.4.3 Logical Operators

Logical operators combine conditional expressions to form compound conditions. The operators are **and, or, not**. The operations result in True or False as per the following truth table (Table 1.2).

Table 1.2 Truth table for logical operations

Operand1	Operand2	Operand1 and Operand2	Operand1 or Operand2	Not Operand1
True	True	True	True	False
True	False	False	True	False
False	True	False	True	True
False	False	False	False	True

Example

```
p=True
q=False
print('p and q is ',p and q)      # logical and operation
print('p or q is ', p or q)       # Logical or operation
print('not p is ',not p)          # logical not operation
```

Output

```
p and q is False
p or q is True
not p is False
```

1.4.4 Bitwise Operators

Numbers are represented as a sequence of bits in the computer memory. Bitwise operators perform operations on the individual bits of the operands.

(i) **Shift operators:** These operators perform operations on individual bits of the operands by shifting the bits to the left or right by specified number of times. When the bits are shifted left, the least significant bits are filled with zeros. Similarly, when the bits are shifted right, the most significant bits are filled with zeros.

For each left shift operation, the value of the operand is doubled as the bits are moved to higher significant positions. Similarly, for each right shift operation, the value of the operand is halved as the bits are moved to less significant positions (Fig. 1.3).

Example

```
print(" Left shift 10 by one position: ", 10 << 1)
print(" Right shift 50 by one position: ",50 >> 1)
```

Output

```
Left shift 10 by one position: 20
Right shift 50 by one position: 25
```

(ii) **Bitwise logical operator** symbols are (Table 1.3)

    &   for **and** operation
    | for **or** operation
    ^   for **exclusive or** operation
    ~   for **not(compliment)** operation

X>>2[X Right shift by 2 times]

X=6 in Binary	0	0	0	0	0	1	1	0	X=6
Right shift by 1 bit : 0 is inserted in the most Significant position and least significant bit is lost.	0	0	0	0	0	0	1	1	X=3
One more Right shift by 1 bit. 0 is inserted in the most significant position and least significant bit is lost.	0	0	0	0	0	0	0	1	X=1

X<<2[X Left shift by 2 times]

X=6 in Binary	0	0	0	0	0	1	1	0	X=6
Left shift by 1 bit : 0 is inserted in the least significant position and most significant bit is lost.	0	0	0	0	1	1	0	0	X=12
One more left shift by 1 bit. 0 is inserted in the least significant position and most significant bit is lost.	0	0	0	1	1	0	0	0	X=24

Fig. 1.3 Shift operations

Table 1.3 Truth table for bitwise operations

Operand1	Operand2	Operand1 & Operand2	Operand1 | Operand2	Operand1 ^ Operand2
0	0	0	0	0
0	1	0	1	1
1	0	0	1	1
1	1	1	1	0

Example

```
x=2      # 2 is internally represented as 0010
y=4      # 4 is represented as 0100
print('x & y : ',x & y)      # bitwise and operation
print('x | y : ',x | y)      # bitwise or operation
print('x ^ y : ',x ^ y)      # bitwise exclusive or
print('~x : ',~x)            # inverting bits
```

Output

```
x & y : 0
x | y : 6
x ^ y : 6
~x : -3
```

1.4.5 Assignment Operators

These operators assign a value of right operand to the left operand. The left operand should be a variable as the value is to be stored in the memory.

(i) **Simple assignment:**

Syntax

variable = expression

First, the *expression* is evaluated and then the result is assigned to the *variable*.

Example

```
radius = 5      # assign constant to variable
area = 3.14 * radius * radius      # assign value of expression
print('Area : ', area)
```

Output

```
Area : 78.5
```

(ii) **Compound assignment:** Assignment operator, =, can be combined with binary arithmetic and bitwise operators. It performs two operations—first the operation specified and then the assignment.

Ex. x += 20 is shorthand notation to x = x+ 20

Here, first addition is performed and then the result is assigned to variable x.

Example

```
x = 10
x += 20      # Addition and assignment
print('Value of x after adding 20 : ',x)
x //= 3      # Integer division and assignment
print('Value of x after integer division by 3 : ',x)
x &= 2       # Bitwise & operation and assignment
print('Value of x after bitwise & with 2 : ',x)
x << = 1     # Left Shift and assignment
print('Value of x after left shift by one position : ', x)
```

Output

```
Value of x after adding 20 : 30
Value of x after integer division by 3 : 10
Value of x after bitwise & with 2 : 2
Value of x after left shift by one position : 4
```

1.4.6   Identity Operators

Check whether operands are the same objects.

The operators are: **is, is not**.

object1 **is** *object2*
object1 **is not** *object2*

The operation returns True or False.

Example

```
print('Data type of 10.5 is float :', type(10.5)  is   float)
x , pi = 10.5, 3.14
print('Whether x & pi are same objects :', x is pi)
y = x
print('Whether x & y are same objects :', x is y)
z = 10.5
print('Whether x & z are same objects :', x is z)
print('Whether x & z are not same objects :', x is not z)
```

Output

> Data type of 10.5 is float : True
> Whether x & pi are same objects : False
> Whether x & y are same objects : True
> Whether x & z are same objects : False
> Whether x & z are not same objects : True

1.4.7   Membership Operators

in, not in operators are called membership operators. It checks if a value exists in iterable objects like string, list, tuple, set, dictionary.

> *value*   **in**   *object_name*
> *value*   **not in**   *object_name*

The operation returns True or False.

Example

> line = 'Programming with Python'
> print(' is "Python " in', '"', line , '" : ' , 'Python' in line)
> odd_num = [11, 21, 33, -9]
> print('is 33 in odd_num : ', 33 in odd_num)
> colors = {'Blue','White','Red','Yello','Pink'}
> print('is "White" not in ',colors,' : ', 'White' not in colors)

Output

> is "Python " in " Programming with Python " : True
> is 33 in odd_num : True
> is "White" not in {'Red', 'Yello', 'Pink', 'White', 'Blue'} : False

1.4.8   Operators Precedence and Associativity

Expression is a combination of constants, variables combined with operators. When multiple operators are present in the expression, the order in which operations are performed is based on precedence and associativity of operators.

Precedence is the priority of operators in performing the operations. When more than one operator is present in the expression, with the same precedence, operations are performed as per associativity rule. Following is the precedence of operators in descending order (Table 1.4).

Table 1.4 Operators precedence and associativity

Operator	Associativity
( )	Left-to-right
**	Right-to-left
unary +, unary - , ~	Right-to-left
*, /, //, %	Left-to-right
+,-	Left-to-right
<<, >>	Left-to-right
>, >= ,<, <=	Left-to-right
==, !=	Left-to-right
is, is not	Left-to-right
in, not in	Left-to-right
&	Left-to-right
^	Left-to-right
|	Left-to-right
!	Right-to-left
&&	Left-to-right
||	Left-to-right
=, +=, -=, *=, /= , //=, %=, &=, ^=, |=, << =, >>=	Right-to-left
Comma	Left-to-right

1.5   Type Conversions

The value of a variable or an expression can be converted to another data type. Type conversion converts the data type of the value but not the data type of the variable.

> **Syntax**

$data\_type(expression)$

data_type to which the value of *expression* to be converted.

(i) Convert **float to int**: Decimal part gets truncated.

Example

```
x=20.9
print('Data type of x : ', type(x))      # display data type of x
print('Converted value : ', int(x))      # convert x value to integer
# data type of x remains unchanged
print('Data type & value of x: ',type(x),x)
```

Output

Data type of x : <class 'float'>
Converted value : 20
Data type & value of x: <class 'float'> 20.9

Example: Convert **float to int** and assign to an integer variable

```
x= 10.89
# convert the value of x to integer and assign to variable y
y= int(x)
print('Data types of x & y : ', type(x), type(y))
print('Values of x and y : ', x , y)
```

Output

Data types of x & y : <class 'float'> <class 'int'>
Values of x and y : 10.89   10

(ii) Convert **int to float**: Zero is added as decimal part.

Example

```
x=10
y=float(x)      # convert int value to float
print('Data type of x & y : ', type(x), type(y))
print('Values of x and y : ', x,y)
```

Output

Data type of x & y : <class 'int'> <class 'float'>
Values of x and y : 10   10.0

(iii) Convert **float to complex:** Float value becomes the real part and the imaginary part is 0.

Example

```
x=10.5
y = complex(x)   # convert float value to complex number
print('Data type of x & y : ', type(x), type(y))
print('Values of x and y : ', x,y)
```

Output

Data type of x & y: <class 'float'> <class 'complex'>
Values of x and y: 10.5   (10.5+0j)

(iv) Converting **complex to *float* or *int*** generates the following error since there are two values in the complex data type, i.e., real and imaginary parts.

Example

```
c=10-5j
f = float(c)
```

Output

```
TypeError     Traceback (most recent call last)
<ipython-input-15-260457d2093e> in <module>()
    1 c=10-5j
—-> 2 f = float(c)

TypeError: can't convert complex to float
```

(v) Convert **string to float** or **int**: String with only *digits* is allowed. Error is generated, if the string contains characters other than digits.

Example

```
s="123"      # here string contains only digits
i =int(s)
print(type(s), type(i))
print(s,i)
```

Output

```
<class 'str'> <class 'int'>
123 123
```

Example

```
s="123a"      # string contains non-digits
i =int(s)
print(type(s), type(i))
print(s,i)
```

Output

```
ValueError     Traceback (most recent call last)
<ipython-input-17-ac180ec5ce25> in <module>()
    1 s="123a"      # string contains non-digits
—-> 2 i =int(s)
    3 print(type(s), type(i))
    4 print(s,i)
    ValueError: invalid literal for int() with base 10: '123a'
```

(vi) Convert **Numeric to string**: Every digit and decimal point becomes a character of the string in the same sequence.

Example

```
a = 10.88
s = str(a)     # numeric to string
print('Data types of a & s : ', type(a), type(s))
print('Values of a & s : ', a,s)
```

Output

```
Data types of a & s: <class 'float'> <class 'str'>
Values of a & s: 10.88   10.88
```

(vii) Convert to a **Boolean:** Any non-zero numeric value is True and zero value is False. Similarly, any non-empty string is True and an empty string is False.

Example

```
x , y , z= 20.78, "", 0j
print('Non-zero numeric value to boolean : ', bool(x))
print('Empty string to boolean : ',bool(y))
print('Zero complex value to boolean : ', bool(z))
```

Output

```
Non-zero numeric value to boolean : True
Empty string to boolean : False
Zero complex value to boolean : False
```

1.6   Statements

Python program consists of statements that perform actions on the data, like assigning value to a variable, making decisions based on the condition, repeating the statements, etc. New line character marks the end of the statement. When a statement runs into multiple lines, use the line continuation character \ after each line.

Example

```
# statement continuation
colors = {'Red', 'Green',\
          'Blue', 'Purple',\
          'Pink'}
print(colors)
```

Output

{'Red', 'Green', 'Pink', 'Blue', 'Purple'}

Python supports the following statements.

- Assignment statement
- Input Statement
- Output Statement
- Conditional statement
- Loop statements
- Control statements

1.6.1   Assignment Statement

Assignment statement is to assign a value to a variable or variables. The value will be stored in the memory location allocated to the variable.

= is the assignment operator

Syntax

variable_name = expression

First, the *expression* on the right-hand side of assignment operator (=) is evaluated and then the result is assigned to the left-hand side *variable_name*.

Example

```
pi = 3.14      # assigns constant value 3.14 to the variable pi
radius = 5     # assigns constant value 5 to the variable radius
# assigns value of RHS expression to variable area
area = pi * radius * radius
print(area)
```

Output

78.5

(i) Python supports multiple assignments in a single statement.

Example

```
x, y ,z = 10,5.97, True
print(type(x),x)
print(type(y),y)
print(type(z),z)
```

Output

<class 'int'> 10
<class 'float'> 5.97
<class 'bool'> True

(ii) Same value can be assigned to multiple variables in a single statement.

Example

sum = count = average = 0
# All the three variables are assigned the same value 0
print(sum, count,average)

Output

0 0 0

1.6.2   Input Statement

Input statement is to assign a value to the variable during the execution of the code using predefined **input()** function.

| Syntax |

variable_name = **input**(" *prompt* ")

prompt is the message displayed to the user when the statement is executed and waits until the user enters the value into the box provided.

Example

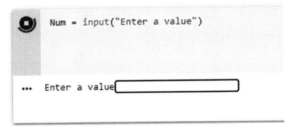

The value entered by the user has to be assigned to a variable otherwise the value is lost.
num = input("Enter a value : ")
print('Data type & value of num : ', type(num), num)

Output

> Enter a value : 10
> Data type & value of num: <class 'str'> 10

The value entered at the keyboard is taken as a string. It is up to the user to convert the value into the required data type.

Example

```
num_str = input("Enter a value")
num_int = int(num_str)
print(type(num_str), type(num_int))
print(num_str, num_int)
```

Output

> Enter a value123
> <class 'str'> <class 'int'>
> 123   123

Difference between assignment statement & input function:

Input() function	Assignment statement
input() function prompts the user to give a value whenever it is executed. So the user has an option to change the value on every execution.	Same value is assigned to the variable, on every execution of the assignment statement.

Multiple values can be accepted in a single input() function using a split( ) function on the input. The delimiter to be used for the split is provided as an argument to split(), in quotes. The default delimiter is space.

Example

```
# Enter multiple values separated by spaces
num1, num2, num3 = input("Enter three values separated by space : ").split()
print(type(num1),num1)
print(type(num2),num2)
print(type(num3),num3)
```

Output

> Enter values separated by space : 10 20 30
> <class 'str'> 10
> <class 'str'> 20
> <class 'str'> 30

Any delimiter can be specified in the split( ) function.

Example

```
num1, num2, num3 = input("Enter 3 values separated by comma : ").split(',')
print(type(num1),num1)
print(type(num2),num2)
print(type(num3),num3)
```

Output

```
Enter values separated by comma : 10,20,30
<class 'str'> 10
<class 'str'> 20
<class 'str'> 30
```

1.6.3 Output Statement

Output statement displays the values on the user monitor/screen, using the print( ) function.

print(*expressions, sep=None, end= None*)

expressions:	Expressions values to be displayed on the monitor.
	In case of multiple expressions, separate them by commas.
	The value of each expression is converted to a string before display.
sep:	Separator to be used between multiple values in the display.
	Default is space.
end:	How to terminate the output. Default in new line \n

Example

```
num = 5
# To display the string followed by value of variable
print("value of num = ", num)      # displays multiple values
```

Output

```
value of num = 5
```

(i) Single print() function can be used to display in multiple lines using new line escape sequence \n in quotes.

Example

```
num1 , num2 = 50 , 100
print(" num1 = " , num1 , "\n num2 = ", num2)
```

Output

> num1 = 50
> num2 = 100

(ii) To display the output of multiple print() functions in the same line, specify **end** parameter value as space.

Example

> # end parameter in the print() function keeps the cursor on the same line
> print("Python ",end="")
> print("Programming")

Output

> Python Programming

(iii) Display multiple values separated by specified **sep** argument value.

Example

> # Display multiple values separated by comma
> breadth, height = 5, 7
> area = 1/2 * breadth * height
> print(breadth, height, area, sep=',')

Output

> 5, 7, 17.5

1.6.4 *Conditional Statement*

In general, statements of the program are executed in sequence called sequential execution. But sometimes, program needs to skip certain statements based on the condition, called conditional statements.

if is Python's conditional statement.

Syntax

> *if condition:*
>   *Statements*   If part
> [**else**:
>   *Statements*]   else part

The part that is enclosed in square brackets is optional.

Statements: one or more Python statements.

if statements can be used in different formats.

(i) Simple **if** statement: Only *if part* exists and no *else part*

Example

```
x = int(input('Enter a number '))
if x > 0:      # x > 0 is condition
        print(x, ' is positive')    # if part
```

Output

```
Enter a number 25
25 is positive
```

(ii) **if-else** statement: Both *if part* and *else part* are present.

Example

```
a , b = input('Enter two values separated by space ').split()
a , b = int(a), int(b)
if a > b:
    print('Bigger value : ', a) # if part with only one statement
else:
    print('Bigger value : ', b) # else part with only one statement
```

Output

```
Enter two values separated by space 20 56
Bigger value: 56
```

if part and *else part* can have multiple statements.

Example

```
a , b = input('Enter two values separated by space').split()
a , b = int(a), int(b)
if a > b:       # if part has multiple statements
    print('Bigger is : ', end=")
    print(a)
else:      # else part has single statement
    print("Bigger is : ", b)
```

Output

```
Enter two values separated by space-16 54
Bigger is: 54
```

(iii) **Nested if:** An **If** statement can have an **if** statement inside its **if** part or **else** part called as *nested if*.

Example

```
num = int(input("Enter a number "))
if num > 0 :
    print(num , " is positive")
else :
    if num < 0 :        # if-else statement in else part
        print(num , " is negative")
    else :
        print("Number is zero")
```

Output

```
Enter a number -20
-20 is negative
```

(iv) **if-elif** statement: *else* and *if* can be combined into *elif*.

Example

```
num = int(input("Enter a number "))
if num > 0 :
  print(num , " is positive")
elif num < 0 :        # else and if are combined
    print(num , " is negative")
else :
    print("Number is zero")
```

Output

```
Enter a number -20
-20 is negative
```

(v) short hand **if- else:** *if* and *else* can be written in a single line when *if* part and *else* part have a single statement.

Example

```
a , b = input("Enter two values separated by space").split()
a , b = int(a) , int(b)
big = a if a > b else b      # single line if-else
print("Bigger is ", big)
```

Output

```
Enter two values separated by space-10 -35
Bigger is -10
```

Note: if statement cannot be empty.

```
if a>b:
```

Output

File "<ipython-input-11-e9e6693e9174>", line 1
   if a>b:
     ^

SyntaxError: unexpected EOF while parsing

To avoid the error, use **pass** statement.

if a>b:
pass

Example

```
a = int(input("Enter a value "))
if a == 0:
    pass
else :
    print(a, ' is non-zero')
```

Output

Enter a value 20
20 is non-zero

1.6.5 Loop Statements

A loop statement repeats a block of statements until the specified condition is satisfied or a certain number of times. Python supports two types of loop statements.

(i) *while* loop,
(ii) *for* loop.

(i) **while loop:** Block of statements enclosed in the loop are repeatedly executed as long as the *condition* is **True**. Once the loop *condition* becomes **False**, the control goes to the next statement after the loop. Statements that form the body of the loop are determined by indentation.

Syntax

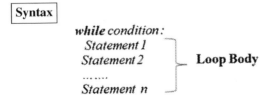

while condition:
   Statement 1
   Statement 2   } **Loop Body**
   ....
   Statement n

Example: Display odd numbers up to 20.

```
i=1
while i<=20 :        #loop is executed as long as condition is true
    print(i, end=' ')      # this statement is in the loop
    i += 2               # this statement is in the loop
# following statement is outside the loop
print("\nThis statement is outside the while loop")
```

Output

```
1 3 5 7 9 11 13 15 17 19
This statement is outside the while loop
```

Note: Statements in the loop are determined based on the indentation.
In the above example, the variable i is called **loop control variable** that forms
a *condition* for the loop, i.e., the value of i determines the number of times the
loop is executed. This variable has to be initialized prior to the loop statement to
avoid generating an error. The *condition* has to be updated in the body of the loop
to avoid infinite looping. If the *condition* is false initially, the body is executed
zero times.

Example

```
while j<=20 :        # loop is executed as long as condition is true
    print(j, end=' ')      # this statement is in the loop
    j += 2             # this statement is in the loop
# following statement is outside the loop
print("\nThis statement is outside the while loop")
```

Output

```
NameError      Traceback (most recent call last)
<ipython-input-8-d48965829e48> in <module>()
---> 1 while j<=20 :
          # loop is executed as long as condition is true
      2 print(j, end=' ')        # this statement is in the loop
      3 j += 2       # this statement is in the loop
      4 print("\nThis statement is outside the while loop")
          # this is outside the loop
NameError: name 'j' is not defined
```

Control Statements *break* and *continue* statements are used in association
with *loop* statements. These are called control statements as they control the loop
execution.
break statement is to exit from the current loop statement.
continue statement is to bypass the current iteration of the loop and continue
with the next iteration.

Unlike other programming languages, Python supports a **while-else** statement.

```
while condition :
    Statement 1
    Statement            Loop body
    Statement  n
else :
    Statements
```

The *else* part of the *while* loop is executed when the loop is terminated normally, i.e., when no *break* is encountered in the loop.

Example: Check if a given number is prime.

```
num = int(input("Enter number : "))
i= 2
while(i <=num//2):
   if num % i == 0:
      print(num, " is not prime")
      break
   i +=1
else:
   print(num, " is prime")
```

Output

```
Enter number : 23
23 is prime
```

Note: Similar to *if* statement, *while* statement with an empty block of statements generates an error irrespective of the condition being true or false.

Example

```
a , b = 10 , 5
while a>b:
```

Output

```
File "<ipython-input-15-00192042912f>", line 2
    while a>b :
             ^
SyntaxError: unexpected EOF while parsing
```

The above error can be avoided using a **pass** statement in the loop.

```
a , b = 10 , 5
while a<b :
    Pass
```

Range Function

range( ) function of Python generates a sequence of integer values based on the parameters specified.

| Syntax |

*range(**start, end, step**)*

The sequence begins with **start** value and continues up to the **end** (not including the **end**) value with an increment of **step** value.

- Start value is optional. When not specified, the default value is 0.
- The step value is also optional. When not specified, the default value is 1.

The range( ) function is usually used in the *for* loop.

(ii) *for* loop

The *for loop* iterates over a sequence object. The number of iterations is determined by the number of items in the sequence object.

| Syntax |

```
for loop_control variable in sequence_object:
    Statement 1
    Statement 2              ⎫
    ........                 ⎬  Loop Body
    Statement n              ⎭

[else

    Statements  ]
```

sequence_object can be any iterable object like range(), list, tuple, dictionary, sets, strings. Values of the *sequence_object* are assigned to the *loop_control_variable* in sequence, on each iteration.

Example 1: Display numbers from 0 to 4.

```
for i in range(5):     # default start value is 0 and step value is 1
    print(i, end=' ')
```

Output

```
0 1 2 3 4
```

Note: 5 is not displayed as end value is not inclusive.

Example 2: Display integers between -5 and 4.

```
for i in range(-5,5):     # default step value is 1
    print(i, end=' ')
```

Output

```
-5 -4 -3 -2 -1 0 1 2 3 4
```

Note: 5 is not displayed as end value is not inclusive.

Example 3: Display items of a list.

```
for item in ['Red','Green','Blue','Black','White']:
    print(item, end=' ')
```

Output

Red Green Blue Black White

Note: Python supports *for-else* statements. *else* part is executed on normal exit from the loop.

Example

```
for i in range(-10, -20, -2):
    print(i, end=' ')
else:
    print("\nThis is else part of the for loop")
```

Output

```
-10 -12 -14 -16 -18
This is else part of the for loop
```

1.7   Random Numbers

A random integer can be generated using the following function.

  randrange(*start, end, step*)

It generates a single random integer based on the parameters specified. In order to use this function, first import *random* module.

  import random

Note: *start, end, step* parameters have the same meaning as in the range() function.

Example 1: Generate a random number between 0 and 4.

```
import random
# any one random number in the sequence 0,1,2,3,4
r1 = random.randrange(5)
print(r1)
```

Output

3

Example 2: Generate a random number between 5 and 19 with a step of 3.

```
# random number in the sequence 5,8,11,14,17
r3 = random.randrange(5,20,3)
print(r3)
```

Output

```
17
```

Example 3: Generate a random number between -5 and -14 with a step of -3.

```
# random number in the sequence -5,-8,-11,-14
r3 = random.randrange(-5,-15,-3)
print(r3)
```

Output

```
-14
```

Exercises

1. Create a menu that provides options for performing the arithmetic operations.
2. Take the age of a person from the user and display whether the person is a child (age < 12) or teenager (age < 18) or adult (age < 50) or a senior citizen (age >= 50).
3. Given the day of a week as an integer, display the name of the day. Assume Sunday is 0.
4. Display the sum of digits of the given number.
5. Display the last digit and first digit of the given number.
6. Accept numbers from the user until 0 is input. Find the sum of the numbers. Use a **while** loop.
7. Take marks of N students from the user and display the Pass percentage. Assume 50 is the pass mark.
8. Given the volume of water in gallons, convert it into liters.
9. Find the acceleration of an object, given time and velocity.
10. Given the memory size in bytes, convert into mega bytes and giga bytes.

Review Questions

(1) What is the output of the following code?

```
X = 20.56
X = "Welcome Python"
print(X)
```

(a) 20.56
(b) Reports an error
(c) Welcome Python
(d) 20.56 Welcome Python

(2) What is the output of the following code?

```
pi = 3.14
print(Pi)
```

(a) NameError: name "Pi" is not defined
(b) 3.14
(c) Pi is a reserved word
(d) Need to import math module to use pi

(3) What is the output of the following code?

```
S = bool("Hello ")
A = bool(0)
print(S and A)
```

(a) True
(b) Hello
(c) False
(d) Reports an error

(4) What is the output of the following code?

```
x = 50
print(x << 2)
```

(a) 12.5
(b) 100
(c) 200
(d) 25

(5) What is the output of the following code?

```
print(200 >> 3)
```

(a) 100
(b) 50
(c) 400
(d) 25

(6) What is the output of the following code?

```
x = 10
y = 15
print(x & y)
```

   (a) True
   (b) 10
   (c) 5
   (d) 25

(7) What is the output of the following code ?

```
A, B = 30 , 12
print(A//B)
```

   (a) 2.5
   (b) 2
   (c) Invalid operator
   (d) 2.0

(8) What is the output of the following code?

```
X = -2.5
print(bool(X))
```

   (a) True
   (b) False
   (c) -2.5
   (d) Reports an error

(9) What is the output of the following code?

```
print(-10 % 3)
```

   (a) -1
   (b) 1
   (c) 2
   (d) -2

(10) What is the output of the following code?

```
print( 10 % -3 )
```

   (a) -1
   (b) 1
   (c) 2
   (d) -2

(11) What is the output of the following code?

```
product = 1
for i in range(5):
     product *= i
print(product)
```

   (a) 0

(b) 120

(c) Reports an error

(d) 13

(12) How many times is the word *Python* displayed?

```
for i in range(5):
  for j in range(1,5):
    print("Python ", end=" ")
```

(a) 5

(b) 25

(c) 10

(d) 20

(13) How many times is the loop repeated?

```
A = 10
while A:
  print(A)
  A -= 2
```

(a) 5

(b) 6

(c) Infinitely

(d) 10

(14) What is the output of the following code?

```
S = 0
while S :
  print("Hello")
else:
  print("Bye")
```

(a) Hello

(b) Bye

(c) Reports an error

(d) 0

(15) What is the output of the following code?

```
import random
x = random.randrange(-5,1)
print(x)
```

(a) -2

(b) 0

(c) -5

(d) Any of the above

(16) ————specifies a code block in Python.

  (a) Parenthesis
  (b) Begin-End
  (c) Indentation
  (d) Quotes

(17) Which of the following is invalid loop statement in Python?

  (a) for
  (b) while
  (c) for-else
  (d) do while

(18) What is the output of the following?

```
a,b,c=5,True,0
if a and b or c:
    print("Yes")
else:
    print("No")
```

  (a) Yes
  (b) No
  (c) Reports an Error
  (d) True

(19) What is the output of the following?

```
if -3:
    print("True")
else:
    print("False")
```

  (a) True
  (b) No
  (c) Reports an Error
  (d) False

(20) What is the output of the following code?

```
c1 = 10+5j
c2=5
print(c1+c2)
```

  (a) Reports an error
  (b) 15+5j
  (c) 15j + 5
  (d) 10 +10j

Chapter 2
Functions

2.1 Introduction

When the given problem is large or complex, it is easy to find the solution by splitting the larger problem into smaller subproblems. This approach will result in a simple and clean solution to the bigger problems. In programming languages, subproblems are implemented as functions in C, methods in C++/Java, procedures in Pascal, and subroutines in Fortran. In a similar fashion, subproblems in Python are implemented using functions.

Functions provide the following benefits:

- Modularity: Divides the larger program into smaller units called functions. Such decomposition makes the code easy to manage, debug, and improves the readability of the code.
- Reusability: Same function can be used multiple times with different input values.
- Reduce the duplication of code.
- Shareability: Functions can be shared and used by others.

For example:

To find the value of N_{C_R}, given N and R.

The problem can be solved in the following way:

1. Write a function to find the factorial for a given number N.
2. Use this factorial function, 3 times with the values N, R, N-R to calculate N_{C_R}.

Implementing functions require the following two steps:

(i) Define the function.
(ii) Call/invoke the function.

© The Author(s) 2024
A. L. Muddana and S. Vinayakam, *Python for Data Science*,
https://doi.org/10.1007/978-3-031-52473-8_2

(i) **Function definition**

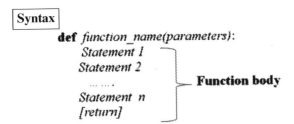

def is a keyword. The statements that constitute the function is called the *function body*. Input values to the function are provided through *parameters* that are optional. When multiple parameters are specified, they are separated by commas. These *parameters* are also known as formal parameters. The values computed in the function body may be passed back to the caller using a *return* statement, which is optional. Execution of the *return* statement terminates the function execution, and control is passed back to the caller.

(ii) **Function call/Function invoke**

Invoking the function executes the function body with the parameters passed in the function call. These parameters are also known as *arguments* or actual parameters.

| Syntax |

    function_name(arguments)

Example: Take the user's name using the input function and greet him.

Function definition

```
def display(name):
   print("Hello ", end=" ")
   print(name)
```

Function call

```
S = input("What is your name: ") # take user name
display(S)     # function call
```

Output

```
What is your name: Arjun
Hello Arjun
```

Function body may include a *return* statement. Values specified in the *return* statement are passed back to the calling point.

Example: Function to calculate factorial of a number.

```
def factorial(num):   # num is parameter to the function
    product = 1
    for i in range(1,num+1):
        product *= i
    # following function returns the value of product to the caller
    return product
```

Function call

```
print(factorial(5))
```

Output

```
120
```

Note: Function call is equivalent to the value returned. Hence, the function call is used in print() to display the returned value. In the above example *num* is the formal parameter and 5 is the actual parameter.

2.2 Properties of Functions

Property 1: Actual parameters can be constants, variables, or expressions.

Example

```
x = int(input("Enter a number : "))
print(factorial(x))   # here actual parameter is a variable
print(factorial(x + 3 ))   # here actual parameter is an expression
```

Output

```
Enter a number: 3
6
720
```

The main advantage of functions is **reusability**, i.e., a function can be called or invoked any number of times with different argument values.

Example: Find the value of N_{C_R}

```
n = int(input("Enter the value of n : "))
r = int(input("Enter the value of r : "))
# following statement calls the function 3 times
ncr = factorial(n) / (factorial(r) * factorial(n - r))
print("ncr = ", ncr)
```

Output

> Enter the value of n : 5
> Enter the value of r : 3
> ncr = 10.0

In the above example, the function **factorial( )** is called three times.

Property 2: A function can have multiple parameters. Return value can be a constant, variable, or expression.

Example: Function to calculate N_{C_R}

```
def ncr(n,r):   # multiple parameters n, r
    # following return statement specifies an expression
    return factorial(n) / (factorial(r) * factorial(n-r))
```

Function call

```
print(ncr(n,r))
```

Output

> 10.0

Property 3: Function parameters are optional and return statements are also optional.

Example

```
# Function with no parameters and no return value
def circle(): # No formal parameter
    radius = float( input("Enter radius : ") )
    area = 3.14 * radius * radius
    circum = 2 * 3.14 * radius
    print(area, circum )
```

Function call

```
circle()
```

Output

> Enter radius : 7
> 153.86, 43.96

Property 4: Function can have multiple return statements.

Example

```
# Function with multiple return statements
def grade(marks):
    if marks>=90 :
        return "Grade A"
    elif marks >= 80 :
```

```
        return "Grade B"
    elif marks>=70 :
        return "Grade C"
    elif marks>= 60 :
        return "Grade D"
    else :
        return "Grade E"
```

Function call

```
print(grade(65))
print(grade(89))
print(grade(40))
```

Output

```
Grade D
Grade B
Grade E
```

Note: Function execution terminates on execution of any one of the return statements.

Property 5: A function can return multiple values. These values are returned as a tuple.

Example: Display area and circumference of a circle given radius.

```
# Function with multiple return values
def circle(radius):   # one formal parameter
    area = 3.14 * radius * radius
    circum = 2 * 3.14 * radius
    return area, circum   # 2 return values
```

Function call

```
circle(7)
```

Output

```
(153.86, 43.96)
```

2.3 Parameters' Mapping

Mapping the actual parameters to the formal parameters can be done in three ways.

(i) *Positional parameters:* Actual and formal parameters are mapped by their positions.

  Example: Find Simple Interest given Principal, Term, and Rate of Interest.

```
def simple_interest(P,T,R):
  SI = (P * T * R) /100
  return SI
```

Function call

```
simple_interest( 2000, 3, 25 )
```

Output

1500.0

In the above function call, actual parameter 2000 corresponds to P, 3 corresponds to T, and 25 corresponds to R.

(ii) *Keyword parameters:* Mapping is done by specifying a formal parameter name in the function call. Hence, actual parameters can appear in any order and need not follow the positions. Parameter names are called keywords and hence the name keyword parameters.

Function call

```
# Actual parameter values are assigned using parameter names
print(simple_interest(T = 4, R = 25, P=2000) )
```

Output

2000.0

(iii) *Default parameters:* Default values can be assigned to the parameters in the function definition, called default parameters. Such parameters values need not be specified in the function call. If not specified, the default value given in the function definition is assumed. If the actual parameter is specified, the specified value is considered, ignoring the default value.

Example: Find Simple Interest given Principal, Term, and Rate of Interest.

```
# Default values of T is 1 & R is 10.
def simple_interest(P,T=1,R=10):
  SI = (P * T * R) /100
  return SI
```

Function calls

```
print(simple_interest(2000)) # T & R have their default values
print(simple_interest(2000,2)) # R has default value 10
# here all the three parameters take specified values
print(simple_interest(2000,2, 20))
```

Output

> 200.0
> 400.0
> 800.0

Default parameters can be specified starting from last to the beginning. Non-default parameters cannot be placed in between the default parameters.

Example: Find Simple Interest given Principal, Term, and Rate of Interest.

```
# Default values of T is 1 & R is 10.
def simple_interest(P=100,T,R=10):
    SI = (P * T * R) /100
    return SI
```

Error

```
File "<ipython-input-30-e0a1f38e1eb1<", line 2
    def simple_interest(P=100,T,R=10):
        ^
SyntaxError: non-default argument followsdefault argument
```

2.4   Parameter Passing Mechanisms

Actual parameter values are passed to the formal parameters in two ways. (i) pass-by-value and (ii) pass-by-reference.

(i) **Pass-by value:** When parameters are passed by value, the value of the actual parameter is copied into the formal parameter variable. Hence, changes made to them inside the function body are not reflected back in the caller. Immutable objects like strings, tuples are passed by value.

Example: Update the parameter in the function.

```
def pass_value(x):
    x = "Hello " + x   # x is modified here
    print("Inside the function definition : ", x)
```

Function call

```
s = input("Enter string : ")      # before function call
pass_value(s)                     # Function call
print("After function call : ", s)
```

Output

> Enter string: Arjun
> Inside the function definition: Hello Arjun
> After function call: Arjun

(ii) **Pass_by reference:** When parameters are passed by reference, formal and actual parameters become aliases and refer to the same memory location. Hence, changes made to the formal parameters inside the function are reflected back in the caller. Mutable objects like lists, sets, and dictionaries are passed by reference. Examples will be given when discussing mutable objects in the subsequent chapters.

2.5   Recursive Functions

Factorial of N is defined as

Method 1: Iterative method

$$N! = N * (N-1) * (N-2) * \ldots * 1$$

Method 2: Recursive method

Factorial can also be defined as

$$N! = N * (N-1)!$$

Here factorial is defined in terms of itself, called *recursive* definition.

(i) Following is the Python function using *Iterative method*.

```
def factorial(N):
    product = 1
    for i in range(1,N+1):
        product *= i
    return product
```

The above function uses a loop to find the factorial, called the iterative method.

(ii) Following is the Python function using *Recursive method*.

```
def factorial(N):
    if N==0 :   # terminating condition
        return 1
    else:
        return N * factorial(N-1)    # function calling itself
```

The above function is called a recursive function as it has a call to itself. In the recursive function definition, there should be a condition to stop calling itself. Such a condition is called a **terminating condition**. If the recursive function does not contain a terminating condition, the function will be infinitely calling itself and control will not come out of the function.

Function call using Method 2:

X = int(input("Enter a positive integer : "))
factorial(X)

Output

Enter a positive integer : 5
120

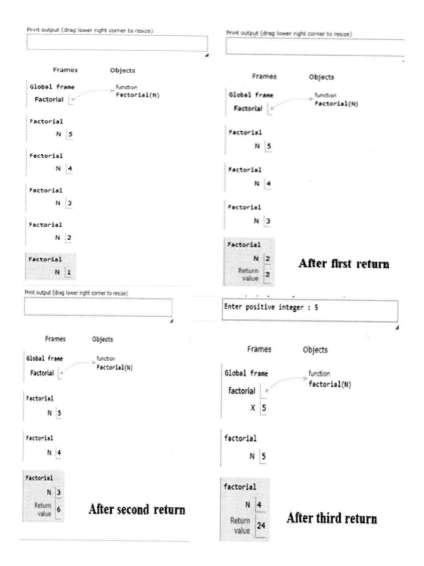

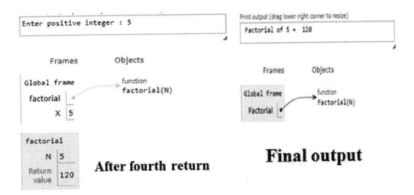

After fourth return   **Final output**

Advantages of recursive function:

- The recursive function is simple to write.
- It requires less code.

Disadvantages of recursive functions:

- During the recursive call, incomplete operation values have to be stored until the terminating condition is reached. It uses a stack data structure to store/push these values. Hence additional memory is required for the stack.
- Once the terminating condition is reached, the values stored on the stack have to be retrieved/popped to complete the operations. Storing and retrieving operations on the stack takes extra time. Hence recursive functions take more execution time compared to iterative functions.

2.6   Lambda Functions

Lambda functions are tiny functions that can have only one statement or expression as its body. The function has no name and hence also called an anonymous function.

Function definition

   variable = **lambda** *formal_parameters: expression*

lambda is a keyword.
expression may include *formal_parameters*. The value of the *expression* is assigned to the *variable*.

Function call

   variable(actual_parameters)

Example: Find the area of a circle given radius.

```
# Lambda function with radius as parameter
circle_area = lambda radius : 3.14 * radius * radius
```

Function call

> circle_area(7)   # Call to lambda function

Output

> 153.86

Lambda function can have zero or more parameters.

Example: Find Euclidean distance given two points.

> # Lambda function with multiple parameters
> dist = lambda x1, y1, x2, y2 : math.sqrt((x2-x1)**2 + (y2-y1)**2)

Function call

> dist(2,2,5,5)   # call to Lambda function

Output

> 4.242640687119285

Example: Find a logarithmic value of 10.

> # Lambda function with zero parameters
> x = lambda : math.log(10)

Function call

> x()   # Call to lambda function with no parameters

Output

> 2.302585092994046

Exercises

Write a Program, Using Functions, for the Following

1. Display a multiplication table of a given number.
2. Generate prime numbers in the specified range.
3. Display Fibonacci numbers up to the given number.
4. Find LCM of two given numbers.
5. Find HCF of the given two numbers.
6. Display the reverse of a given number.
7. Check if the given number is perfect.
8. Find sum of the series $1 / 1! + 2 / 2! + 3 / 3! + \ldots$

Write Recursive Functions, for the Following

1. Find the sum of the first N natural numbers.
2. Find the sum of the digits of a number.
3. Display multiples of 3 between two specified numbers.
4. Find GCD of two given numbers.
5. Find the nth Fibonacci number.
6. Check if the given number is prime.
7. Given the decimal number convert it to binary.

Write Lambda Functions for the Following

1. Find the sigmoid value for a given x value.
2. Check if given number is divisible by 7 and 5.
3. Find the slope of a given line.
4. Convert the temperature from Celsius to Fahrenheit.
5. Find compound interest.
6. Find the area of a right-angle triangle.
7. Find the sum of the numbers in a given range.

Review Questions

(1) What is the output of the following code?

```
def test_fun(a, b=5, c=10):
    return a+b+c
print(test_fun(20, 1))
```

(a) 35
(b) 15
(c) 31
(d) Error is generated

(2) What is the output of the following code?

```
def test_fun(x=4,y):
    print(x+y)
test_fun(-3)
```

(a) 1
(b) -1
(c) 7
(d) Error is generated

(3) What is the output of the following code?

```
f = lambda a, b : a % b
print(f(10, 3))
```

(a) 1
(b) 3
(c) 3.33
(d) Error is generated

(4) What is the output of the following code?

```
def test_fun(radius):
  print(radius, end=' ')
  print(3.14*radius*radius, end=' ')
print(test_fun(10))
```

(a) 10 314.0
(b) 10 314.0 None
(c) 10 3.14
(d) Error is generated

(5) What is the output of the following code?

```
def rec_fun(n):
  if n<=5:
    return
  else :
    return n * (n-1)
print(rec_fun(4))
```

(a) None
(b) 24
(c) Get into infinite loop
(d) Error is generated

(6) Which of the following statements is not true with the functions?

(a) Function body should have at least one return statement
(b) Function can return multiple values
(c) Function body cannot be empty
(d) Function can have multiple parameters

(7) What is the output of the following code?

```
def test_fun( t1, t2 ):
  t1 += t2
  return t1
test_fun((1,2,3), (4,5,6,7))
```

(a) (1, 2, 3)
(b) (1, 2, 3, 4, 5, 6, 7)
(c) (4, 5, 6, 7)
(d) Error is generated

(8) What is the output of the following code?

```
def test_fun( a, b ) :
  return a - b
print( test_fun(b=10, a= -5) )
```

(a) -15
(b) 5
(c) 15
(d) Error is generated

(9) What is the minimum number of arguments to be provided in function call?

```
def test_fun(a, b, c= 10):
  return a*b*c
```

(a) 0
(b) 1
(c) 2
(d) 3

(10) What type of object is returned by the following function?

```
def test_fun(a, b):
  return a+b, a*b
test_fun(10,20)
```

(a) Two integer values
(b) List
(c) Tuple
(d) Set

Chapter 3
Strings

Characters are the symbols used in writing the code. As computers can only store and process binary data, these characters are converted into a binary form called encoding. Binary data is again converted back to character form to present it to the user, called decoding. ASCII and Unicode are the popular encoding methods.

A string is a sequence of characters enclosed in single or double quotes. It is a sequence data type where individual characters can be accessed using its index. Python does not support character data type. A single character in quotes is also treated as a string of length one. A String object is immutable, i.e., once created, it cannot be modified. However, it can be assigned to another string variable.

String objects are used in Natural Language Processing, Search Engines, Chatbots, Information Retrieval Systems, etc.

3.1 Create String Objects

A string object is a sequence of characters of the character set. The character set includes alphabets, digits, operators, delimiters, special characters, etc.

(i) **Create an empty string object**

An empty string object can be created in two ways:

(a) Using empty quotes (single or double).
(b) Using string class, *str*.

© The Author(s) 2024
A. L. Muddana and S. Vinayakam, *Python for Data Science*,
https://doi.org/10.1007/978-3-031-52473-8_3

Example

```
# create empty string using single quotes
s1 = ' '
print("Data type of s1 : ", type(s1))
print("String s1 : ", s1)
# create empty string using str class
s2 = str()
print("Data type of s2 : ", type(s2))
print("String s2 : ", s2)
```

Output

Print output (drag lower right corner to resize)

```
Data type of s1 :   <class 'str'>
String s1 :
Data type of s2 :   <class 'str'>
String s2 :
```

Frames   Objects

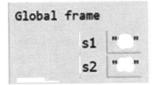

(ii) **Create a non-empty string object**
A non-empty string object can be created by enclosing the sequence of characters in single or double quotes which can then be assigned to a variable.

Example

```
# string enclosed in double quotes
s1 = "Hello World"
# string enclosed in single quotes
s2 = 'Hello World'
print("Data type of s1 : ", type(s1))
print("String is : ", s1)
print("Data type of s2 : ", type(s2))
print("String is : ",s2)
```

Output

Print output (drag lower right corner to resize)

```
Data type of s1 :  <class 'str'>
String is :  Hello World
Data type of s2 :  <class 'str'>
String is :  Hello World
```

Frames   Objects

Global frame

s1	"Hello World"
s2	"Hello World"

(iii) **Create multiline strings**

If a string runs into multiple lines, it is to be enclosed in triple quotes (single or double).

Example

```
# Multiline string
s = '''Python supports
multiline strings
enclosed in triple
   quotes
either single or double quotes
'''

print(s)
```

Output

```
Python supports
multiline strings
enclosed in triple quotes
either single or double quotes
```

Escape Sequences in String

When the string is enclosed in single quotes, if the string itself contains single quotes as one of its characters, it is to be preceded by escape character backslash \.

If the string is enclosed in single quotes and the string itself contains double quotes, the escape character is not required.

The same rule is applicable when the string is enclosed in double quotes.

Example

```
# Double quoted text in single quotes string
s = 'Python is "Object oriented" language'
print(s)
# Single quoted text in double quotes string
s = "Python is 'Object oriented' language"
print(s)
# Same type of quotes require escape character
s = "Python is \"Object oriented\" language"
print(s)
```

Output

```
Python is "Object oriented" language
Python is 'Object oriented' language
Python is "Object oriented" language
```

len() function on strings returns the number of characters in the string, including spaces.

Syntax

len(*string_object*)

Example

```
# len() function
s1 = 'Hello How are you?'
print("Number of characters in s1 : ", len(s1))
```

Output

```
Number of characters in s1 : 18
```

3.2   Accessing String Objects

String object being a sequence data type, its characters can be accessed using the index. The index is also called a subscript.

String	H	e	l	l	o		H	a	i	!
+ve index	0	1	2	3	4	5	6	7	8	9
-ve index	-10	-9	-8	-7	-6	-5	-4	-3	-2	-1

Fig. 3.1 Indexing string

(i) Indexing

Individual characters of a string are accessed using the index called indexing. The index ranges from zero to (length-1). The negative index can also be used that refers to the characters from the back of the string. The index of the last character is -1, last but one character is -2, and so on.

Syntax

> string_object[*index*]

Index values for the string "Hello Hai!" is as shown in Fig. 3.1.

Example

```
# Indexing
s1 = 'Hello How are you?'
# Access first character
print("First character is : ", s1[0])
# Access last character
print("Last character is : ", s1[-1])
# Access third character from last
print("Third character from last is : ", s1[-3])
```

Output

> First character is : H
> Last character is : ?
> Third character from last is : o

(ii) Slicing

A substring of a string can be extracted by specifying the start index, stop index, and step value. This operation is called slicing. The stop index is not inclusive, i.e., the character at the stop index is not included in the substring.

Syntax

> string_object[*start:stop:step*]
> The default value of *stop* is the end of the string.

The default value of *start* is the beginning of the string.
The default value of *step* is 1.

Example

```
# Slicing
str1 = 'Hello How are you?'
print("First three characters : ", str1[:3])
print("Last three characters : ", str1[-3:])
print("Characters from index 2 to 7 : ", str1[2:8])
print("Alternate characters : ", str1[: :2])
print("String in reverse order : ", str1[: : -1])
```

Output

```
First three characters : Hel
Last three characters : ou?
Characters from index 2 to 7 : llo Ho
Alternate characters : HloHwaeyu
String in reverse order : ?uoy era woH olleH
```

Note 1: Indexing or slicing will not modify the original string.
    print("Characters of string: ", s1)

Output
    Characters of string: Hello How are you?

Note 2: Specifying an index that is out of range generates an error.
    print(str1[20])

Output

```
IndexError                    Traceback (most recent call last)
< ipython-input-10-c9c04a693aa6> in <module>()
——> 1 print(str1[20])

IndexError: string index out of range
```

3.3 Operations on Strings

String objects are immutable, i.e., once created, the object cannot be changed or modified. Hence operations like addition, deletion, and modification of elements are not permitted on strings. However, deletion of the entire string is possible, which will be discussed in subsequent sections.

Example

```
# change a character
s1 = 'Hello How are you?'
s1[3] = 'L'
```

Output

```
TypeError                    Traceback (most recent call last)
<ipython-input-19-b8ded2f6c70b> in <module>()
        1 S1 = 'Hello How are you?'
——> 2 S1[3] = 'L'
```

TypeError: 'str' object does not support item assignment.

(i) **String concatenation**

Combines two or more strings. It can be done in multiple ways.

(a) Using + operator

Returns a new string by concatenating the string operands.

(b) Using *join(string_list)* method.

It requires string arguments to be specified as a list.

Returns a new string by concatenating the strings in the *string_list*.

Example

```
# string concatenation
s1 = 'Python'
s2 = ' Programming'
s3 = ' is fun'
print('Concatenation using + operator : ',s1 + s2 + s3)
# concatenation using join() method
print('Concatenation using join method : ',' '.join([s1, s2, s3]))
```

Output

```
Concatenation using + operator : Python Programming is fun
Concatenation using join method : Python Programming is fun
```

(ii) **Repetition operator ***

Concatenates multiple copies of the same string.

*string_object * number_repetitions*

Returns a new string object.

Example

```
str1 = 'Hello '
print(str1*3)
```

Output

> Hello Hello Hello

(iii) **Membership Testing**
in operator checks whether a substring is present in the given string.
> *sub_string **in** string_object*

Returns True or False.

Example

```
# Membership testing using in operator
s= 'Python programming is simple'
print('programming' in s)
```

Output

> True

3.4   Methods on Strings

Python provides a number of methods on string objects to perform different operations. Commonly used methods are

(i) *string_object.lower()*
Returns a new string with all the characters converted to lowercase.
(ii) *string_object.upper()*
Returns a new string with all the characters converted to uppercase.
(iii) *string_object.capitalize()*
Returns a new string with only the first character capitalized.
(iv) *string_object.title()*
Returns a new string by capitalizing the first character in each word.
(v) *string_object.casefold()*
Ignore the case while comparing the strings.

Example

```
str1 = "programming with python"
print("Capitalize all the characters : ", str1.upper())
print("Capitalize only first character : ", str1.capitalize())
print("Capitalize first character of each word : ", str1.title())
```

Output

Capitalize all the characters : PROGRAMMING WITH PYTHON
Capitalize only first character : Programming with python
Capitalize first character of each word : Programming With Python

(vi) *string_object.isdigit()*
Returns *True* if the string contains only digits and *False* otherwise.
(vii) *string_object.isalpha()*
Return *True* if the string contains only alphabets and *False* otherwise.
(viii) *string_object.isalnum()*
Returns *True* if the string contains alphabets or digits and *False* otherwise.

Example

```
str1 = "123"
print('whether str1 contains only digits ?: ', str1.isdigit())
print('Are all characters of str1 alphabets?: ', str1.isalpha())
str2="12A"
print('All characters of str2 alphabets or digits?:', str2.isalnum()))
```

Output

whether str1 contains only digits ?: True
Are all characters of str1 alphabets?: False
All characters of str2 alphabets or digits?: True

(ix) *string_object.split(delimiter)*
Splits the string into substrings, using the specified *delimiter.*
The default *delimiter* is space.
Returns list of substrings.

Example

```
s1 = "programming is fun"
print("List of substrings separated by space: ", s1.split())
s2 = "python: C++: Java"
print("List of substrings separated by colon: ", s2.split(':'))
s3 = "ram@gmail.com"
print("List of substrings separated by @: ", s3.split('@'))
```

Output

List of substrings separated by space: ['programming', 'is', 'fun']
List of substrings separated by colon: ['python', ' C++', ' Java']
List of substrings separated by @: ['ram', 'gmail.com']

(x) strip() method removes leading and trailing spaces in the string.
string_object.strip()

Example

```
# Remove leading and trailing spaces
s1 = " Hello , How are you? "
print(s1.strip())
```

Output

Hello, How are you?

(xi) *string_object.replace(arg1,arg2)*
Returns a new string by replacing *arg1* with *arg2* in the *string_object*.
But the original string will not change as string objects are immutable.

Example

```
# Replace the characters
s = "Good Morning"
print("Replacing o with # : ", s.replace('o','#'))
print("Replacing with a substring : ", s.replace('Morning','Evening'))
print("String after replace : ",s)
```

Output

Replacing o with # : G##d M#rning
Replacing with a substring : Good Evening
String after replace : Good Morning

(xii) *string_object.startswith(prefix) , string_object.endswith(suffix)*
Returns Boolean value based on whether the *string_object* starts or ends with
the specified *prefix* or *suffix* string.

Example

```
s1 = 'Hi, I am Good'
print('Whether the string starts with Hi: ', s1.startswith('Hi'))
print('Whether the string ends with dot: ', s1.endswith('.'))
```

Output

Whether the string starts with Hi: True
Whether the string ends with dot: False

(xiii) *string_object.count(sub_string,start,end)*
Returns the frequency of *sub_string* in the *string_object*.
Search begins at the start index and stops at the end-1 index.
start & end arguments are optional. Default value for *start* is 0 and *end* is last index.

Example

s = 'Hi, How are you? How do you do'
print('Count of "How" in the string: ',s.count('How'))
print('Count of "How" after 10th index: ', s.count('How',10))
print('Count of "How" between 10 & 15th index:',s.count('How',10,15))

Output

Count of "How" in the string: 2
Count of "How" after 10th index: 1
Count of "How" between 10 & 15th index: 0

(xiv) *string_object.find(sub_string)*
Returns the lowest index at which *sub_string* is present in the string_object. Returns -1 if not present.

Example

s = 'Hi, How are you? How do you do'
print('First occurrence of "How" in the string: ', s.find('How'))
print('First occurrence of "how" in the string: ', s.find('how'))

Output

First occurrence of "How" in the string: 4
First occurrence of "how" in the string: -1

(xv) *string_object.*format(*arg1,arg2, ..*)
string_object contains text along with placeholders specified as { }
arg1,arg2…are the arguments whose values are inserted into the placeholders.
Returns formatted string object.
Mapping of the arguments to placeholders can be done as follows:

   (a) **Positional formatting**: Arguments and placeholders are mapped by their positions.
   (b) **Index-based formatting**: The placeholder contains the index of the argument. The corresponding value of the argument is inserted at the placeholder.

(c) **Keyword formatting**: Argument names are called keywords. These keywords are specified inside the placeholder where the corresponding value
is replaced.

Example

```
name = input('Enter your name : ')
mail_id = input('Enter mail Id : ')
x = 'Dear { }, received your mail id { }'.format(name,mail_id)
print('Positional formatting :',x)
y = 'Dear {1},received your mail id {0}'.format(mail_id, name)
print('Index based formatting:',y)
z = 'Dear {nm},received your mail id {m}'.format(m=mail_id, nm=name)
print('Keyword formatting:',z)
```

Output

```
Enter your name: Arjun
Enter mail Id: arjun@gmail.com
Positional formatting : Dear Arjun, received your mail id arjun@gmail.com
Index based formatting: Dear Arjun, received your mail id arjun@gmail.com
Keyword formatting: Dear Arjun, received your mail id arjun@gmail.com
```

Numeric values can be formatted by specifying data type and precision. The value
is rounded to a specified number of decimal places.

Example

```
item = 'Apple'
price = 55.98
print('price of { } is {:.1f} '.format(item, price))
```

Output

```
price of Apple is 56.0
```

3.5   Iterating Through String Objects

As the string object is a sequence data type, elements can be iterated using a *for* loop.

Example

```
# Iterating through string
s = 'Python programming is simple'
print('Accessing each character : ')
for i in s:
```

```
    print(i, end=' ')
print('\Accessing each word : ')
for i in s.split():
    print(' ',i,)
```

Output

```
Accessing each character :
P y t h o n p r o g r a m m i n g i s s i m p l e
Accessing each word :
  Python
  programming
  is
  simple
```

3.6   Type Conversions

String objects can be converted to other data types.

```
new_data_type(String_object)
```

(i) String objects can be converted into list, tuple, set objects. Each character of the string is treated as an element in the new object.

Example

```
s1 = "Python"
print("String to List: ", list(s1))
print("String to Tuple: ", tuple(s1))
print("String to set: ", set(s1))
```

Output

```
String to List: ['P', 'y', 't', 'h', 'o', 'n']
String to Tuple: ('P', 'y', 't', 'h', 'o', 'n')
String to set: {'P', 'o', 'y', 'n', 't', 'h'}
```

(ii) String objects can be converted to a Boolean data type. Any non-empty string is **True** and an empty string is **False**.

Example

```
# String to boolean
s1 = 'Python'
s2 = ''
print('Non-empty string to boolean : ', bool(s1))
print('Empty string to boolean : ', bool(s2))
```

Output

> Non-empty string to boolean: True
> Empty string to boolean: False

(iii) String objects can be converted to int, float, or complex data types provided the characters are permitted in the corresponding data type.

Example

```
# string to numeric data types
s1 = "123"
i = int(s1)
print("Data type and value of i : ", type(i), i)
s2 = "3.14"
f = float(s2)
print("Data type and value of f : ", type(f), f)
s3 = "3-5j"
c = complex(s3)
print("Data type and value of c : ", type(c), c)
```

Output

> Data type and value of i: <class 'int'> 123
> Data type and value of f: <class 'float'> 3.14
> Data type and value of c: <class 'complex'> (3-5j)

Exercises

1. Write a function to count the number of words and lines in a multiline string.
2. Write a function to count the number of vowels in the string.
3. Write a function to count the number of articles in the string.
4. Write a function to check if a string is a palindrome.
5. Write a function that returns the string in reverse order.
6. Find the number of Gmail IDs in a multiline string.
7. Find the frequency of each vowel in the string.
8. Accept N names from the user and display the capitalized name.
9. Write a function to create a string by replacing digits with # character.
10. Write a function that returns the number of digits in the string.

Review Questions

(1) What is the output of the following code?

print('Python is {1} object-oriented {0}'.format('language','an'))

(a) Python is an object-oriented language
(b) Python is object-oriented language
(c) Python is language
(d) Error is generated

(2) What is the output of the following code?

print('Python is high-level {0} and object-oriented {0}'.
format('language','an'))

(a) Python is high-level and object-oriented language
(b) Python is high-level and an object-oriented language
(c) Python is high-level language and object-oriented language
(d) Error is generated

(3) What is the output of the following code?

print('{1} % {2} = {0}'.format(20%7, 20, 7))

(a) 20
(b) 7
(c) 20 % 7 = 6
(d) Error is generated

(4) What is the output of the following code?

'Language'.replace('g','G')

(a) LanGuage
(b) LanguaGe
(c) lanGuaGe
(d) LanGuaGe

(5) What is the output of the following code?

'Python is simple, Python is easy'.find('Python')

(a) 6
(b) 0
(c) 19
(d) 24

(6) What is the output of the following code?

print(len('Python is simple'))

(a) 3
(b) 14

(c) 16

(d) 17

(7) Extracting a substring from a given string is known as

(a) Indexing

(b) Slicing

(c) Splitting

(d) Formatting

(8) Which of the following methods returns a list of substrings of a given string?

(a) split()

(b) replace()

(c) strip()

(d) find()

(9) Which of the following is a string concatenation operator?

(a) **

(b) *

(c) +

(d) /

(10) Which of the following is false?

(a) String objects are mutable

(b) An empty string can be created using str()

(c) Multiline strings are created using triple quotes

(d) A backslash is used as an escape sequence for strings

Chapter 4
Built-in Data Structures: Lists

A data structure is a collection of organized data stored in computer memory and the operations permitted on the data. These operations help in writing efficient programs by providing fast access to the data. Python provides built-in data structures as well as constructs to create user-defined data structures. Python provides *class* construct to define user-defined data structures.

Python **built-in data structures** include lists, tuples, dictionaries, sets, and strings. These basic data structures cover most of the real-world data structures for data manipulations.

The basic built-in data structures differ in the following ways:

 (i) whether the object can be changed after creating it, called ***mutability***.
(ii) whether the elements of the object can be accessed based on their position in the object, called ***sequence*** object.

List

A list is a built-in data structure in Python. List object is a collection of ordered elements. Python provides a number of library functions and methods for manipulating the list object. The elements can be of the same or heterogeneous data types. The list object is **mutable**, *i.e.*, elements can be added, deleted, or modified. It is like a dynamically sized array in other programming languages like C++ and Java. List objects are widely used in data science.

List elements are enclosed in square brackets [   ] and separated by commas.

© The Author(s) 2024
A. L. Muddana and S. Vinayakam, *Python for Data Science*,
https://doi.org/10.1007/978-3-031-52473-8_4

Example

```
# List of integers separated by ,
even_num= [2,4,8,10]
print(even_num)
```

Output

```
[2, 4, 8, 10]
```

4.1   Create List Objects

(i) An **empty list** can be created in two ways:

(a) using pair of square brackets,
(b) using constructor of *list* class.

Example

```
# Create an empty list
l1 = []          # using pair of square brackets
print("Creating empty List using square brackets : ", l1)
l2 = list()     # using constructor of list class
print("Creating empty List using constructor : ", l2)
```

Output

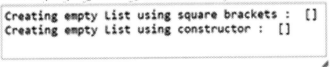

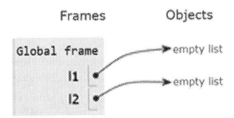

(ii) **Non-empty list** object: Non-empty list object is created by enclosing the elements in square brackets. Elements are separated by commas.

List elements can be of any data type like integer, float, Boolean, complex, strings, lists, tuples, dictionaries, sets, *etc.*, or a mix of different data types.

Example: List of complex numbers

```
complex_list = [ 10+2j, -7j, 20-5j]
print(complex_list)
```

Output

```
[(10+2j), (-0-7j), (20-5j)]
```

Example: List of strings

```
strings_list = [ "Ram", "Laxman", "Bharat"]
print(strings_list)
```

Output

```
['Ram', 'Laxman', 'Bharat']
```

List elements **need not be of the same data type**. It can be a combination of different data types.

Example

```
# List elements with different data types
mixed_list = [ 10, True, 10+4j, "Arjun", 3.14]
print(mixed_list)
```

Output

```
[10, True, (10+4j), 'Arjun', 3.14]
```

Built-in library function, *len( )* determines the number of elements or length of the list.

| **Syntax** |

```
len(list_object)
```

Example

```
# len() function
print("Length of strings list : ", len(strings_list))
print("Length of Complex numbers list : ", len(complex_list))
print("Length of Mixed list : ", len(mixed_list))
```

Output

```
Length of strings list : 3
Length of Complex numbers list : 3
Length of Mixed list : 5
```

4.2   Indexing and Slicing

(i) **Indexing:** A list is a sequence object, *i.e.*, elements in the list are ordered. Hence elements are accessed using index or subscript. Indices range from 0 to (length-1).

Example

```
odd_num =[1,3,5,7,9,11,13,15]
print("List elements are : ", odd_num)
```

Output: List elements are : [1, 3, 5, 7, 9, 11, 13, 15]

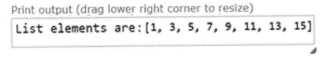

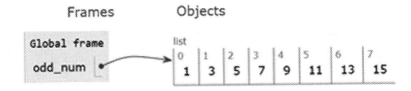

Example

```
# Accessing first element of the list
print("First element of the list : ",odd_num[0])
# Accessing third element of the list
print("Third element of the list : ",odd_num[2])
```

Output

```
First element of the list : 1
Third element of the list : 5
```

List elements can also be accessed from the back using a negative index. Index value –1 refers to the last element, –2 refers to the last but one element, and so on.

Example

```
# Accessing elements using negative index
print("Last element of the list: ", odd_num[-1])
print("Third element from back of the list: ", odd_num[-3])
```

Output

> Last element of the list: 15
> Third element from back of the list: 11

(ii) **Slicing** is extracting a sub-sequence of a list.

> | Syntax |

> *list_name[start:stop:step]*

start & step values are optional. The default *start* value is 0 and the default *step* value is 1. *stop* index not inclusive.

Example

```
# slicing
odd_num =[1,3,5,7,9,11,13,15]
print("List elements are : ", odd_num)
print("First five elements : ", odd_num[0:5])
# omitting start index assumes index 0
print("First five elements : ", odd_num[:5])
# omitting stop index assumes end of list
print("From 5th element onwards : ", odd_num[5:])
# using step size
print("Alternative elements up to fifth :", odd_num[0:5:2])
# using negative index
print("Last five elements : ", odd_num[-5:])
```

Output

> List elements are : [1, 3, 5, 7, 9, 11, 13, 15]
> First five elements : [1, 3, 5, 7, 9]
> First five elements : [1, 3, 5, 7, 9]
> From 5th element onwards : [11, 13, 15]
> Alternative elements up to fifth : [1, 5, 9]
> Last five elements : [7, 9, 11, 13, 15]

Note: *stop* index is not inclusive.

4.3 Nested Lists

An element of a list can be another list object called a nested List. It is also known as a list of lists.

Example

```
# List of Lists – nested lists
nested_list = [ [1,2,3], "Arjun", [True, False]]
print(nested_list)
print("Number of elements in the list : ", len(nested_list))
```

Output

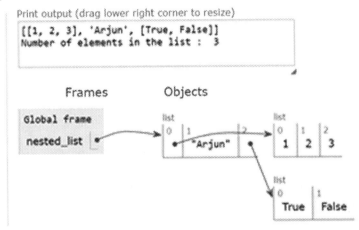

In the above example, the list has only three elements—the first element is a list of integers, the second is a string, and the third element is a list of Booleans.

Indexing and slicing of nested lists Indexing/slicing of nested list objects requires two subscripts—first subscript for the outer list and the second subscript for the inner list.

Example

```
# Indexing and slicing of nested list
print("Third element is : ", nested_list[2])
# Third member of first element
print("Third member of first element is : ", nested_list[0][2])
# last two elements of the list
print("Elements other than first are : ", nested_list[1:])
```

Output

```
Third element is: [True, False]
Third member of first element is : 3
Elements other than first are : ['Arjun', [True, False]]
```

4.4 Methods on List Objects

List objects are mutable, *i.e.*, elements can be inserted, deleted, or modified.

(i) **Insertion:** Element can be inserted at any position of a list. This operation can be done using different methods.

   (a) **append():** Insert an element as the last element of the list.

   | Syntax |

   > *list_object.***append***(element)*

   (b) **insert():** Insert an element at the specified index position.

   | Syntax |

   > *list_object.***insert***(index, element)*

   Example

```
# Appending element
colors = ["Red", "Green"]
print("List elements are : ", colors)
# append an element
colors.append("Blue")
print("List elements after appending : ", colors)
# Inserting as first element
colors.insert(0,"White")
print("List elements after inserting at the beginning, : ", colors)
```

   Output

```
List elements are : ['Red', 'Green']
List elements after appending : ['Red', 'Green', 'Blue']
List elements after inserting at the beginning, : ['White', 'Red',
'Green', 'Blue']
```

   Note: append() and insert() methods can add only one element to the list.

   (c) **extend()** method can append one or more elements to the list.

Syntax

*list_object.***extend**(*list_of_elements*)

Example

```
# Extend the list with one or more elements
pandavas = [" Dharmaraj", "Bheem", "Arjun"]
print("Pandavas before extending : ", pandavas)
pandavas.extend(["Nakul", "Sahadev"])
print("Pandavas after extending : ", pandavas)
```

Output

Print output (drag lower right corner to resize)

```
Pandavas before extending :  [' Dharmaraj', 'Bheem', 'Arjun']
Pandavas after extending :  [' Dharmaraj', 'Bheem', 'Arjun', 'Nakul', 'Sahadev']
```

Frames   Objects

Global frame
pandavas → list
               0   1   2   3   4
               " Dharmaraj" "Bheem" "Arjun" "Nakul" "Sahadev"

Difference between append() and extend()

append() method adds only one element at the end of the list. When the element to be appended is a list object, it is added as a single element at the end. Whereas for extend() method, elements of the list are added one by one at the end.

Example

```
# Append takes the list as single element and add at the end
pandavas = [" Dharmaraj", "Bheem", "Arjun"]
print("Pandavas before appending : ", pandavas)
pandavas.append(["Nakul", "Sahadev"])
print("Pandavas after appending : ", pandavas)
```

Output

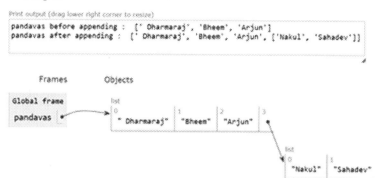

(d) **List concatenation:** A list can be appended to another list using the + operator called concatenation.

| Syntax |

list_object1 + list_object2

Returns a new list after appending each element of *list_object2* to *list_object1*.
list_object1 and list_object2 are not modified.

Example

```
# List concatenation
pandavas = [" Dharmaraj", "Bheem", "Arjun"]
l2 = ["Nakul", "Sahadev"]
print("Concatenation: " , pandavas + l2)
print("pandavas after concatenation: ", pandavas)
print("l2 after concatenation: ", l2)
```

Output

```
Concatenation: [' Dharmaraj', 'Bheem', 'Arjun', 'Nakul', 'Sahadev']
pandavas after concatenation: [' Dharmaraj', 'Bheem', 'Arjun']
l2 after concatenation: ['Nakul', 'Sahadev']
```

Note: Neither of the lists gets modified after concatenation. To update the list, use assignment.

Example

```
# To update the list, reassign after concatenation
pandavas = pandavas + l2
print("After concatenation and reassignment : ", pandavas)
```

Output

> After concatenation and reassignment : [' Dharmaraj', 'Bheem',
> 'Arjun', 'Nakul', 'Sahadev']

(ii) **Deletion:** Elements of a list object can be deleted. Python provides the following
methods to delete elements of a list object.

   (a) **remove()** method deletes the first occurrence of the specified element from
   the list. It returns the modified list.

   Syntax

   > *list_object.**remove**(element)*

   Example

   > # Delete a specified element from the list
   > even_num= [2,4,6,8,4,10]
   > print("List before deletion :", even_num)
   > even_num.remove(4)
   > print("List after deletion :", even_num)

   Output

   > List before deletion: [2, 4, 6, 8, 4, 10]
   > List after deletion: [2, 6, 8, 4, 10]

   If the specified element is not in the list, an error is generated.

   Example

   > # Error if specified element is not in the list
   > print("List elements are : ", even_num)
   > even_num.remove(20)

   Output

   > List elements are : [2, 6, 8, 4, 10]
   > _____
   > ValueError   Traceback (most recent call last)
   > < ipython-input-33-7f04c5e03f0d > in <module>()
   >   1 # Error if specified element is not in the list
   >   2 print("List elements are : ", even_num)
   > —-> 3 even_num.remove(20)
   >
   > ValueError: list.remove(x): x not in list

(b) **pop()** method removes the element at the specified index. The deleted element is returned by the method.

Syntax

*list_object.***pop**(*index)*

index is optional. If not specified, last element is deleted.

Example

```
even_num= [2,4,6,8,4,10]
print(' Deleted element : ', even_num.pop() )
print("List elements after popping last element : ", even_num)
even_num.pop(2)
print("List elements after popping element at index 2 : ", even_num)
```

Output

```
Deleted element: 10
List elements after popping last element : [2, 4, 6, 8, 4]
List elements after popping element at index 2 : [2, 4, 8, 4]
```

(c) **del:** deletes the element at the specified index. This is same as pop() with index as argument but does not return the deleted element.

Syntax

del *list_object*[*index*]

Example

```
even_num = [2,4,6,8,10,12]
print("List elements before deletion : ", even_num)
del even_num[3]
print("After deletion at 3rd index using del : ", even_num)
even_num.pop(3)
print("After deletion at 3rd index using pop : ", even_num)
```

Output

```
List elements before deletion : [2, 4, 6, 8, 10, 12]
After deletion at 3rd index using del : [2, 4, 6, 10, 12]
After deletion at 3rd index using pop : [2, 4, 6, 12]
```

del can also be used to delete a sub-sequence of a list.

Syntax

> **del** *list_object[start:stop]*

stop index is not inclusive

Example

> even_num = [2,4,6,8,10,12]
> print("List elements before deletion : ", even_num)
> del even_num[1:3]   # stop index not included
> print("List elements after deletion : ", even_num)

Output

Print output (drag lower right corner to resize)

```
List elements before deletion :   [2, 4, 6, 8, 10, 12]
List elements after deletion :   [2, 8, 10, 12]
```

(d) **clear()** method removes all the elements of the list, but the list object exists.

Syntax

> *list_object.***clear()**

Example

> # Delete all elements in the list
> rating = [4,3,5,2,1,4,5,1,2,5]
> print("List elements are : ", rating)
> rating.clear()
> print("List after clear method :", rating)

Output

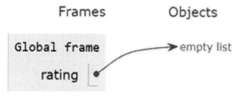

(iii) **Modifying list object:** Value of an element, at the specified index, can be modified by reassigning a new value.

| Syntax |

   list_object[index]=new_value

Example

   even_num = [2,4,6,8,10,12]
   print("List elements before modifying : ", even_num)
   even_num[4] = 20
   print("List after modifying element at 4th index : ", even_num)

Output

   List elements before modifying : [2, 4, 6, 8, 10, 12]
   List after modifying element at 4th index : [2, 4, 6, 8, 20, 12]

(iv) **count()** method returns the number of times an element occurs in the list. Returns zero if the element is not in the list.

| Syntax |

   *list_object.***count**(*element*)

Example

   # Frequency of element in the list
   rating = [4,3,5,2,1,4,5,1,2,5]
   print("Frequency of 5 : ", rating.count(5))
   print("Frequency of 1 : ", rating.count(1))
   print("Frequency of 10 : ", rating.count(10))

Output

> Frequency of 5 : 3
> Frequency of 1 : 2
> Frequency of 10 : 0

(v) **sort()** method orders the list elements in either ascending or descending order.

| Syntax |

> *list_object.***sort**(*reverse*)

Default value of the *reverse* parameter is **False**, which sorts the elements in ascending order. When *reverse* is set to **True**, elements will be sorted in descending order.
list_object gets modified in the sorted order.

Example

```
# Sorting list elements
num = [10,-4,0,5,100,-39]
print("List before sorting :", num)
num.sort()
print("List after sorting in ascending order: ", num)
num.sort(reverse=True)
print("List after sorting in descending order: ", num)
```

Output

> List before sorting : [10, -4, 0, 5, 100, -39]
> List after sorting in ascending order: [-39, -4, 0, 5, 10, 100]
> List after sorting in descending order: [100, 10, 5, 0, -4, -39]

(vi) **reverse()** method reverses the order of list elements.

| Syntax |

> *list_object.***reverse**()

list_object gets modified with elements in the reverse order.

Example

```
# Reverse list elements
num = [10,-4,0,5,100,-39]
print("List elements are :", num)
num.reverse()
print("List elements after reverse() : ", num)
```

Output

> List elements are : [10, -4, 0, 5, 100, -39]
> List elements after reverse() : [-39, 100, 5, 0, -4, 10]

(vii) **copy()** method creates a copy of the list object that can then be assigned to a new list object.

| Syntax |

*list_object.***copy()**

Example

```
# copy method
num = [10,-4,0,5,100,-39]
print("Elements of num : ", num)
num_copy = num.copy()
print("Elements of num_copy : ", num_copy)
```

Output

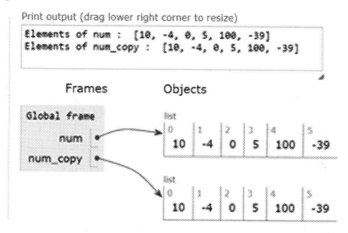

The copy() operation is a **shallow copy**, *i.e.*, if the original list is modified, the copy will not be affected and *vice versa*.

Example

```
# Shalow copy
num = [10,-4,0,5,100,-39]
num_copy = num.copy()
num.append(25)
num_copy.append(500)
print("num list after appending 25 to num : ", num)
print("num_copy after appending 500 to num_copy: ", num_copy)
```

Output

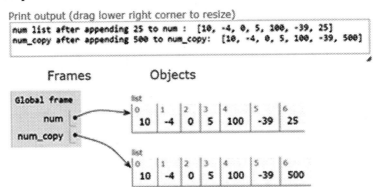

Print output (drag lower right corner to resize)

```
num list after appending 25 to num :  [10, -4, 0, 5, 100, -39, 25]
num_copy after appending 500 to num_copy:  [10, -4, 0, 5, 100, -39, 500]
```

4.5   Functions on List Objects

(i) Python provides the following summary statistical functions on list objects.

Syntax

    sum(*list_object*)   returns *sum* of list elements
    max(list_object)   returns *maximum* element of the list
    min(*list_object*)   returns *minimum* element of the list

Example

```
l1 = [10,0,-5,37,-20]
print("List elements : ", l1)
print("Sum of list element : ", sum(l1))
print("Maximum of list elements : ", max(l1))
print("Minimum of list elements : ", min(l1))
```

Output

```
List elements : [10, 0, -5, 37, -20]
Sum of list element : 22
Maximum of list elements : 37
Minimum of list elements : -20
```

(ii) **Enumerations:** The enumeration operation associates each element of the iterable object with an integer value. The initial value of the integer can be specified as an argument.

Syntax

enumerate(*iterable_object, start=0*)

start: Initial integer value. Default value is 0
Returns an enumerated object which can be used in *for* *loop* or convert into a list, tuple, dictionary, set.

Example: Assign integer value to days of the week-days object.
```
week_days=['Monday','Tuesday','Wednesday','Thursday','Friday']
enum_week_days = enumerate(week_days,1)
print('Data type of enumerate object: ', type(enum_week_days))
# following statement use enumerate object in for loop
for ele in enum_week_days :
  print(ele, end=' ')
```

Output

```
Data type of enumerate object: <class 'enumerate'>
(1, 'Monday') (2, 'Tuesday') (3, 'Wednesday') (4, 'Thursday')
(5,'Friday')
```

Example: Convert enumerate object to list

```
spring = ['March','April','May']
spring_enum = enumerate(spring, start=3)
# following statement converts enumerate object to list
print( list(spring_enum))
```

Output

```
[(3, 'March'), (4, 'April'), (5, 'May')]
```

(iii) **zip():** This function associates corresponding values of the arguments to create a single iterable zip object.

Syntax

zip(*iterable_objects*)

iterable_objects: The number of *iterable_objects* can be two or more.
Returns a zip object where each element is a tuple of corresponding elements of the *iterable_objects*. It can then be converted to a list, tuple, set, dictionary, *etc.*

Example

> performance = ['Outstanding','Good','Average', 'Poor']
> grades = ['O','A','B','F']
> perf_zip = zip(performance, grades)
> print('Data type of perf_zip : ', type(perf_zip))
> print(list(perf_zip))

Output

> Data type of perf_zip : <class 'zip'>
> [('Outstanding', 'O'), ('Good', 'A'), ('Average', 'B'), ('Poor', 'F')]

(iv) **map()** applies the specified function on each element of the iterable object.

> **Syntax**

> **map**(*function, iterable_object*)

Returns map object, which is iterable. It can then be converted to a list.

Example

> lst = [2,4,6,8]
> map_lst = map(lambda x : x**3, lst)
> print('Original object : ', lst)
> print('Mapped object : ', list(map_lst))

Output

> Original object : [2, 4, 6, 8]
> Mapped object : [8, 64, 216, 512]

(v) **reduce()** function is to reduce the iterable object elements into a single value. First, the specified function is applied on the first two elements that return a result. Then the function is repeated on the result of the previous step and the next element in the sequence. This is repeated until the last element of the list. The final result is returned.

> **Syntax**

> **reduce**(*function, iterable_object*)

reduce() function is available in the ***functools*** module of Python. This module has to be imported before using the function.

Example: Find the product of elements of the list object.

```
from functools import reduce
lst = [1,2,3,4,5]
red_lst = reduce(lambda x, y : x*y , lst)
print(red_lst)
```

Output

    120

(vi) **any() & all()**

any() function returns True if any of the elements in the list object is True. Returns False otherwise.

all() function returns True if every element in the list object is True. Returns False otherwise

> **Syntax**

    any(*list_object*)
    all(*list_object*)

Note: Any non-zero numeric value is True and zero is False. A non-empty object is True and an empty object is False.

Example

```
lst1 = [ 3.14, '', 0]
# if any of list element is True- 3.14 is True
print(any(lst1))
lst2 = [3.14, 'Python', 0]
# if all of the list element are True- 0 is False
print(all(lst2))
```

Output

    True
    False

4.6   List Objects in *for* Loops

Each element of a list object can be accessed in sequence, using *for* loops.

Example

```
l1 = [10,0,-5,37,-20]
# Accessing list elements using for loop
print("List elements are :", end=' ')
for element in l1 :
    print(element, end=' ')
```

Output

List elements are : 10 0 -5 37 -20

4.7 List Comprehensions

List comprehensions provide a simple, compact, and fast way of generating new list objects, using an existing iterable object like a list, string, *etc.* It uses *for* loops inside square brackets to generate the elements.

Example 1:

```
# List comprehension : Generating odd numbers from 10 to 20
odds = [element for element in range(10, 20) if element%2==1]
print("Data type of odds: ", type(odds))
print("List elements are : ",odds)
```

Output

Data type of odds: <class 'list'>
List elements are: [11, 13, 15, 17, 19]

Example 2: Generating list using nested loops

```
# List comprehension using nested loops
l1 = [ i + j for i in range(1,5) for j in [10,20,30]]
print("List elements: ", l1)
```

Output

List elements: [11, 21, 31, 12, 22, 32, 13, 23, 33, 14, 24, 34]

Example 3: Generating nested lists

```
# List comprehensions to generate nested lists
nest_lst = [ [i for i in range(1,j+1)] for j in range(1,6) ]
print("Nested list using list comprehension: \n ",nest_lst)
```

Output

Nested list using list comprehension:
[[1], [1, 2], [1, 2, 3], [1, 2, 3, 4], [1, 2, 3, 4, 5]]

Exercises

1. Write a user-defined function to display the sum of elements of a list using *for* loop.
2. Display the square and cube of integers from 1 to 10 using list comprehension.
3. Display odd elements of a given list using list comprehension.
4. Write a function to check if the number is prime. Create a list of prime numbers up to 50 using the prime function and list comprehension.
5. Write a user-defined function to display the number of complex numbers in a list.
6. Given a list of Boolean values, find the number of True and number of False values.
7. Given a list of student grades, count the number of students in each grade.
8. Given a list of integers, remove the negative values.
9. Given a list of real values, round each value to one decimal place, using list comprehensions.
10. Given the marks of students in the class, find the class average. Use reduce() function.

Review Questions

(1) Which of the following is not true about the lists?

(a) mutable
(b) sequence object
(c) element values can be modified
(d) elements cannot be accessed using the index

(2) Which of the following functions is not for adding elements to lists?

(a) add( )
(b) extend( )
(c) append( )
(d) insert( )

(3) What is the output of the following code?

```
data = [10,9,8,7,6,5]
del data[:4]
print(data)
```

(a) [10,9,8,7,6,5]
(b) [10,9,8,7]
(c) [5]
(d) [6,5]

(4) What is the output of the following code?

```
data =['Blue','Red','Green','Gray']
print(max(data))
```

(a) Blue
(b) Red
(c) Gray
(d) Error reported

(5) What is the output of the following code?

```
data =[1,3,[1,2],7]
print(data[2])
```

(a) 3
(b) 1,2
(c) [1,2]
(d) 2

(6) What is the output of the following code?

```
data =[1,3,7]
x = [10,20]
print( data+x )
```

(a) [1, 3, 7, 10, 20]
(b) [1, 3, 7, [10, 20]]
(c) [1, 3, 7]
(d) [10, 20]

(7) Code to extract last element of the following list is

```
data =[1,3,[1,2],7]
```

(a) data[-1]
(b) data[-0]
(c) data[0]
(d) None of these

(8) What is the output of the following code?

```
data = [1, 7, -5, 0, 25, 6]
data.reverse()
print(data)
```

   (a) [6, 25, 0, -5, 7, 1]
   (b) [-5, 0, 1, 6,7, 25]
   (c) [7, 1, 0, -5, 6, 25]
   (d) [25, 7, 6, 1, 0, -5]

(9) What is the output of the following code?

```
data = list(range(1,10,3))
print(data[-2])
```

   (a) 8
   (b) 9
   (c) 7
   (d) 4

(10) What is the output of the following code?

```
data=[3,2,5,6]
data.insert(2,8)
print(data)
```

   (a) [3, 2, 5,8, 6]
   (b) [3, 2, 8, 5, 6]
   (c) [3 ,8 ,2 ,5 ,6]
   (d) [3, 2, 5, 6, 8]

Chapter 5
Built-in Data Structure: Tuple

Tuple is one of the built-in data structures in Python. A tuple object is an ordered sequence of elements of the same or heterogeneous data types. As the elements are ordered, elements are accessed using the index, which is similar to a list. But tuple object is immutable, i.e., once the object is created, it cannot be changed by addition, deletion, or modification operations.

Tuple elements are enclosed in a pair of parentheses and separated by commas.

Comparing a Tuple and a List

Tuple	List
Tuple is a sequence type object, i.e., elements are accessed using the index	List is also a sequence type object where elements are accessed using the index
Elements can be of the same or heterogeneous data types. Tuples usually contain elements of heterogeneous data types	Elements can be of the same or heterogeneous data types. Lists usually contain elements of homogeneous data types
Elements are enclosed in pair of parentheses ( )	Elements are enclosed in pair of square brackets [ ]
Tuple objects are immutable, i.e., once created, the object cannot be modified	List objects are mutable, i.e., elements can be added, deleted, or modified
Accessing elements is faster due to its static nature	Accessing elements is comparatively slow
Tuples have limited built-in functions as insertion, deletion, or modifications are not possible	Lists have many built-in functions to perform various operations

© The Author(s) 2024
A. L. Muddana and S. Vinayakam, *Python for Data Science*,
https://doi.org/10.1007/978-3-031-52473-8_5

5.1   Create Tuple Objects

(i) **Empty tuple** can be created in two ways:

    (a) Using empty pair of parentheses.
    (b) By creating an object of the tuple class.

Example

```
# Create empty tuple using pair of parenthesis
t1 = ()
print("Data type of t1 : ",type(t1))
print("Elements of t1 : ", t1)
# Create empty tuple using tuple class constructor
t2= tuple()
print("Data type of t2 : ",type(t2))
print("Elements of t2: ", t2)
```

Output

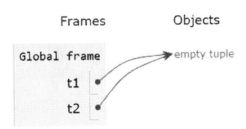

```
Print output (drag lower right corner to resize)
Data type of t1 :   <class 'tuple'>
Elements of t1 :   ()
Data type of t2 :   <class 'tuple'>
```

```
        Frames                  Objects

    Global frame          empty tuple
            t1
            t2
```

(ii) **Create a non-empty tuple object** Tuple objects can have multiple elements
of the same or different data types enclosed in parentheses and separated by
commas. Duplicate elements are permitted.

Example

```
# Create tuple of complex numbers
tuple_complex = ( 1+2j, 3-8j, 2.5+6j)
print("Elements are : ",tuple_complex)
```

Output

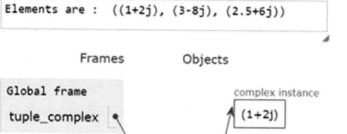

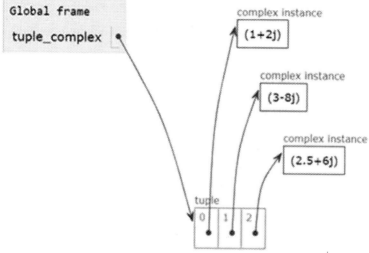

Tuple elements can be of heterogeneous data types.

Example

```
# Create tuple of heterogeneous data types
tuple_mixed = (10, 3.14, True, 10-4j, "Arjun")
print("Tuple elements are : ", tuple_mixed)
```

Output

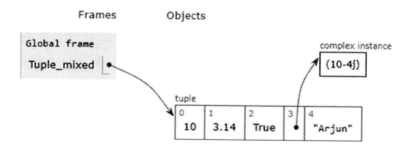

In the above example, the tuple object has constants, a Boolean value, a complex number, and a string.

(a) When a variable is assigned multiple values separated by commas, the variable is treated as a tuple.

Example

    t1 = 8.5, "A Grade"
    print("Data type : ", type(t1))
    print("Elements are : ", t1)

Output

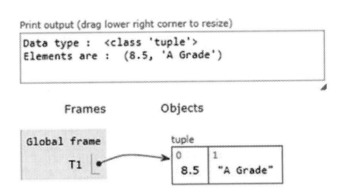

(b) When a variable is assigned a single value followed by a comma, it is also treated as a tuple.

Example

    t= 20,
    print("Data type : ", type(T2))
    print("Elements are : ", T2)

Output

Print output (drag lower right corner to resize)

    Data type :   <class 'tuple'>
    Elements are :   (20,)

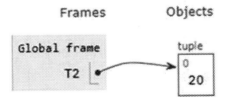

Note: Tuple objects are immutable: Once the object is created it cannot be changed by adding, deleting, or modifying the elements.

Example

```
tuple_mixed = (10, 3.14, True, 10-4j, "Arjun")
print("Elements are : ", tuple_mixed)
tuple_mixed[2] = 100
```

Output

```
Elements are : (10, 3.14, True, (10-4j), 'Arjun')
```

```
TypeError       Traceback (most recent call last)
<ipython-input-1-679ecf3267ca> in <module>()
    1 tuple_mixed = (10, 3.14, True, 10-4j, "Arjun")
    2 print("Elements are : ", tuple_mixed)
—-> 3 tuple_mixed[2] = 100

TypeError: 'tuple' object does not support item assignment
```

5.2   Indexing and Slicing

A tuple is a sequence data type, i.e., elements are ordered. Hence, the elements can be accessed using index/subscript. Indexing and slicing of tuple objects are similar to that of lists objects. The index ranges from 0 to length-1.

Example

```
# Indexing & Slicing
tuple_mixed = (10, 3.14, True, 10-4j, "Arjun")
print("Elements are : ", tuple_mixed)
print("First element is : ", tuple_mixed[0])
print("Second element from last is : ", tuple_mixed[-2])
print("Last three elements are : ", tuple_mixed[-3:])
print("Second to fourth elements are : ", tuple_mixed[1:4])
```

Output

```
Elements are : (10, 3.14, True, (10-4j), 'Arjun')
First element is : 10
Second element from last is : (10-4j)
Last three elements are : (True, (10-4j), 'Arjun')
Second to fourth elements are : (3.14, True, (10-4j))
```

5.3   Nested Tuples

Elements of a tuple object can be another tuple object, known as a nested tuple. Indexing and slicing of nested tuple objects require two indices, the first index for the outer tuple object and the second index for the inner tuple object.

Example

```
# Nested tuple
tuple_nested = (1,(8.5, "Grade A"), 2, (6,4, "Grade B"))
print("Elements are : ", tuple_nested)
# Indexing & Slicing
print("Last element is : ", tuple_nested[-1])
print("Second element first value is : ", tuple_nested[1][0])
```

Output

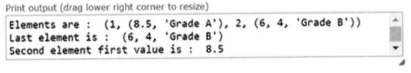

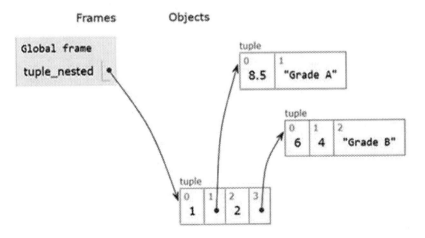

5.4   Operations on Tuples

Following operations can be applied on tuple objects.

(i) **Concatenation:** Binary operator +, creates a new tuple by concatenating the elements of the right operand tuple to the elements of the left operand tuple. Neither of the operand tuples gets modified (tuples are immutable).

Example

    t1 = (5,10,15,20,25)
    t2 = (50,55)
    t3 = t1+t2
    print('Concatenation of tuples : ', t3)

Output

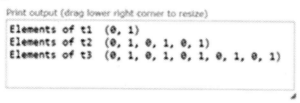

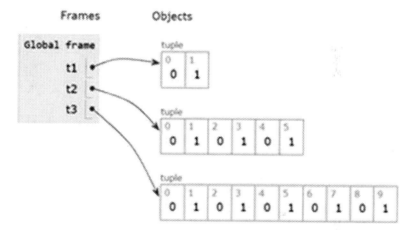

(ii) **Multiplication**: Binary operator, *, returns a new tuple by repeating the operand tuple elements by specified number of times. Number of repetitions can be specified either as left or as right operand to *.

Example

    # Create tuples using repetitions
    t1 = (0,1)
    t2 = t1 * 3
    t3 = 5 * t1
    print("Elements of t1 ", t1)
    print("Elements of t2 ", t2)
    print("Elements of t3 ", t3)

Output

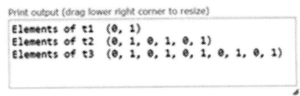

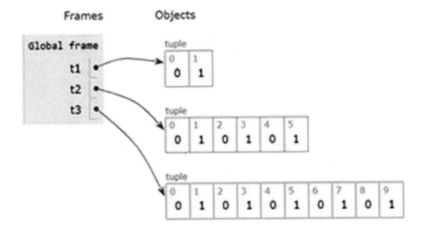

(iii) **Membership operator**: The *in* operator checks if an element is a member of the tuple. It returns a Boolean value.

Example

pandavas = ('Dharmaraj', 'Bheem', 'Arjun', 'Nakul', 'Sahadev')
print('Nakul' in pandavas)
print('Karna' in pandavas)

Output

True
False

5.5   Functions on Tuples

Tuple objects being immutable, limited number of library functions are provided for the commonly used operations.

(i) **len**(*tuple_object*)
returns a number of elements in the *tuple_object*.

(ii) **sum**(*tuple_object*)

    returns sum of elements of the *tuple_object*. It requires the tuple elements to be of numeric data types (int, float, complex).

(iii) **min**(*tuple_object*)

    returns the minimum element of the *tuple_object*. Tuple elements must be integer, float, string data types.

(iv) **max**(*tuple_object*)

    returns maximum elements of the *tuple_object*. Tuple elements must be integer, float, string data types.

Example

```
# Functions on Tuples
tuple_int = (10, 0,-5,29,56,-100)
tuple_num = (3.14, 0, 50, -10.5)
tuple_complex = ( 1+2j, 3-8j, 2.5+6j)
tuple_strings = ("Bheem", "Nakul", "Arjun")
print("Length of tuple_strings : ", len(tuple_strings))
print("Minimum element in tuple_int : ", min(tuple_int))
print("Maximum element in tuple_num : ", max(tuple_num))
print("Maximum element in tuple_strings:", max(tuple_strings))
print("Sum of tuple_num elements : ", sum(tuple_num))
print("Sum of tuple_complex elements :", sum(tuple_complex))
```

Output

```
Length of tuple_strings : 3
Minimum element in tuple_int : -100
Maximum element in tuple_num : 50
Maximum element in tuple_strings: Nakul
Sum of tuple_num elements : 42.64
Sum of tuple_complex elements : (6.5+0j)
```

(v) **Sorting**: Elements of a tuple object can be sorted in ascending or descending order.

| **Syntax** |

sorted(*tuple_object, reverse*)

reverse argument value can be True or False. The default value is False. If set to True, the elements are sorted in descending order.

tuple_object passed as an argument does not get modified. The function returns the sorted tuple which can then be assigned to another tuple object.

Example

tuple_num = (3.14, 0, 50, -10.5)
print("Tuple elements : ", tuple_num)
print("Elements in sorted order : ", sorted(tuple_num))
print("Elements in descending sorted order : ",
sorted(tuple_num, reverse=True))
# Original list does not change
print("Tuple elements after sorting : ", tuple_num)

Output

To have an argument *tuple_object* in sorted order, assign it to the same variable after applying the function.

Example

tuple_num = sorted(tuple_num)
print("Elements after sorting and reassigning : ", tuple_num)

Output

Elements after sorting and reassigning : [-10.5, 0, 3.14, 50]

Note: Comparison operations are not supported for complex and Boolean values. Hence, tuple objects having complex or Boolean values cannot be sorted.

(vi) **Reversing order of tuple elements:** The order of elements can be reversed using the **reversed()** function.

Syntax

reversed(*tuple_object*)

Returns a reversed object, which can then be converted to a tuple. *tuple_object* does not get modified (*tuples* are immutable).

Example

```
# Reverse tuple elements
tuple_int = (10, 0,-5,29,56,-100)
print("Tuple elements : ", tuple_int)
tuple_reverse = reversed(tuple_int)
print("After reversed() function : ", tuple_reverse)
print("convert reversed object to tuple: ", tuple(tuple_reverse))
# original tuple does not change
print("Elements of original tuple -> tuple_int :", tuple_int)
```

Output

```
Tuple elements : (10, 0, -5, 29, 56, -100)
After reversed() function : <reversed object at 0x7f0373554690>
convert reversed object to tuple : (-100, 56, 29, -5, 0, 10)
Elements of original tuple -> tuple_int : (10, 0, -5, 29, 56, -100)
```

(vii) **any()**

Syntax

any(*tuple_object*)

The function returns true if any one of its elements is true. It is false otherwise. Any non-empty object is true. Empty objects like the empty string, 0 numeric value are false.

Example

```
t1 = (10, 0, False, "Hello")
t2 = (0, False, "")
print("Any one of the element of t1 is True : ", any(t1))
print("Any one of the element of t2 is True : ", any(t2))
```

Output

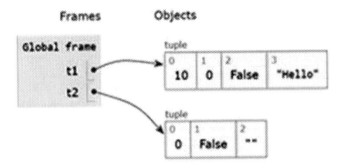

(viii) **all()**

Syntax

all(*tuple_object*)

Returns true if all the tuple elements are true. It is false otherwise.

Example

t1 = (10, 3-2j, True, "Hello")
t2 = (0, 3-2j, True, "Hello") # First element 0 is False
print("Whether all the elements of t1 are True : ", all(t1))
print("Whether all the elements of t2 are True : ", all(t2))

Output

Whether all the elements of t1 are True : True
Whether all the elements of t2 are True : False

5.6   Methods on Tuple Objects

Tuple being an immutable object, very few methods are applicable.

(i) **count()**

tuple_object.**count**(*element*)

Returns the number of times the *element* occurred in the *tuple_object*. Return zero if the element is not in the tuple.

Example

rating = (4,3,5,2,1,4,5,1,2,5)
print("Frequency of 5 rating : ", rating.count(5))
print("Frequency of 1 rating : ", rating.count(1))
print("Frequency of 0 rating : ", rating.count(0))

Output

Frequency of 5 rating : 3
Frequency of 1 rating : 2
Frequency of 0 rating : 0

(ii) **index()**: Finds the index of the first occurrence of the specified element in the given range of indices of a tuple object.

tuple_object.**index**(*element, start, end*)

element: The element to be searched for
start: Index from where to start the search. It is optional and the default value is 0.
end: Index till where the search is to be performed. *end* value not inclusive. It is optional and the default value is the length of the tuple. If *end* is specified, *start* should also be specified.
Returns index of the first occurrence of the element. If not found, it throws an error.

Example

rating = (4,3,5,2,1,4,5,1,2,5)
print("First occurrence of 5 : ", rating.index(5))
print("First occurrence of 4 from index 2 : ", rating.index(4,2))
print("First occurrence of 2 between the index 0 and 3 : ", rating.index(2, 0,3))

Output

First occurrence of 5 : 2
First occurrence of 4 from index 2 : 5

ValueError   Traceback (most recent call last)
<ipython-input-17-92452159b955> in <module> ()
     2 print("First occurrence of 5 : ", rating.index(5))
     3 print("First occurrence of 4 from index 2 : ",
rating.index(4,2))
—-> 4 print("First occurrence of 2 between the index 0 and 3 : ",
rating.index(2, 0,3))

ValueError: tuple.index(x): x not in tuple

5.7   Type Conversions

Iterable objects like lists, strings, can be converted into tuple objects using tuple()
function.

(i) **List to Tuple**: Each element of the list becomes an element of the tuple in the
same order.

    | **Syntax** |

        tuple(*list_object*)

Example

# List to Tuple
rating_list = [4,3,5,2,1,4,5,1,2,5]
rating_tuple = tuple(rating_list)
print("Object Data types are : ", type(rating_list),
type(rating_tuple))
print(rating_tuple)

Output

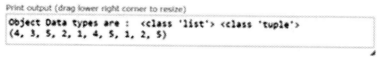

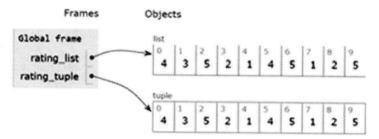

(ii) **Tuple to List**: Each element of the tuple becomes an element of the list in the same order.

| Syntax |

list(*tuple_object*)

Example

```
# Tuple to List
grades_tuple = (9.4, 6.7, 8, 5.6, 7.2)
grades_list = list(grades_tuple)
print("Object Data types are : ", type(grades_tuple),
type(grades_list))
print("Elements of grades_list : ", grades_list)
```

Output

Object Data types are : <class 'tuple'> <class 'list'>
Elements of grades_list : [9.4, 6.7, 8, 5.6, 7.2]

(iii) **String to Tuple**: Each character of the string becomes an element of the tuple in the same sequence.

| Syntax |

tuple(*string_object*)

Example

```
# String to tuple
s1 = "Hello World"
t1 = tuple(s1)
print("Object Data types are : ", type(s1), type(t1))
print("Elements of Tuple : ", t1)
```

Output

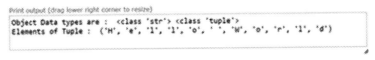

(iv) **Tuple to String**: Elements of the tuple can be concatenated using join() method to form a string.

| Syntax |

"".join(*tuple_object*)

Example

```
# Tuple to String
t1 = ( 'P', 'y', 't', 'h', 'o', 'n')
t2= ( "Hello", "Arjun", "Awesome!")
s1 = "".join(t1) # elements of the tuple are joined without space
s2= " ".join(t2) # elements of the tuple are joined with space
print("Tuple t1 converted to string : ",s1)
print("Tuple t2 converted to string : ",s2)
```

Output

```
Tuple t1 converted to string : Python
Tuple t2 converted to string : Hello Arjun Awesome!
```

(v) **Tuple to Boolean**

| Syntax |

bool(*tuple_object*)

The function returns *true* if the *tuple_object* is non-empty and *false* otherwise.

Example

```
# Tuple into boolean
t1 = ()
t2= (10,3.14,0)
# Empty object is False
b1 = bool(t1)
print("Value of b1 : ",b1)
# Non-empty object is True
b2 = bool(t2)
print("Value of b2 : ",b2)
```

Output

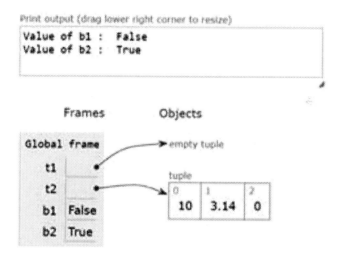

Note: Tuple objects can also be converted into other objects like sets that will be discussed in subsequent chapters.

5.8   Iterating Tuple Objects

Each element of the tuple object can be accessed in *for* loops using *in* operator.

Example

```
# Using in operator
t1 = (10, 3-2j, True, "Hello")
for element in t1:
    print(type(element))
```

Output

<class 'int'>
<class 'complex'>
<class 'bool'>
<class 'str'>

5.9   Unpacking

Tuple elements can be assigned to individual variables by unpacking the tuple object. This is done by assigning tuple objects to multiple variables. Number of variables on the left-hand side of the assignment operator should be same as the number of elements in the tuple.

Example

```
# unpacking tuple elements
t1= (8.5, 'A')
cgp, grade = t1
print("CGP : ", cgp)
print("Grade : ", grade)
```

Output

```
CGP : 8.5
Grade : A
```

Example

```
t1= (8.5, 'A', 'Arjun')
cgp, grade = t1
print("CGP : ", cgp)
print("Grade : ", grade)
```

Output

```
ValueError      Traceback (most recent call last)
<ipython-input-3-01a4010845a9> in <module>()
     1 t1= (8.5, 'A', 'Arjun')
—-> 2 cgp, grade = t1
     3 print("CGP : ", cgp)
     4 print("Grade : ", grade)
```

ValueError: too many values to unpack (expected 2)

Note: In the above example the tuple object has three elements but only two variables are provided in unpacking.

5.10 Enumerations

Enumeration operation on tuple objects is the same as on the list objects. It creates a tuple of (*element, index*) pairs for each element of the tuple. Index starts from *start_index* and is incremented for each subsequent element. It returns an enumerated object which can then be converted to a tuple using type conversions.

Syntax

> **enumerate**(*tuple_object, start_index*)

start_index is optional and default value is 0.

Example

```
# Enumerations
days=('Tuesday', 'Wednesday', 'Thursday', 'Friday', 'Saturday')
t = enumerate(days,2)
print("Data type of t : ", type(t))
print("After Converting Enumerated to tuple : \n", tuple(t))
```

Output

```
Data type of t : < class 'enumerate' >
After Converting Enumerated to tuple :
((2, 'Tuesday'), (3, 'Wednesday'), (4, 'Thursday'), (5, 'Friday'), (6,
'Saturday'))
```

5.11 Zipping

Syntax

> **zip**(*tuple_object1, tuple_object2*)

Creates a new tuple by pairing the corresponding elements of the argument tuple objects. It returns a zip object which can then be converted to a tuple.

Example

```
# Zip two tuples
cgp=(5,6,7,8,9)
grades=('D', 'C', 'B', 'A', 'O')
result= zip(cgp,grades)
print("Data type of Result : ", type(result))
print("After converting Zip object to tuple : ",tuple(result))
```

Output

Print output (drag lower right corner to resize)

Data type of Result : <class 'zip'>
After converting Zip object to tuple :   ((5, 'D'), (6, 'C'), (7, 'B'), (8, 'A'), (9, 'D'))

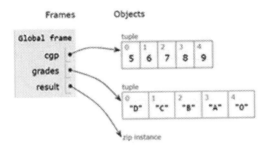

Exercises

1. Create a tuple object by taking input from the user.
2. Accept the name of the weekday from the user and display the number of the day in the week. Exit when an invalid day name is given as input. Assume 0 for Sunday.
3. Given two tuple objects, create a new tuple object by adding the corresponding values of the input tuples.
4. Generate a new tuple by removing duplicate elements of the input tuple.
5. Take input containing CGP of students, separated by space. Write a user-defined function to count the number of students who got more than 7 CGP. Use tuple object.
6. Take input containing grades of students, separated by space. Display count of each grade.
7. Take four subject marks of each of N students and create a tuple containing the total marks of each student.
8. Given a tuple object, check if it is a nested tuple.
9. Write a function to check if all the elements of the input tuple are of the same data type.
10. Display the data types of the elements of a tuple.

Review Questions

(1) Which of the following is not a tuple?

(a) (3.14,)
(b) (5, 3.14)
(c) (10, [1,2])
(d) 3.14

(2) What is the output of the following code?

```
t = (4,5,6,7,8)
print(t[2:-1])
```

(a) (6, 7)
(b) (4, 5)
(c) (7, 8)
(d) Generates error

(3) What is the output of the following code?

```
t = (3, 'Python', (1,2,4), True)
print(len(t))
```

(a) 7
(b) 4
(c) 5
(d) Generates error

(4) What is the output of the following code?

```
t = (3, 'Python', (1,2,4), True)
print(t[1][-1])
```

(a) True
(b) n
(c) (1,2,4)
(d) 4

(5) What is the output of the following code?

```
print(list(tuple('Hello')))
```

(a) ('H', 'e', 'l', 'l', 'o')
(b) ['H', 'e', 'l', 'l', 'o']
(c) ['Hello']
(d) ('Hello')

(6) What is the output of the following code?

```
t = tuple('Welcome Python')
print(t.count('o'))
```

(a) 2
(b) 0
(c) 1
(d) Generates error

(7) What is the output of the following code?

```
sorted(tuple('python'))
```

(a) ['hnopty']
(b) ('h', 'n', 'o', 'p', 't', 'y')
(c) ['hnopty']
(d) ['h', 'n', 'o', 'p', 't', 'y']

(8) What is the output of the following code?

```
a, b = (2, (5,10))
print(b * a)
```

(a) (5, 10, 5, 10)
(b) 30
(c) (5, 5, 10, 10)
(d) (15,15)

(9) What is the output of the following code?

```
t = (3, 'Python', (1,2,4), True)
print(max(t))
```

(a) 4
(b) True
(c) y
(d) Error is generated

(10) What is the output of the following code?

```
t = ( 10, –5, 3.14, True)
print(sum(t))
```

(a) 8.14
(b) 9.14
(c) 5
(d) Error is generated

Chapter 6
Built-in Data Structure: Sets

Set is a Python built-in data structure that is similar to mathematical sets. A set is a collection of items and the items are unordered. The items are also called as elements. Elements in the set are unique, meaning that sets have no duplicate elements. Elements may be of different data types, but must be of immutable types like constant, string, tuple, etc. Set objects are generally used when duplicates are to be removed from lists and tuples. Similar to lists, tuples, strings, etc., set objects are also iterable with a *for* loop. Membership testing of an element in the set object is better optimized compared to list objects.

The set elements are enclosed in curly braces { } and separated by commas.

6.1 Create Set Objects

(i) **Empty set** is created using the constructor of the *set* class.

Example

```
# Create an empty set
s1 = set()
print("Data type of s1 : ", type(s1))
print("Elements of s1 : ",s1)
```

© The Author(s) 2024
A. L. Muddana and S. Vinayakam, *Python for Data Science*,
https://doi.org/10.1007/978-3-031-52473-8_6

Output

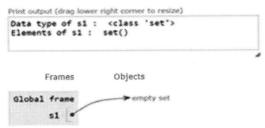

Unlike other data structures like lists, tuples, an empty set cannot be created using the empty brackets { }, since the same brackets are also used for dictionary objects.

Example

```
# empty { } creates an empty Dictionary object but not set object
s2 = {}
print("Data type of s2 : ", type(s2))
print("Elements of s2 : ",s2)
```

Output

```
Data type of s2 : <class 'dict'>
Elements of s2 : { }
```

(ii) Create a **non-empty set** by enclosing the elements in { }. If any duplicate elements are specified, they automatically get removed.

Example

```
s1 ={2,5,3,70,6,0,1,2,6,3}   # 10 elements
print(type(s1))
# Duplicates will be removed
print("Number of elements in the set : ", len(s1))
print("Set elements are : ",s1)   # duplicates are removed
```

Output

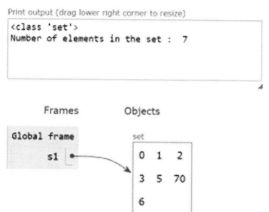

Print output (drag lower right corner to resize)

```
<class 'set'>
Number of elements in the set :  7
```

Frames   Objects

Global frame   set

s1 ●   0 1 2

                3 5 70

                6

6.2 Properties of Sets

(i) **No duplicate elements**: Set does not contain duplicate elements. If specified, they are automatically removed. In the above example, elements 2, 3, 6 are repeated twice which are removed. Hence, the number of elements is 7 instead of 10.

(ii) **Set elements can only be immutable objects** like constants, strings, tuples but not mutable objects like lists, sets, dictionaries.

Example

```
# set elements can not be mutable objects
s2 = {3.14, "Apple", True, ["A Grade", "B Grade"] }
print("Elements of set : ", s2)
```

Output

TypeError   Traceback (most recent call last)
< ipython-input-3-58782a8688a9 > in < module >()
    1 # Sets can not have mutable elements like Lists, Dictionaries, Sets
—-> 2 s2 = {3.14, "Apple", True, ["A Grade", "B Grade"] }
    3 print("Elements of set : ", s2)

TypeError: unhashable type: 'list'

In the above example, an error is generated as one of the elements is a list object which is mutable.

(iii) **Set elements are unordered**: There is no order among the set elements. Hence, elements cannot be accessed using an index.

(iv) A single set object can have a combination of different immutable objects.

Example

```
# set elements are of mixed data types
s1 = { 3.14, "Apple", True, 10+5j, ("A Grade", "B Grade") }
print("Elements of set : ", s1)
```

Output

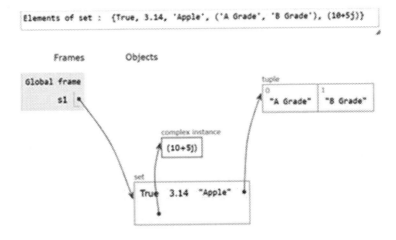

In the above example,

- The set object has different data types like a constant, Boolean value, string, tuple, and a complex number.
- The order in which elements are specified in the assignment is different from what is stored in the object, as the set elements are unordered.

6.3   Membership Testing

As the set elements are unordered, the elements of a set cannot be accessed using the index. But elements can be accessed using **in** operator.

Example

```
# round off the grades
grades = {7.5, 8.0, 6.4, 9.6, 5.3}
for element in grades:
    print(round(element,0), end=" " )
```

Output

5.0 6.0 8.0 8.0 10.0

in operator checks, if an element is in the set. It returns *True* if the element is in the set and *False* otherwise.

| Syntax |

element **in** *set_object*

Example

```
# Membership testing results in True or False
colors = { "Red", "Green", "Blue", "Yellow"}
x = "Green"
print("Whether Black is member of the set : ", "Black" in colors)
print("Whether Green is member of the set : ", x in colors)
```

Output

Whether Black is member of the set : False
Whether Green is member of the set : True

6.4 Functions on Set Objects

Python provides number of predefined functions on set objects. Following are the aggregation functions on sets.

(i) **len**(*set_object*) returns number of elements in the set.
(ii) **max**(*set_object*) returns maximum elements in the set.
(iii) **min**(*set_object*) returns minimum elements in the set.
(iv) **sum**(*set_object*) returns sum of all the elements in the set.

Example

```
grades = {7.5, 8.0, 6.4, 9.6, 5.3, 7.5}
print('Data type of grades object : ', type(grades))
print("Set elements are : ",grades)
print('Number of elements in the set : ', len(grades))
print('Maximum element in the set : ', max(grades))
print('Minimum element in the set : ', min(grades))
print('Sum of set elements : ', sum(grades))
```

Output

> Data type of grades object : <class 'set'>
> Set elements are: {5.3, 6.4, 7.5, 8.0, 9.6}
> Number of elements in the set : 5
> Maximum element in the set : 9.6
> Minimum element in the set : 5.3
> Sum of set elements : 36.8

Note: sum() function can be applied to a set having only numeric elements. **min()**, **max()** functions can be applied on sets with only numeric elements or sets with only string elements.

6.5   Methods on Set Objects

Set objects are mutable. New elements can be added or existing elements can be deleted but the value of an element cannot be modified. Following are the methods to add elements or delete elements from the set.

(i) **Addition**: Add elements to the set.

(a) **add()** method adds the specified element to the set object.

> set_object.**add**(*element*)

> *element* to be added
> The method returns the modified *set_object*.

Example

```
# add an element
odd_num = { 21,15,7, 19}
print("Set elements are : ", odd_num)
odd_num.add(11)
odd_num.add(50)
print("Set elements after adding 11,50: ", odd_num)
```

Output

> Set elements are : {7, 15, 19, 21}
> Set elements after adding 11,50: {7, 11, 15, 19, 50, 21}

(b) **update()** method adds multiple elements to the set object

> set_object.**update**(*object*)

> *object* can be a list, tuple, set, dictionary, string.
> Returns updated set_object.

Example

```
# add multiple elements to the set
odd_num = { 21,15}
print("Set elements are : ", odd_num)
odd_num.update({15,23})      # update using set object
print("Set elements after updating with set object : ", odd_num)
odd_num.update([27,29])      # update using list object
print("Set elements after updating with list object : ", odd_num)
```

Output

Set elements are : {21, 15}
Set elements after updating with set object : {23, 21, 15}
Set elements after updating with list object : {15, 21, 23, 27, 29}

(ii) **Deletion**: Delete elements from the set.

(a) **remove()** method deletes the specified element from the set.

   *set_object.**remove**(element)*

Returns the modified set_object.
Raises an error if the *element* does not exist in the set.

Example

```
# remove method on sets
odd_num = { 21,15,9,7,19}
print("Set elements are : ",odd_num)
odd_num.remove(21)
print("Set elements after removing 21 : ", odd_num)
odd_num.remove(50)      # error if element is not in the set
```

Output

Set elements are : {7, 9, 15, 19, 21}
Set elements after removing 21 : {7, 9, 15, 19}

```
KeyError      Traceback (most recent call last)
<ipython-input-7-4b474c41d6f9> in <module>()
    4 Odd_num.remove(21)
    5 print("Set elements after removing 21 : ", Odd_num)
—-> 6 Odd_num.remove(50)
    7
KeyError: 50
```

(b) **discard()** method is similar to the **remove()** method which deletes the specified element. But the difference is, no error is generated if the element does not exist in the set.

*set_object.***discard**(*element*)

Returns the modified *set_object*.

Example

```
# discard method on sets
odd_num = { 21, 15, 9, 7, 19}
print("Set elements are : ",odd_num)
odd_num.discard(21)
print("Set elements after removing 21 : ", odd_num)
odd_num.discard(50)     # generates no error
print("Set elements after discard 50 : ",odd_num)
```

Output

```
Set elements are : {7, 9, 15,19, 21}
Set elements after removing 21 : {7, 9, 15, 19}
Set elements after discard 50 : {7, 9, 15, 19}
```

(c) **pop()** method deletes an arbitrary element from the set. It returns the deleted element and the *set_object* is also updated. It raises an error if the set is empty.

*set_object.***pop**()

Example

```
# pop method on sets
odd_num = { 15, 21, 19}
print("Set elements are : ",odd_num)
print("Deleted element is : ", odd_num.pop())
print("Set elements after pop : ", odd_num)
print("Deleted element is : ", odd_num.pop())
print("Deleted element is : ", odd_num.pop())
print("Set elements after pop : ", odd_num)
odd_num.pop()       # error if empty set
```

Output

```
Set elements are : {19, 21, 15}
Deleted element is : 19
Set elements after pop : {21, 15}
Deleted element is : 21
```

Deleted element is : 15
Set elements after pop : set()

KeyError   Traceback (most recent call last)
<ipython-input-2-96b802048700> in <module>()
      7 print("Deleted element is : ", odd_num.pop())
      8 print("Set elements after pop : ", odd_num)
----> 9 odd_num.pop() # error if empty set

KeyError: 'pop from an empty set'

(d) To **delete multiple elements** from the set.

set_object.difference_update(*elements_to_be_deleted*)

Returns the modified *set_object*.
No error is generated if elements do not exist in the set.

Example

```
# Delete multiple values
Odd_num = {21,15,17, 13, 9, 7, 19}
print("Set elements are : ", Odd_num)
Odd_num.difference_update( {13, 21} )
print("Set elements after deleting 13 & 21 : ", Odd_num)
```

Output

Set elements are : {7, 9, 13, 15, 17, 19, 21}
Set elements after deleting 13 & 21 : {7, 9, 15, 17, 19}

(e) **clear()** method deletes all elements of the set, but the set object exists.

set_object.**clear()**

Example

```
# clear method on sets
odd_num = {21, 15, 17, 13, 9, 7, 19}
print("Set elements are : ",odd_num)
odd_num.clear()      # all elements are deleted
print("Set elements after clear operation : ", odd_num)
```

Output

Set elements are : {7, 9, 13, 15, 17, 19, 21}
Set elements after clear operation : set()

Note: There is no way of changing the value of a particular element, i.e., the value of an element cannot be modified.

6.6   Operations on Sets

Set operations like union, intersection, difference, etc. can be applied to set objects using predefined methods or using the operators. These operations are similar to mathematical set operations.

Consider the below set objects for the set operations:

left_op = {3, 5, 7, 9, 12, 15}
right_op= {21, 15, 12, 18}

(i) **Union** operation returns a new set object that contains elements of both the operand sets. This can be done using the **union()** method or the | (pipe symbol) operator. The operand sets do not get modified after the operation.

Example

# Set Union
print("Union operation using union() method : ", left_op.union(right_op))
print("Union operation using | operator : ", left_op |right_op)
print("Elements of left_op after the operation : ", left_op)
print("Elements of right_op after the operation : ", right_op)

Output

Union operation using union() method : {3, 5, 7, 9, 12, 15, 18, 21}
Union operation using | operator : {3, 5, 7, 9, 12, 15, 18, 21}
Elements of left_op after the operation : {3, 5, 7, 9, 12, 15}
Elements of right_op after the operation : {18, 12, 21, 15}

(ii) **Intersection** operation returns a new set object containing elements that are common to both the operand sets. This can be done using the **intersection()** method or **&** operator. The operands do not get modified after the operation.

Example

# Set intersection
print("Using intersection()
method:",left_op.intersection(right_op))
print("Using & operator : ",left_op & right_op)
print("Elements of left_op after the operation: ", left_op)
print("Elements of right_op after the operation: ", right_op)

Output

Using intersection() method: {12, 15}
Using & operator : {12, 15}
Elements of left_op after the operation: {3, 5, 7, 9, 12, 15}
Elements of right_op after the operation: {18, 12, 21, 15}

(iii) **intersection_update()** method updates the left operand set with the elements that are common to both the operand sets. Return value is None.

Example

```
# Set intersection update
print("Intersection_updatereturns:",
    left_op.intersection_update(right_op))
# Left operand set gets modified
print("Elements of left_op :",left_op)
# Right operand set not modified
print("Elements of right_op :",right_op)
```

Output

```
Intersection_update returns: None
Elements of left_op : {12, 15}
Elements of right_op : {18, 12, 21, 15}
```

(iv) **Difference** operation returns a new set object containing the elements that are in the left operand set but not in the right operand set. Neither of the operand sets is modified.

This can be done using **difference()** method or − operator.

Example

```
# Set difference
left_op = { 3, 5, 7, 9, 12, 15}
right_op = { 21, 15, 12, 18}
print("Using difference() method : ",
left_op.difference(right_op))
print("Using - operator :",left_op - right_op)
# operand sets are not modified
print("Elements of left_op : ", left_op)
print("Elements of right_op : ", right_op)
```

Output

```
Using difference() method : {9, 3, 5, 7}
Using - operator : {9, 3, 5, 7}
Elements of left_op : {3, 5, 7, 9, 12, 15}
Elements of right_op : {18, 12, 21, 15}
```

(v) **difference_update()** method updates the left operand set with the elements that are in the left operand but not in the right operand set. Return value is None.

Example

```
# Set difference update
left_op = { 3, 5, 7, 9, 12, 15}
right_op = { 21, 15, 12, 18}
print("Using difference_update(): ",
left_op.difference_update(right_op))
# Left operand set modified
print("Elements of left_op : ", left_op)
# Right operand set not modified
print("Elements of right_op : ", right_op)
```

Output

```
Using difference_update(): None
Elements of left_op : {3, 5, 7, 9}
Elements of right_op : {18, 12, 21, 15}
```

(vi) **symmetric_difference()** returns a new set with elements that are in either the left operand set or right operand set but not both. Neither of the operand sets is modified.

Example

```
# Symmetric difference
left_op = { 1, 3, 5, 7, 9, 12, 15}
right_op = { 21, 15, 12, 18}
print("Symmetric Difference : ",
left_op.symmetric_difference(right_op))
# Left operand set not modified
print("Elements of left_op :",left_op)
# Right operand set not modified
print("Elements of right_op :", right_op)
```

Output

```
Symmetric Difference : {1, 3, 5, 7, 9, 18, 21}
Elements of left_op : {1, 3, 5, 7, 9, 12, 15}
Elements of right_op : {18, 12, 21, 15}
```

(vii) **symmetric_difference_update()** The left operand set is updated with the elements that are either in the left operand set or in the right operand set but not in both. Return value is None.

Example

```
# Symmetric difference update
left_op = { 1, 3, 5, 7, 9, 12, 15}
right_op = { 21, 15, 12, 18}
```

```
print('Return value :
',left_op.symmetric_difference_update(right_op))
# Left operand set is modified
print("Elements of left_op :", left_op)
# Right operand set is not modified
print("Elements of right_op :", right_op)
```

Output

```
Return value : None
Elements of left_op : {1, 3, 5, 7, 9, 18, 21}
Elements of right_op : {18, 12, 21, 15}
```

In the above example, the common elements 12 and 15 are deleted from the left operand, but the right operand is unchanged.

(viii) **copy()** method creates a shallow copy of the set object. Original and copy objects are unaffected by adding or deleting elements to either of the objects.

Example

```
colors = { "Red", "Green", "Blue", "Yellow"}
colors_new = colors.copy()      # make copy of colors
colors.add('Pink')
colors_new.remove('Green')
print('colors :',colors)
print('colors_new :',colors_new)
```

Output

```
colors : {'Pink', 'Yellow', 'Blue', 'Red', 'Green'}
colors_new : {'Red', 'Yellow', 'Blue'}
```

(ix) **Set comparisons:** Relational operators check, if the sets are the same or one is a subset or a superset of the other. The operation results in **True** or **False**.

operand1 relational_operator operand2
== whether both the operand sets have the same elements
!= whether both the operand sets do not have the same elements
< whether *operand1* is a proper subset of *operand2*
<= whether *operand1* is a subset of *operand2*
> whether *operand1* is a proper superset of *operand2*
>= whether *operand1* is a superset of *operand2*

Example

```
# Set comparisons using relational operators
colors = { "Red", "Green", "Blue", "Yellow"}
rgb = {"Blue"', "Red", "Green"}
print("rgb is proper subset of colors: ", rgb<colors)
print("rgb is subset of colors: ", rgb<=colors)
print("colors is proper superset of rgb: ", colors>rgb)
print("colors is superset of rgb: ", colors>=rgb)
print("whether both the sets are same: ", rgb==colors)
print("whether both the sets are not same: ", rgb!=colors)
```

Output

```
rgb is proper subset of colors: True
rgb is subset of colors: True
colors is proper superset of rgb: True
colors is superset of rgb: True
whether both the sets are same: False
whether both the sets are not same: True
```

(x) **subset and superset:** Python provides issubset() and issuperset() methods to check if one set is a subset or superset of the other set.

(a) **set_object1.issubset**(set_object2)
Returns **True** if all the elements of *set_object1* are present in *set_object2* and **False** otherwise.
This operation is the same as the relational operator <=.

(b) *set_object1*.**issuperset**(*set_object2*)
Returns **True** if all the elements of *set_object2* are present in *set_object1* and **False** otherwise.
This operation is the same as the relational operator >=.

Example

```
# Subset & superset
colors = { "Red", "Green", "Blue", "Yellow"}
rgb = {"Blue", "Red", "Green"}
print("Check for subset using <= operator : ", rgb<=colors)
print("Check for subset using issubset() method :
",rgb.issubset(colors))
print("Check for superset using >= operator: ",
colors.issuperset(rgb))
print("Check for superset using issuperset() method: ",
colors>=rgb)
```

Output

Check for subset using <= operator : True
Check for subset using issubset() method : True
Check for superset using >= operator: True
Check for superset using issuperset() method: True

(xi) **isdisjoint()** method checks if two sets have no common elements.

Example

op1={10,20,30}
op2={40,50,60}
op3={20,10,30}
print("Are the sets op1 & op2 disjoint : ", op1.isdisjoint(op2))
print("Are the sets op1 & op3 disjoint : ", op1.isdisjoint(op3))

Output

Are the sets op1 & op2 disjoint : True
Are the sets op1 & op3 disjoint : False

6.7 Type Conversions

Iterable objects like lists, tuples, dictionaries, and strings can be converted into a set
object. Duplicate elements are removed in the resultant set.

Example

```
# Type conversions
lst = [2,5,3,70,6,0,1,2,6,3]
st1 = set(lst)
print("List to Set : ", st1)      # Duplicates are removed
str1 = "Hello World"
st2 = set(str1)
print("String to Set : ", st2)      # Duplicates are removed
tp = (8.5, 7.4, 4.3, 6.2, 4.3, 8.5)
st3 = set(tp)
print("Tuple to Set : ", st3)      # Duplicates are removed
grades = {'O': 90, 'A':80,'B':70}
print("Dict Keys are formed into set : ",set(grades))
print("Dict values are formed into set",set(grades.values()))
print("Dict items are formed into set : ",set(grades.items()))
```

Output

List to Set : {0, 1, 2, 3, 5, 70, 6}
String to Set : {'l', 'W', 'r', ' ', 'd', 'e', 'o', 'H'}
Tuple to Set : {8.5, 4.3, 6.2, 7.4}
Dict Keys are formed into set : {'B', 'A', 'O'}
Dict values are formed into set {80, 90, 70}
Dict items are formed into set : {('B', 70), ('O', 90), ('A', 80)}

6.8   Set Comprehensions

Similar to list, tuple, and dictionary comprehensions, set comprehensions also provide a simple and concise way of creating set objects. It uses *for* loop in the curly braces { } to generate elements of the set.

Example: Create a set having squares of numbers from 5 to 10.

```
st = {i*i for i in range(5,11)}
print("Set elements : ", st)
```

Output

Set elements : {64, 36, 100, 81, 49, 25}

Example: Create a set with square roots of list elements, rounded to 2 decimal places.

```
import math
st = { round(math.sqrt(i),2) for i in [10, 20,30,40,50]}
print("Set elements : ", st)
```

Output

Set elements : {3.16, 4.47, 5.48, 6.32, 7.07}

Example: Generate set object using nested for loop.

```
st ={ i+j for i in range(1,6) for j in [10,20,30,40,50] if (i+j) % 3 ==0 }
print("Set elements : ",st)
```

Output

Set elements : {33, 42, 12, 45, 15, 51, 21, 54, 24}

6.9   Frozen Sets

Set objects are mutable. But it can be made immutable using the frozenset() function.

frozenset(*iterable_object*)

Iterable_object can be a set, tuple, dictionary, list etc.
Returns a frozen set object initialized with the elements of *iterable_object*.
If *iterable_object* is not specified, empty frozen set is returned.

(i) Create a frozen set object

Example

```
# create frozen set from list, dictionary
lst = [1,3,5,7]
frozen_lst = frozenset(lst)
print('Frozen set from list : ', type(frozen_lst), frozen_lst)
dct = {'A':'Good', 'B':'Average', 'C':'Satisfactory' }
frozen_dct = frozenset(dct)
print('Frozen set from dictionary : ',type(frozen_dct),
frozen_dct)
```

Output

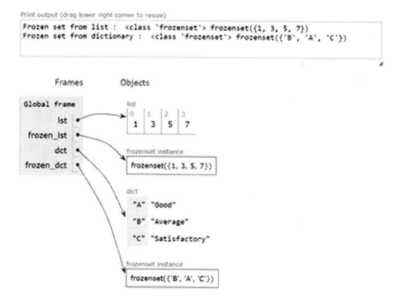

As shown in the above code, when a dictionary object is used to initialize the frozen set object, dictionary keys become elements of the frozen set.

(ii) The frozen set object is **immutable**.

Example

```
# frozen set object is immutable
frozen_set.add(9)
```

Output

```
AttributeError      Traceback (most recent call last)
<ipython-input-7-5392b2f37111> in <module> ()
    1 # frozen set object is immutable
—-> 2 frozen_set.add(9)
```

AttributeError: 'frozenset' object has no attribute 'add'

The above code generates an error when add operation is applied.

(iii) Frozen sets are generally used as keys for dictionaries or elements of a normal set object.

Example

```
# frozen set elements are added to set object
lst = [1,3,5,7]
frozen_lst = frozenset(lst)
st = {10,20,30}   # set object
# adding elements of frozen set to mutable set object
st.update(frozen_lst)
print('Elements of st : ', st)
```

Output

```
Elements of st : {1, 3, 20, 5, 7, 10, 30}
```

(iv) **Operations** on frozensets: All the operations on normal set objects that do not modify the operand set object are applicable to frozen set objects also. Union, intersection, difference, symmetric_difference, copy, issubset, issuperset, and isdisjoint are all applicable to frozen sets also. But set update operations like add, update, remove, pop, delete, difference_update, symmetric_difference_update, intersection_update, etc. are not applicable on frozen sets.

Exercises

1. Write a set comprehension to generate a set with multiples of 10 between 100 and 200.
2. Generate a set of prime numbers less than 100 using set comprehension.
3. Given a string, find the vowels present in the string.
4. Create a frozen set of names consisting of more than five characters. Accept the names from the user. Use set comprehension.
5. Given a list of colors by the user, write a function that returns a frozen set of RGB colors.
6. Given a list of student name and programming language known by the student, create a set of students who knows Java programming language.
7. Take two strings from the user and find a number of distinct characters in the strings.
8. Generate a set of real values from a given input set. Use list comprehension.
9. Find second and third highest elements of a set.
10. Display set elements in ascending order.

Review Questions

Consider the following sets and answer questions below.

    s1 = { 'Red','Green', 'Blue', 'Black'}
    s2 = { ('White','Black') }

(1) What is the output of the following?

print (s1 | s2)

(a) {'White', 'Black', 'Red', 'Blue', 'Green'}
(b) {('White', 'Black'), 'Red', 'Blue', 'Green', 'Black'}
(c) ['White', 'Black' , 'Red', 'Blue', 'Green']
(d) ('White', 'Black' , 'Red', 'Blue', 'Green')

(2) What is the output of the following?

print(s1[:2])

(a) Black
(b) Green
(c) Blue
(d) Error is generated

(3) What is the output of the following?

  print(s2-s1)

  (a) {'Red', 'Green', 'Blue'}
  (b) { }
  (c) {('White', 'Black')}
  (d) {'White' }

(4) What is the output of the following?

  x = (s1 | s2) x.remove('Black') print(x)

  (a) None
  (b) {'Red', 'Green', 'Blue', ('White', 'Black') }
  (c) { 'Red', 'Green', 'Blue', 'White' }
  (d) {'Red', 'Green', 'Blue', ('White') }

(5) What is the output of the following?

  print(s1 & s2)

  (a) { 'Black' }
  (b) set()
  (c) None
  (d) {('White', 'Black') }

(6) What is the output of the following?

  print(tuple(s1))

  (a) ('Red', 'Blue', 'Black', 'Green')
  (b) (('Red', 'Blue',)')
  (c) ('Red', 'Blue', 'Green')
  (d) (('Red', 'Blue', 'Black', 'Green'))

(7) Which of the following is not true about sets?

  (a) Sets elements are mutable objects
  (b) Sets are unordered
  (c) Sets do not allow duplicates
  (d) Set elements can be combination of different types of immutable objects

(8) Which of the following method is used to insert elements into a set?

  (a) discard()
  (b) remove()
  (c) update()
  (d) pop()

(9) Which of the following operators are used to check if two sets are the same or subset of one another?

  (a) Arithmetic
  (b) Relational
  (c) Membership
  (d) None

(10) Which of the following set is invalid?

  (a) {'Python', 0, ('Red', 1, 2)}
  (b) {'Python', True, 1 }
  (c) { }
  (d) set( )

Chapter 7
Built-in Data Structure: Dictionary

Dictionary is one of the Pythons' built-in data structures. A dictionary is a collection of data stored as key–value pairs, enclosed in curly brackets. Key, value are separated by colon and key–value pairs are separated by commas. Unlike other built-in data structures where each element is a single value, a dictionary element is a pair of key and value. The dictionary object maps a set of unique keys to a set of values. Hence, a dictionary is also referred to as an associative array in other programming languages. Initially, the dictionary object was an unordered collection but from Python version 3.7 onwards, it is an ordered collection of key–value items, i.e., the object maintains the insertion order. The dictionary object is mutable with no duplicate keys.

7.1   Create Dictionary Objects

(i) **Create an empty dictionary object:** Empty object can be created in two ways:

    (a) Using a pair of curly brackets.
    (b) Using constructor of the dictionary class.

Example

```
# Create empty Dictionary
dct1 = { }
print("Data type of dct1 : ", type(dct1))
print("Elements of dct1 : ", dct1)
dct2 = dict()
print("Data type of dct2 : ", type(dct2))
print("Elements of dct2 : ", dct2)
```

© The Author(s) 2024
A. L. Muddana and S. Vinayakam, *Python for Data Science*,
https://doi.org/10.1007/978-3-031-52473-8_7

Output

```
Print output (drag lower right corner to resize)
Data type of dct1 :  <class 'dict'>
Elements of dct1 :  {}
Data type of dct2 :  <class 'dict'>
Elements of dct2 :  {}
```

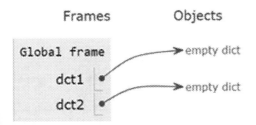

(ii) **Create a non-empty dictionary object:** Key and value are separated by a colon. The *key: value* pairs are separated by commas and enclosed in curly brackets { }.

Example

```
dct = {"Name": "Arjun", "Age": 25, "Gender":"Male"}
print("Elements are : ", dct )
```

Output

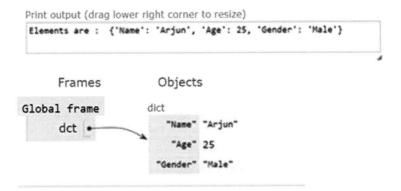

In the above example,

> *keys* are Name, Age, Gender.
> *Values* are Arjun, 25, Male.

len() function on dictionary object gives number of elements, i.e., key:value pairs in the object.

| Syntax |

  len(*dict_object*)
Example

    # len() : number of key, value pairs
    print("Number of elements in the dictionary : ", len(dct))

Output

    Number of elements in the dictionary : 3

7.2 Properties of Dictionary Objects

  (i) *Keys* of a dictionary object should be **unique**. If duplicate keys are specified, only one key exists and the latest value is associated with the key.

Example

    dct = {"Name": "Arjun", "Age": 25, "Gender":"Male", 'Name' : 'Bheem'}
    print(dct)

Output

    {'Name': 'Bheem', 'Age': 25, 'Gender': 'Male'}

 (ii) Dictionary objects are **mutable—key : value** pairs can be added or deleted from a dictionary object. Examples are provided in Sect. 7.4.
(iii) **Keys must be immutable objects** like constants, strings, tuples, etc., whereas values can be mutable or immutable objects.

    days = {("Saturday","Sunday"): "Weekend" , 90: "A Grade", "B Grade" :
    7}

In the above example, keys are

    ("Saturday","Sunday") is a tuple
    90 is a constant
    "B Grade" is a string

7.3   Accessing the Elements

(i) Values associated with keys, of a dictionary object, can be accessed in two ways

Syntax

(a) *dict_object*[*key*]
(b) *dict_object*.**get**(*key*)

Example

dct = {"Name": "Arjun", "Age": 25, "Gender":"Male"}
print("Using key as index : ", dct['Age'])
print("Using get() method : ", dct.get('Age'))

Output

Using key as index : 25
Using get() method : 25

(ii) Following methods access elements of a dictionary object:

Syntax

(a) *dict_object*.**keys()**   returns the keys
(b) *dict_object*.**values()**   returns the values
(c) *dict_object*.**items()**   returns *key :* value pairs.

Note: The *key:*value pairs are called items of the dictionary object.

Example

dct = {"Family":"Pandavas", "Name":"Arjun", "Siblings" : 4}
print("Keys : ",dct.keys())
print("Values : ", dct.values())
print("Key-Value pairs: ", dct.items())

Output

Keys : dict_keys(['Family', 'Name', 'Siblings'])
Values : dict_values(['Pandavas', 'Arjun', 4])
Key-Value pairs: dict_items([('Family', 'Pandavas'), ('Name', 'Arjun'), ('Siblings', 4)])

7.4 Operations on Dictionary Objects

Dictionary objects are mutable, i.e., elements can be added, deleted, or modified.

(i) **Add** an element to the dictionary by specifying the *key* in [ ] and assigning a *value*.

Example

```
# add an element
dct = {"Family":"Pandavas", "Name":"Arjun","Siblings" : 4 }
dct['Guru'] = "Dronacharya"
print("After addition : ", dct)
```

Output

After addition : {'Family': 'Pandavas', 'Name': 'Arjun', 'Siblings': 4, 'Guru': 'Dronacharya'}

(ii) **Modify** the value of the given key using the assignment.

Example

```
# Modify the value of given key
dct = {"Family":"Pandavas", "Name":"Arjun","Siblings" : 4 }
dct['Siblings'] = 5
print("After modification are: ", dct)
```

Output

After modification: {'Family': 'Pandavas', 'Name': 'Arjun', 'Siblings': 5}

(iii) **Delete** a specified key–value pair. This can be done in multiple ways:

(a) **del** *dict_object[key]*
Returns *dict_object* after deleting specified *key–value* pair.
(b) *dict_object*.**pop**(*key*)
Returns the value corresponding to the deleted key:value pair and *dict_object* is modified.
(c) *dict_object*.**popitem**()
Deletes the last key:value pair,
Returns deleted key:value pair as a tuple and the *dict_object* is modified.
(d) *dict_object*.***clear*()**
Deletes all the items of the dictionary but the object exists.
Returns empty *dict_object*.

Example

dct= {"Family":"Pandavas", "Name":"Arjun", "Skill": "Shooter", "Siblings" :
4}
Delete using del
del dct['Skill']
print("After deletion using del : ", dct)
# Delete using pop()
print('Value corresponding to deleted key using pop : ',dct.pop('Siblings'))
print("After deletion using pop : ", dct)
# Delete last element using popitem()
print('Value corresponding to deleted key using popitem(): ',dct.popitem())
print("After deleting last element using popitem : ",dct)
# Delete all the elements
dct.clear()
print("After clear() operation : ",dct)

Output

After deletion using del : {'Family': 'Pandavas', 'Name': 'Arjun', 'Siblings':
4}
Value corresponding to deleted key using pop : 4
After deletion using pop : {'Family': 'Pandavas', 'Name': 'Arjun'}
Value corresponding to deleted key using popitem(): ('Name', 'Arjun')
After deleting last element using popitem : {'Family': 'Pandavas'}
After clear() operation : { }

(iv) **del** *dict_object*

deletes the entire object from memory and the object does not exist anymore.

Example

dct_new = {1:"One", 2:"Two", 3:"Three"}
# Remove object
del dct_new
print("After del : ",dct_new)

Output

NameError   Traceback (most recent call last)
<ipython-input-24-a2faf664f778> in <module>()
    2 # Remove object
    3 del dct_new
—-> 4 print("After del operation : ",dct_new)

NameError: name 'dct_new' is not defined

(v) **copy dictionary object to another dictionary object**

Syntax

*dict_object.**copy()***

Returns a dictionary that can be assigned to an object. The operation is a shallow copy, i.e., updates made to the original object will not be reflected in the copy and *vice versa*.

Example

```
# Copy operation
dct = {"Name":"Arjun", "Skill": "Shooter"}
dct_dup = dct.copy()
print("Elements of dct : ", dct)
print("Elements of dct_dup : ", dct_dup)
dct.popitem()
print("dct after deleting last item from dct : ", dct)
print("dct_dup after deletion from dct : ", dct_dup)
dct_dup.pop("Name")
print("dct_dup after deleting Name from dct_dup : ", dct_dup)
print("dct after deletion from dct_dup : ", dct)
```

Output

```
Elements of dct : {'Name': 'Arjun', 'Skill': 'Shooter'}
Elements of dct_dup : {'Name': 'Arjun', 'Skill': 'Shooter'}
dct after deleting last item from dct : {'Name': 'Arjun'}
dct_dup after deletion from dct : {'Name': 'Arjun', 'Skill': 'Shooter'}
dct_dup after deleting Name from dct_dup : {'Skill': 'Shooter'}
dct after deletion from dct_dup : {'Name': 'Arjun'}
```

(vi) **Update** a dictionary object with items of another dictionary object.

Syntax

*dict_object1.**update**(dict_object2)*

Items of *dict_object2* are added to *dict_object1*.
dict_object2 does not change but *dict_object1* gets updated.

Example

```
# Update operation
capitals = {"USA":"Washington"}
asia = {"India": "Delhi"}
capitals.update(asia)
print("capitals after update() : ", capitals)
print("asia after update() : ", asia)
```

Output

>   capitals after update() : {'USA': 'Washington', 'India': 'Delhi'}
>   asia after update() : {'India': 'Delhi'}

(vii) Dictionary object can be created by specifying only keys using fromkeys() method.

| Syntax |

>   *dict.**fromkeys**(key_list, default_value)*

key_list : list of keys
default_value : Same value is assigned to all the keys.
>   It is optional. If not specified, it is None.
>   Default values can be changed later, by updating the object.
Returns a dictionary which can then be assigned to a variable.

Example

```
# Create dictionary using keys
k = ["Name", "RNo", "Mail Id"]
dct = dict.fromkeys(k)
print("Data type of dct : ", type(dct))
print("Elements of dct : ", dct)
```

Output

```
Print output (drag lower right corner to resize)
Data type of dct :   <class 'dict'>
Elements of dct :   {'Name': None, 'RNo': None, 'Mail Id': None}
```

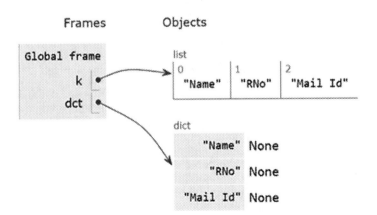

Example

```
marks = ["DBMS", "Python", "OS"]
dct = dict.fromkeys(marks, 40)
print("Data type of dct : ", type(dct))
print("Elements of dct : ", dct)
```

Output

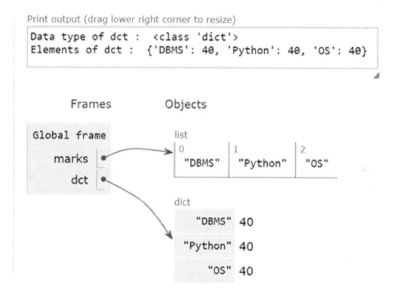

```
Print output (drag lower right corner to resize)
Data type of dct :   <class 'dict'>
Elements of dct :   {'DBMS': 40, 'Python': 40, 'OS': 40}
```

In the above example, 40 is assigned as the default value for all the keys.

7.5   Iterating Dictionary Objects

Each item of a dictionary can be accessed using *in* operator in the *for* loops. It can be done in the following ways:

(i) To access only keys of the dictionary object, use *dict_object* name in *for* loop.

Example

```
capitals = {"India": "Delhi", "USA":"Washington", "Japan":"Tokyo",
"China":"Beijing"}
# Access only keys of the dictionary
for element in capitals:
    print(element, end = ' ')
```

Output

India USA Japan China

(ii) To access only values of the dictionary, use *dict_object.values()* in the loop.

Example

```
capitals = {"India": "Delhi", "USA":"Washington", "Japan":"Tokyo",
"China":"Beijing"}
# Access only values of the dictionary
for element in capitals.values():
    print(element, end= ' ')
```

Output

Delhi Washington Tokyo Beijing

(iii) To access key–value pairs of the dictionary, use *dict_object.items()* in the loop.

Example

```
capitals = {"India": "Delhi", "USA":"Washington", "Japan":"Tokyo",
"China":"Beijing"}
# Access key,value pairs of the dictionary
for element in capitals.items():
    print(element)
```

Output

```
('India', 'Delhi')
('USA', 'Washington')
('Japan', 'Tokyo')
('China', 'Beijing')
```

7.6 Dictionary Comprehension

Comprehension is a concise way of creating a dictionary object, by enclosing *for* loop in curl brackets. It can include conditions to select the required elements.

Example

```
odd_squares = {i: i**2 for i in range(5,10) if i%2==1}
print("Data type : ", type(odd_squares))
print("Elements are : ", odd_squares)
```

Output

> Data type : <class 'dict' >
> Elements are : {5: 25, 7: 49, 9: 81}

Example: Create dictionary using zip object.

> country = ['India','USA','Japan']
> capital = ['New Delhi','Washington','Tokyo']
> con_cap = {element[0]: element[1] for element in zip(country,capital)}
> print(type(con_cap))
> print(con_cap)

Output

> <class 'dict'>
> {'India': 'New Delhi', 'USA': 'Washington', 'Japan': 'Tokyo'}

7.7 Type Conversions

Dictionary objects can be converted to other data types like lists, tuples, sets, etc., using the constructor of that class.

| Syntax |

> *data_type*(*dict_object*)

(i) **Dictionary to list object:** When a dictionary name is specified, the keys of the dictionary form a list.

Example

```
# dictionary to list
capitals = {"India": "Delhi", "USA":"Washington", "Japan":"Tokyo"}
print("Data type of capitals : ", type(capitals))
lst = list(capitals)
print("Elements of list : ", lst)
```

Output

> Data type of capitals : <class 'dict'>
> Elements of list : ['India', 'USA', 'Japan']

(ii) **Create a list of values of the dictionary object.**

Example

```
# Form list of dictionary values
lst = list(capitals.values())
print("Data type of lst : ", type(lst))
print("Elements of lst : ", lst)
```

Output

```
Data type of lst : <class 'list'>
Elements of lst : ['Delhi', 'Washington', 'Tokyo']
```

(iii) **Create a list of key–value pairs of the dictionary object.**

Example

```
# Form list of key-values of dictionary
lst = list(capitals.items())
print("Data type of lst : ", type(lst))
print("Elements of lst : ", lst)
```

Output

```
Data type of lst : <class 'list'>
Elements of lst : [('India', 'Delhi'), ('USA', 'Washington'), ('Japan',
'Tokyo')]
```

(iv) **zip object to a dictionary. zip()** function maps corresponding elements of two objects and returns an iterator. The iterator can then be converted into a dictionary or a tuple or a list.

Example

```
cgp = [10,9,8]
grades = ("O","A+","A")
Performance = zip(cgp, grades)
print("Data type of performance : ", type(Performance))
# Converting zip object into dictionary
performance = dict(performance)
print("Data type of performance : ", type(performance))
print("Elements of Performance : ", performance)
```

Output

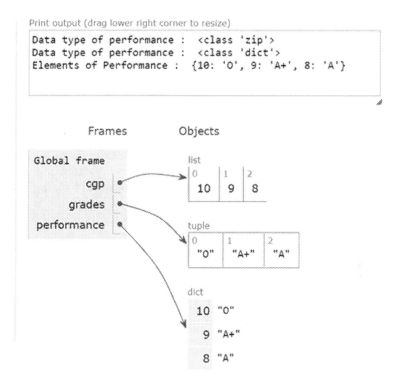

```
Print output (drag lower right corner to resize)
Data type of performance :   <class 'zip'>
Data type of performance :   <class 'dict'>
Elements of Performance :   {10: 'O', 9: 'A+', 8: 'A'}
```

(v) **Similarly, keys, values, items of a dictionary object can also be converted to a tuple or a set.**

Example

```
capitals = {"India": "Delhi", "USA":"Washington", "Japan":"Tokyo"}
print("Data type of capitals : ", type(capitals))
# Dictionary keys to tuple
tpl = tuple(capitals)
print("Elements of the tuple : ", tpl)
# Dictionary items to set
st = set(capitals.items())
print("Elements of set st : ", st)
```

Output

```
Data type of capitals : <class 'dict'>
Elements of the tuple : ('India', 'USA', 'Japan')
Elements of set st : {('USA', 'Washington'), ('India', 'Delhi'), ('Japan', 'Tokyo')}
```

Exercises

1. Write a function that displays the keys of a dictionary object that are strings.
2. Write a function that displays the dictionary items that have a list as a value.
3. Create a dictionary with five subject marks of a student and then add an item with total marks.
4. Take names of N students from the user. Create a dictionary with a name as the key and the number of vowels in the name as its value.
5. Create a dictionary of names and CGPs of N students taken from the user. Write a function that displays the names of students who secured more than 7 CGP.
6. Take names of N students from the user. Create a dictionary with a name as the key and the length of the name as the value. Write a function that returns a dictionary after deleting items having names with more than 5 characters.
7. Write a function that deletes the dictionary items with string as its value.
8. Create a dictionary of five courses and the number of students enrolled. Write a function that returns the dictionary after deleting the courses with less than 20 enrollments.
9. Accept lists of phone numbers, primary names, and secondary names of N students from the user. Write a function that returns a dictionary of phone numbers and names. Names are formed by concatenating primary and secondary names.
10. Write a function that takes two dictionary objects and returns a new object that includes the items of both. If the keys are the same, the corresponding value is a tuple of values of both the input dictionaries.

Review Questions

(1) What is the output of the following code?

```
months = {'Dec': 12, 'Jan':1,'Jun':6}
print(months[0])
```

   (a) Dec
   (b) 12
   (c) Jan
   (d) Error is generated

(2) What is the output of the following code?

```
months = {'Dec': 12, 'Jan':1,'Jun':6}
print('Mar' in months)
```

   (a) False
   (b) 0
   (c) True
   (d) Error is generated

(3) What is the output of the following code?

```
d1 = {'Name': 'Karna', 'Phone': 9999}
d2 = d1.copy()
d2['Mother'] = 'Kunthi'
print(d1)
```

   (a) {'Name': 'Karna', 'Phone': 9999, 'Mother': 'Kunthi'}
   (b) {'Name': 'Karna', 'Phone': 9999}
   (c) {'Phone': 9999, 'Name': 'Karna', 'Mother': 'Kunthi'}
   (d) Error is generated

(4) What is the output of the following code?

```
months = {'Dec': 31, 'Jan':31,'Jun':30, 'Mar': 31}
months.popitem()
print(months)
```

   (a) {'Jan': 31, 'Jun': 30, 'Mar': 31}
   (b) {'Dec': 31, 'Jan': 31, 'Jun': 30}
   (c) {'Jan': 31, 'Jun': 30, 'Mar': 31}
   (d) {'Dec': 31, 'Jan': 31, 'Mar': 31}

(5) What is the data type of the variable, d, in the following code?

```
d = {(ele, ele+1) for ele in [5,10,15]}
```

   (a) tuple
   (b) dictionary
   (c) list
   (d) set

(6) What is the output of the following code?

```
d = {'Country' : 'India', 'Capital': 'New Delhi', 'Currency':'Rs', 'Capital':
'Delhi'}
print(d.get('Capital'))
```

   (a) New Delhi
   (b) Delhi
   (c) 2
   (d) Error is generated

(7) What is the output of the following code?

```
prices = {'Banana': 50 , 'Apple': 70 , 'Orange': 65 }
prices_new = {'Apple': 80, 'Grapes':90}
prices.update(prices_new)
print(prices)
```

   (a) {'Banana': 50, 'Apple': 70, 'Orange': 65 }

(b) {'Banana': 50, 'Apple': 70, 'Orange': 65, 'Grapes': 90}
(c) {'Apple': 80, 'Grapes':90}
(d) {'Banana': 50, 'Apple': 80, 'Orange': 65, 'Grapes': 90}

(8) What is the output of the following code?

```
d1 = { 'Banana': 50 , 'Apple': 70 , 'Orange': 65 }
d2 = { 'Orange': 75, 'Grapes': 100 }
print(d1 + d2)
```

(a) {'Banana': 50, 'Apple': 70, 'Orange': 140 }
(b) {'Banana': 50, 'Apple': 70, 'Orange': 75, 'Grapes': 100 }
(c) {'Banana': 50, 'Apple': 70, 'Orange': 140, 'Grapes': 100 }
(d) Error is generated

(9) What is the output of the following code?

```
fruits = { 'Banana': 50 , 'Apple': 70 , 'Orange': 65 }
print(len(fruits))
```

(a) 6
(b) 3
(c) 23
(d) Error is generated

(10) What is the output of the following code?

```
fruits = { 'Banana': 50 , 'Apple': 70 , 'Orange': 65 }
print(set(fruits))
```

(a) {'Banana', 'Apple', 'Orange'}
(b) { 50, 70, 63 }
(c) { 'Banana': 50 , 'Apple': 70 , 'Orange': 65 }
(d) { 'Apple': 70, 'Banana': 50 , 'Orange': 65 }

Chapter 8
Files

8.1 Introduction

Standard input and output functions accept user data from the console and display the data to the console. These values are stored in the variables of the program and are lost when the program terminates. When data to be taken from the console is large or when the data is to be saved even after the program terminates, it has to be stored in a permanent and non-volatile memory like secondary storage. The data is stored as a file on the secondary storage devices. A file is a container that stores the related information on secondary storage devices like hard disk, CD, pen drive, etc. Python supports reading from or writing data into files, called file handling. Python provides a number of library functions for performing different file operations like reading, writing, appending, etc.

Python supports two types of files.

(i) Text file—It is a sequence of lines where each line is a sequence of characters. Lines are delimited by a special character called newline (\n).
(ii) Binary files—It is a sequence of bytes which can only be interpreted by appropriate application or machine.

Examples of binary files include command files, executable files, compressed files, audio files, video files, etc. This chapter discusses the handling of text files.

8.2 File Handling

File handling requires the following sequence of steps:

- Opening the file.
- Performing operations like read, write, etc.
- Closing the file.

© The Author(s) 2024
A. L. Muddana and S. Vinayakam, *Python for Data Science*,
https://doi.org/10.1007/978-3-031-52473-8_8

8.2.1 Opening the File

A file has to be opened before performing any operation on the file like reading, writing, etc.

open() is a Python built-in function to open the file. The function returns a file object, also called file handle or file descriptor. For all the subsequent file operations, this file object is to be used and not the file name provided in the open() function.

| Syntax |

   open(*file_path, mode*)

file_path argument specifies the name and location of the file on the secondary storage device. File_path can be specified in two ways.

 (i) relative path—file location is specified starting from the current directory.
(ii) absolute path—file location is specified starting from the root directory.

mode argument specifies whether the file is used for reading, writing, or for both read and write operations. Different values for ***mode*** parameter are

r	opens the file for reading Error is generated if the file does not exist This is the default mode

w	opens the file for writing
	If the file exists, the contents are erased and the writing starts from
	   the beginning of the file
	In case the file does not exist, a new file is created and the data
	   is added

a	opens the file for adding data at the end of the existing file In case the file does not exist, a new file is created and data is added

x	creates a file Error is generated if the file already exists
r+	open the file for both reading and writing operations The file pointer is positioned at the beginning of the file Error is generated in case the file does not exist
w+	open the file for both reading and writing operations The file pointer is positioned at the beginning of the file If the file does not exist, a new file is created If the file already exists, the file contents are erased
a+	open the file for both reading and writing operations The file pointer is positioned at the end of the file If the file does not exist, a new file is created If the file already exists, the file is appended with new content
t	treats the file as a text file. This is the default file type
b	treats the file as binary

Example

> fp = open('/content/sample_data/olympics.txt')

In the above example, fp is the file object. As the **mode** argument is not specified, default values are assumed, i.e., read operation, and text file formats are assumed.

8.2.2   Closing the File

Once we are done with accessing the file, it needs to be closed. Close operation releases the resources tied up with the file like freeing the memory utilized by the file.

| Syntax |

> *file_object*.**close**()

Example

> fp.close()

Once the file is closed, no more read/write operations are permitted. To perform read/write operations, the file needs to be opened again in the appropriate mode.

Even though Python provides garbage collector to cleanup the unused objects, it is a good practice to close the files once done with the file operations.

An opened file is associated with a file pointer at which reading or writing takes place which can then be repositioned as required.

8.2.3   Writing Data into Files

Python provides the following functions to write data into files:

(i) **write**()

| Syntax |

> *file_object*.**write**(*string*)

string value is written to the file referenced by the *file_object*. If the file already exists, the file is truncated and new contents are written. In case the file does not exist, a new file is created.

Example 1: Write into a non-existing file.

```
from os.path import exists
print("Does the file exists :",exists('sample.txt'))
# write into new file
fd= open('sample.txt','w')
fd.write('Python is a high-level programming language\n')
fd.write('Programming with python is fun\n')
fd.write('Python is an interpreted language\n')
fd.close()
```

Output

Does the file exists : False

To display the contents of the file, use the read() function. An explanation on read() function will be given in the subsequent section.

Example

```
from os.path import exists
print("Does the file exists :",exists('sample.txt'))
# read the file contents
fd= open('sample.txt','r')
print('File contents : \n', fd.read())
fd.close()
```

Output

Does the file exists : True
File contents :
Python is a high-level programming language
Programming with Python is fun
Python is an interpreted language

Example 2: Write into the existing file.

```
from os.path import exists
print("Does the file exists :",exists('sample.txt'))
# write into existing file
fd= open('sample.txt','w')
fd.write('Python is an object-oriented language\n')
fd.close()
# open the file in read mode
fd= open('sample.txt','r')
print('File contents : \n', fd.read())
fd.close()
```

Output

Does the file exists : True
File contents :
Python is an object-oriented language

Note: New data overwrites existing file contents.
(ii) **writelines()**

Syntax

*file_object.**writelines**(string_list)*

It is similar to the write() function, except that the argument is a list of strings.

Example

```
from os.path import exists
print("Does the file exists :",exists('sample.txt'))
fd= open('sample.txt','w')
fd.writelines(['Python is a high-level programming
    language\n','Programming with python is fun\n' ])
fd.close()
# open the file in read mode
fd= open('sample.txt','r')
print('File contents : \n', fd.read())
fd.close()
```

Output

Does the file exists : True
File contents :
Python is a high-level programming language
Programming with python is fun

(iii) **append the file**

This is also a write operation. When the file is opened in append (a) mode, the file handle is positioned at the end of the file. All subsequent **write** operations like write(), writelines() functions, add the data at the end of the file in case the file exists. If the file does not exist, a new file is created and the data is written into the file.

Example

```
from os.path import exists
print("Does the file exists :",exists('sample.txt'))
# open the file in read mode
fd= open('sample.txt','r')
print('Existing file contents : \n', fd.read())
```

```
fd.close()
# open file in append mode
fd= open('sample.txt','a')
fd.write('One line appened\n')
fd.writelines(['Second line appened\n','Third line appened\n' ])
fd.close()
# open the file in read mode
fd= open('sample.txt','r')
print('File contents after append : \n', fd.read())
fd.close()
```

Output

Does the file exists : True
Existing file contents :
Python is a high-level programming language
Programming with python is fun
File contents after append :
Python is a high-level programming language
Programming with python is fun
One line appened
Second line appened
Third line appened

8.2.4   Get File Pointer Position

Every opened file is associated with a pointer that points to the position in the file where reading or writing takes place, called a file pointer. The **tell()** function returns the file pointer position

Syntax

file_object.tell()

8.2.5   Reading Data from Files

The contents of a file can be accessed using the following functions. The functions return the number of bytes read from the file. Following are the functions to read from file

(i) *file_object*.**read()**
   Reads data from the current file pointer position till the end of the file. Returns the number of bytes read.

(ii) *file_object*.**read(size)**

Returns the specified number of characters from current file pointer position.

(iii) *file_object*.**readline()**

Returns the current line from file pointer position

Example

```
fd = open('sample.txt','r')
print('When a file is opened in read mode, the file pointer is at :
    ',fd.tell())
print('5 Characters from current file pointer position :
    ',fd.read(5))
print('Now the file pointer is at : ',fd.tell())
print('Characters in the current line from the current file pointer
    :\n\n',fd.readline())
print('Now the file pointer is at : ',fd.tell())
print('Data from current file pointer position till end of
    file:\n\n',fd.read())
fd.close()
```

Output

```
When a file is opened in read mode, the file pointer is at : 0
5 Characters from current file pointer position : Pytho
Now the file pointer is at : 5
Characters in the current line from the current file pointer :

n is a high-level programming language

Now the file pointer is at : 44
Data from current file pointer position till end of file:
Programming with Python is fun
One line appened
Second line appened
Third line appened
```

8.2.6 *Changing the File Pointer Position*

seek() function changes the position of the file pointer.

| Syntax |

file_object.seek(*offset, whence*)

offset indicates how much to move from current position

whence is a reference point for the offset with the following values

0 indicates the beginning of the file
1 indicates the current file pointer position
2 indicates the end of the file
The default value is 0.
Returns new file pointer location

Note: For text files, *whence* value cannot be 1 or 2 except when offset is 0.

Example

```
fd = open('sample.txt','r')
print('File pointer is at : ', fd.tell())
fd.seek(5)     # change file pointer to position 5
print('Data from 5th character till end of line:\n',fd.readline())
print('Now the file pointer is at : ', fd.tell())
fd.seek(0,2)     # change file pointer to end of file
print('The file pointer is at ', fd.tell(), 'after moving to end of the file ')
fd.close()
```

Output

File pointer is at : 0
Data from 5th character till end of line:
n is a high-level programming language

Now the file pointer is at : 44
The file pointer is at 131 after moving to end of the file

8.2.7   Read and Write to Files

Both read and write operations can be performed on an open file using r+, w+, and a+ modes.

In r+ and w+ modes, initially, the file pointer is at the beginning of the file, whereas the file pointer is at the end of the file when opened in a+ mode.

r+ mode generates an error if the file does not exist, whereas a new file is created in w+ and a+ modes.

Example 1: Perform read and write using w+

```
fd = open('/content/sample_new.txt','w+')
print('File pointer is at ', fd.tell(), ' when opened with w+ ')
fd.write("No variable declarations in Python\nPython is a
   dynamically typed language\n")
print("After the write operation, the file pointer is at :",fd.tell())
fd.seek(0,0)     # position file pointer to beginning of file
print("First line of the file is : \n ",fd.readline())     # read first line
fd.close()
```

Output

> File pointer is at 0 when opened with w+
> After the write operation, the file pointer is at : 74
> First line of the file is :
> No variable declarations in Python

Example 2: Perform read and write using r+

```
fd = open('/content/sample_new.txt','r+')
print('File pointer is at ', fd.tell(), ' when opened with r+ ')
print("File contents : \n",fd.read())
print('File pointer is at',fd.tell(), ' after read operation')
fd.write("New line\n")
print("File pointer after write : ",fd.tell())
fd.seek(0,0)     # position the file pointer to beginning of file
print("File contents : \n",fd.read())
fd.close()
```

Output

> File pointer is at 0 when opened with r+
> File contents :
> No variable declarations in Python
> Python is a dynamically typed language
>
> File pointer is at 74 after read operation
> File pointer after write : 83
> File contents :
> No variable declarations in Python
> Python is a dynamically typed language
> New line

Example 3: Perform read and append using a+

```
fd = open('/content/sample_new.txt','a+')
print('File pointer is at ', fd.tell(), ' when opened with a+ ')
print("read() function does not return any data when file pointer is at
    the end of file : \n",fd.read())
print('File pointer is at',fd.tell(), ' after read operation')
fd.write("One more line added\n")
print("File pointer after write : ",fd.tell())
fd.seek(0,0)      # position the file pointer to beginning of file
print("File contents : \n",fd.read())
fd.close()
```

Output

> File pointer is at 83 when opened with a+
> read() function does not return any data when file pointer is at the end of file :
> File pointer is at 83 after read operation
> File pointer after write : 103
> File contents :
> No variable declarations in Python
> Python is a dynamically typed language
> New line
> One more line added

8.3   Working with Files and Directories

Files are stored on secondary storage devices like a hard disk. To manage large number of files, hierarchical organization is one of the approaches to store and handle the files. Files are grouped into directories. A directory is also called a folder. Each directory contains files and subdirectories in it. Python provides an *os* module to work with directories and files. This module provides an interface between Python and the operating system.

Following are the functions of *os* module to work with files and directories.

First *os* module has to be imported to use the functions

    import os

Get the current working directory

    os.getcwd()

Change the directory

    os.chdir('directory_path')

Display files and subdirectories of a directory

    os.listdir('directory_path')

Create a new directory

    os.mkdir('path')

Check if the **path** specified as argument is a directory or a file. It returns True or False

    os.path.isdir('path')
    os.path.isfile('path')

Remove a directory. The directory must be empty to remove it.

    os.rmdir('path')

Rename a file

    os.rename('old_filename', 'new_file_name')

Delete a file

    os.remove('path')

Get the size of directory or file in terms of bytes

    os.path.getsize('path')

Get access/modified time of a file

    os.path.getatime('file_path'))
    os.path.getmtime('file_path'))

These functions return the number of seconds passed since 1 January 1970. To convert that value into date and time format, use *fromtimestamp()* function of **datetime** module.

Example

```
import datetime
t = os.path.getatime('/content/sample_data/sample.txt')
dt = datetime.datetime.fromtimestamp(t)
print("Date time :",dt)
print("Date :",dt.date())
print("Time : ",dt.time())
print("Years:",dt.year," Months:",dt.month, " Days:",dt.day)
print("Hours:",dt.hour,"Minutes:",dt.minute, " Seconds:",dt.second)
```

Output

```
Date time : 2022-05-02 09:18:01.447931
Date : 2022-05-02
Time : 09:18:01.447931
Years: 2022   Months: 5   Days: 2
Hours: 9   Minutes: 18   Seconds: 1
```

8.4   Case Study: File Handling

Consider the following files containing student data.

details.csv: The file contains student details like Roll No., Name, and Mail_id.

First_sem.csv, Second_sem.csv, Third_sem.csv: Each file contains Roll No. and grade points obtained by the students in the corresponding semester.
Following file operations and data analysis are performed.

(i) Move to the directory containing these files.

```
import os
os.chdir('/content/sample_data/Marks')
print(os.getcwd())
```

Output

/content/sample_data/Marks

(ii) List the files in the current folder.

```
os.listdir(os.getcwd())
```

Output

['Third_sem.csv', 'First_sem.csv', 'details.csv', 'Second_sem.csv']

(iii) Display column names and the number of lines in each of the four files.

```
for f in os.listdir(os.getcwd()):
    fp = open(f,'r')
    cols = fp.readline()
    print('File Name : ',f)
    print(' Column Names : ', cols, end=' ')
    lines=fp.readlines()
    print(' Number of lines : ',len(lines))
    fp.close()
```

Output

```
File Name : Third_sem.csv
  Column Names : Rno,sem3_gp
    Number of lines : 33
File Name : First_sem.csv
  Column Names : Rno,sem1_gp
    Number of lines : 33
File Name : details.csv
  Column Names : Rno,Name,Mail_id
    Number of lines : 33
```

File Name : Second_sem.csv
Column Names : Rno,sem2_gp
Number of lines : 33

(iv) Create a new file, *perform.csv*, with the columns of the four files- rno, name, sem1_gp, sem2_gp, sem3_gp.

```
fp=open('/content/sample_data/perform.csv','w')
fpd= open('/content/sample_data/Marks/details.csv','r')
fp1= open('/content/sample_data/Marks/First_sem.csv','r')
fp2= open('/content/sample_data/Marks/Second_sem.csv','r')
fp3= open('/content/sample_data/Marks/Third_sem.csv','r')
while True:
    details= fpd.readline()
    if details =='':
      break
  # use strip() function to remove newlines
    rno = details.split(',')[1].strip()
    one= fp1.readline().strip()
    two = fp2.readline().split(',')[1].strip()
    three = fp3.readline().split(',')[1].strip()
    line=(rno,one, two,three)
  # create record by concatenating the required data        from the files
    line = ','.join(line)
    line=line+'\n'
    fp.write(line)
fp.close()
fpd.close()
fp1.close()
fp2.close()
fp3.close()
```

(v) From the *perform.csv* file, extract those students who got more than 9 grade points in all three semesters.

```
fp=open('/content/sample_data/perform.csv','r')
next(fp)
while True:
    line=fp.readline()
    if line=='':
      break
    (name,rno, gp1,gp2,gp3) = line.split(',')
    if float(gp1)>9 and float(gp2)>9 and float(gp3)>9 :
        print(name, gp1, gp2,gp3)
fp.close()
```

Output

> Kaila Kavya 9.43 9.2 9.33
> Chittimalla Aravind 9.14 9.11 9.6

(vi) Extract the students who got 0 grade point in any of the three semesters.

```
fp=open('/content/sample_data/perform.csv','r')
next(fp)
while True:
    line=fp.readline()
    if line=='':
      break
    (name,rno, gp1,gp2,gp3) = line.split(',')
    if float(gp1)==0 or float(gp2)==0 or float(gp3)==0 :
      print(name, gp1, gp2,gp3)
fp.close()
```

Output

> Vadde Shirisha 8.35 8.14 0
> Rishi Kanth Reddy 8.46 7.82 0
> Nallama Veena Anusha 7 0 0
> Rakesh Daddali 7.43 0 7.7

(vii) Find the average grade point of all three semesters and display the students whose average is below 5.

```
with open('/content/sample_data/perform.csv','r') as fp:
    next(fp)
    while True:
        line=fp.readline()
        if line=='':
          break
        (name,rno, gp1,gp2,gp3) = line.split(',')
        avg = round((float(gp1)+float(gp2)+float(gp3))/3,2)
        if avg<5:
          print(name, avg)
```

Output

> Nallama Veena Anusha 2.33

(viii) Find the top scorers of each semester and append them to ***perform .csv*** file.

```
fp=open('/content/sample_data/perform.csv','r+')
fp.readline()
high1=high2=high3=0
while True:
```

```
          line=fp.readline()
          if line=='':
            break
          (name,rno, gp1,gp2,gp3) = line.split(',')
          #print(line)
          gp1 = float(gp1)
          gp2=float(gp2)
          gp3=float(gp3)
          if gp1>high1:
            high1=gp1
            name1= name
          if gp2>high2:
            high2=gp2
            name2=name
          if gp3>high3:
            high3=gp3
            name3=name
      print('First sem highest : ',name1, high1)
      line1= 'First sem highest : '+name1+' '+ str(high1)+'\n'
      print('Second sem highest : ',name2, high2)
      line2= 'Second sem highest : '+name2+' '+str(high2)+'\n'
      print('Third sem highest : ',name3, high3)
      line3= 'Third sem highest : '+name3+' '+ str(high3)+'\n'
      print(fp.tell())
      fp.writelines([line1, line2, line3])
      fp.close()
```

Output

```
First sem highest : Vijay Paul Reddy Nakkala 9.68
Second sem highest : Kaila Kavya 9.2
Third sem highest : Chittimalla Aravind 9.6
1491
```

(ix) Display the last three lines of the *perform.csv* file, which is the top scorers.

```
fp = open('/content/sample_data/perform.csv','r')
# extract all the lines
lines=fp.readlines()
# take last three lines
last3_lines = lines[-3:]
# display last 3 lines
for i in range(3):
   print(last3_lines[i])
fp.close()
```

Output

> First sem highest : Vijay Paul Reddy Nakkala 9.68
> Second sem highest : Kaila Kavya 9.2
> Third sem highest : Chittimalla Aravind 9.6

Exercises

1. Take the name, phone number, and mail ID of ten of your friends from the console and store them in a file named friends.txt in the current directory.
2. Add 5 more friends' data to the above file.
3. Count the number of words in the above file.
4. Create a file named primes.txt having prime numbers below 100.
5. Find the sum of the numbers in primes.txt file.
6. Write 5 to 10 multiplication tables into a file.
7. Find the number of vowels in a file.
8. Find the frequency of the given word in a file.
9. Write fruit names and the corresponding prices in a file.
10. Read numbers from a text file and create a new file with divisors of each number in a separate line.

Review Questions

(1) Access modes to perform both read and write operations in existing file is

    (a) r+
    (b) r+ and w+
    (c) w+ and a+
    (d) r+ and a+

(2) seek() function to move the file pointer to the beginning of the file is

    (a) seek(0)
    (b) seek(0,2)
    (c) seek(0,1)
    (d) None of the above

(3) File pointer is at .... when the file is opened in write mode.

    (a) Beginning of the file
    (b) End of the file
    (c) Current position
    (d) Random position

(4) Which of the following is an absolute file path?

    (a) c:\usr\sample.txt

    (b) sample.txt

    (c) data\sample.txt

    (d) mydata\data\sample.txt

(5) Which of the following reads first five characters of the file when the file is opened in append mode.

    (a) read(5)

    (b) seek(0) ; read(5)

    (c) read(5); seek(0,0)

    (d) read()

(6) Which of the following functions write data into a file?

    (a) write()

    (b) writeline()

    (c) writelines()

    (d) both a and c options

(7) Which of the following is an invalid mode to open a file?

    (a) w

    (b) a+

    (c) aw

    (d) w+

(8) Which of the following is a binary file?

    (a) .exe

    (b) .doc

    (c) .pdf

    (d) .txt

(9) Which of the following is not a correct open statement to read from a file?

    (a) open('sample.txt','r')

    (b) open('sample.txt','w+')

    (c) open('sample.txt','w')

    (d) open('sample.txt','a+')

(10) Function that returns current file pointer position.

    (a) seek()

    (b) tell()

    (c) read()

    (d) write()

Chapter 9
Data Manipulations with Pandas

9.1 Introduction

Pandas is a widely used Python package for data manipulations and analysis. It is built on top of the NumPy module. NumPy is used to work with multidimensional arrays more efficiently. Pandas is a handy tool for data analysis tasks like cleaning, handling missing data, data normalization, data visualizations, and loading and saving data. Pandas objects deal with tabular data. Columns are called attributes having a name. Rows also have names called row indices or row labels. Pandas package provides library functions and methods for basic and advanced operations on the tabular data.

Pandas provide two powerful data structures for creating and manipulating data.

 (i) *Series* is a data object with one column.
(ii) *Dataframe* is a two-dimensional data object with one or more columns. Columns can be of heterogeneous data types.

This chapter focuses on dataframes, as it is widely used in data science.

9.2 Dataframes

First, the package needs to be imported before working on a dataframe object.

> *import pandas as pd*

To know the version of the pandas package, use

> \# Pandas version
> *pd.__version__*

© The Author(s) 2024
A. L. Muddana and S. Vinayakam, *Python for Data Science*,
https://doi.org/10.1007/978-3-031-52473-8_9

9.2.1   Create Dataframes

Dataframes can be created using the *DataFrame()* function of Pandas.

| Syntax |

pandas.*DataFrame(data, index, columns, dtype, copy)*
data: Specified as list, dictionary, numpy array, series object, another dataframe object etc.

index: List of row labels. It is optional. If not specified,

the labels are integers ranging from 0 to (number_of_rows-1).

columns: List of column names. It is optional. If not specified,

they are integers ranging from 0 to (number_of_cols-1).

dtype: List of data types of each column.

(i) Create an empty dataframe

Example

```
import pandas as pd
df = pd.DataFrame()
print(type(df))
print(df)
```

Output

```
<class 'pandas.core.frame.DataFrame'>
Empty DataFrame
Columns: []
Index: []
```

(ii) Create a dataframe from a list object. Each sublist in the list will form a row of the dataframe.

Example

```
# Dataframe from a list with column names
students = [['Python',87],['Maths',75], ['English',91]]
df = pd.DataFrame(students, columns=['Subject','Marks'])
print(df)
```

Output

	Subject	Marks
0	Python	87
1	Maths	75
2	English	91

Note: Since row labels are not specified, the default labels are 0, 1, 2.

(iii) Create a dataframe from a dictionary.

Example

```
# Create dataframe from dictionary with row labels
students = { "Rno": [10,25,33,46], "Names": ["Ram", "Arjun",
"Krishna","Laxman"]}
df = pd.DataFrame(students, index =['a','b','d','s'])
print("Dataframe is : \n")
print(df)
print('No. of rows : ', len(df))
```

Output: Dataframe is:

	Rno	Names
a	10	Ram
b	25	Arjun
d	33	Krishna
s	46	Laxman
No. of rows:	4	

In the above example,

Rno, Names are column names
a,b,d,s are the row indices/row names/row labels.

Note: len(*data_frame*) returns the number of rows in the dataframe.

9.2.2 Attributes of a Dataframe

An attribute is the property or characteristic of an object. Each object may have a number of attributes. For example, a table object has attributes like height, width, length, color etc. Similarly, a dataframe object has the following attributes.

Syntax

data_frame.**attribute_name**

(i) *data_frame*.**shape**
Returns the number of rows and number of columns of the *data_frame*.
(ii) *data_frame*.**ndim**
Returns number of dimensions in the dataframe.
(iii) *data_frame*.**size**
Returns an integer indicating the number of elements in the dataframe.
(iv) *data_frame*.**columns**
Returns column names of the *data_frame*.
(v) *data_frame*.**index**
Returns the row labels of the dataframe as a range.

Example

> print('Shape of the dataframe : ', df.shape)
> print('Number of dimensions : ', df.ndim)
> print('Size of the dataframe : ', df.size)
> print('Column names : ', df.columns)
> print('Row Labels : ', df.index)

Output

> Shape of the dataframe : (4, 2)
> Number of dimensions : 2
> Size of the dataframe : 8
> Column names : Index(['Rno', 'Names'], dtype='object')
> Row Labels : Index(['a', 'b', 'd', 's'], dtype='object')

Note: By default, row labels range from 0 to 4 (stop index 4 is not inclusive) with a step of 1. But in the above example, the row labels are ['a', 'b', 'd', 's'], as specified while creating the dataframe.

(vi) *data_frame*.**dtypes**

> Returns the data type of each column.

Example

> print('Data types of the columns :\n', df.dtypes)

Output

> Data types of the columns:
> Rno   int64
> Names   object
> dtype: object

(vii) *data_frame*.**values**

> Return values of the data frame as a two-dimensional numpy array.

Example

> print('Dataframe values as Numpy array :\n',df.values)

Output

> Dataframe values as Numpy array:
> [[10 'Ram']
> [25 'Arjun']
> [33 'Krishna']
> [46 'Laxman']]

9.2.3 Add Columns

Following are the methods of adding new columns to an existing dataframe.

(i) Appending a column

| Syntax |

*data_frame['**new_col**'] = **col_values***
Example

```
# Add Quality column as last one
df["Quality"] = ["Governance", "Archery", "Flute","Trust"]
print('Dataframe after adding a column : \n',df)
```

Output

Dataframe after adding a column:

	Rno	Names	Quality
a	10	Ram	Governance
b	25	Arjun	Archery
d	33	Krishna	Flute
s	46	Laxman	Trust

(ii) Add new column at specified position using **insert** method

| Syntax |

*data_frame.**insert** (index, col_name, values)*
Example

```
df.insert(2, "Cgp", [7.4,6.9,8.2,7.12])
print('Dataframe after inserting column :\n',df)
```

Output

Dataframe after inserting column:

	Rno	Names	Cgp	Quality
a	10	Ram	7.40	Governance
b	25	Arjun	6.90	Archery
d	33	Krishna	8.20	Flute
s	46	Laxman	7.12	Trust

Note: "Cgp" column is inserted at column index 2.

9.2.4 Accessing Data

Data from specified rows and columns can be accessed, using the following methods.

(i) Access specific columns

(a) Access data of a single column

> ### data_frame['column_name']

Returns entire column as series object.

Example

```
# Access single column
print(df["Quality"])
print(type(df["Quality"]))
```

Output

```
a Governance
b Archery
d Flute
s Trust
Name: Quality, dtype: object <class 'pandas.core.series.Series'>
```

(b) To access data from multiple columns, specify the column names as a list.

> ### data_frame[[column_list]]

Returns a dataframe object containing specific columns data.

Example

```
# Access multiple columns data
print(df[["Names","Quality"]])
```

Output

	Names	Quality
a	Ram	Governance
b	Arjun	Archery
d	Krishna	Flute
s	Laxman	Trust

(ii) Reset row indices to default values starting from 0.

> ### data_frame.reset_index(*inplace, drop*)

By default, the current row index is added as a new column. To avoid that, set the values for *inplace* and *drop* arguments *to* **True**.

Example

df.reset_index(inplace=True,drop=True)
print(df)

Output

	Rno	Names	Cgp	Quality
0	10	Ram	7.40	Governance
1	25	Arjun	6.90	Archery
2	33	Krishna	8.20	Flute
3	46	Laxman	7.12	Trust

(iii) Access rows

 (a) Access first N rows

 data_frame.head(N)

 (b) Access last N rows

 data_frame.tail(N)

Note: Default value of N is 5

Example

# Access first 3 rows
print('First 3 rows :\n',df.head(3))
# Access last 3 rows
print('Last 3 rows :\n',df.tail(3))

Output

First 3 rows:

	Rno	Names	Cgp	Quality
0	10	Ram	7.4	Governance
1	25	Arjun	6.9	Archery
2	33	Krishna	8.2	Flute

Last 3 rows:

	Rno	Names	Cgp	Quality
1	25	Arjun	6.90	Archery
2	33	Krishna	8.20	Flute
3	46	Laxman	7.12	Trust

(iv) Access rows by specifying row index range

data_frame[start:stop]

Example

print('Rows with index 2 and 3 :\n',df[2:4])
# Access all the rows upto index 3(not including 3)
print('Rows upto index 3 :\n',df[:3])
# all the rows from index 2
print('Rows from index 2 onwards :\n', df[2:])

Output

Rows with index 2 and 3:

	Rno	Names	Cgp	Quality
2	33	Krishna	8.20	Flute
3	46	Laxman	7.12	Trust

Rows upto index 3:

	Rno	Names	Cgp	Quality
0	10	Ram	7.4	Governance
1	25	Arjun	6.9	Archery
2	33	Krishna	8.2	Flute

Rows from index 2 onwards:

	Rno	Names	Cgp	Quality
2	33	Krishna	8.20	Flute
3	46	Laxman	7.12	Trust

(v) Access rows by specifying list of row indices

data_frame.iloc[[indices_list]]

Example

print('Row at index 2 followed by row at index
1:\n',df.iloc[[2,1]])

Output

Row at index 2 followed by row at index 1:

	Rno	Names	Cgp	Quality
2	33	Krishna	8.2	Flute
1	25	Arjun	6.9	Archery

(vi) Access data of specific rows and columns

data_frame[col_names][row_start:row_stop]

Example

Access first 3 rows of Quality column
print('First 3 rows of Quality and Names columns: \n',df[['Quality',
'Names']][:3])

Output

First 3 rows of Quality and Names columns:

	Quality	Names
0	Governance	Ram
1	Archery	Arjun
2	Flute	Krishna

(vii) The specific rows and columns data can also be accessed using the following loc() method.

data_frame.loc[row_start:row_stop, [col_names]]

row_stop is inclusive.

Example

df.loc[:3, ['Quality','Names']]

Output

	Quality	Names
0	Governance	Ram
1	Archery	Arjun
2	Flute	Krishna
3	Trust	Laxman

9.2.5 Adding Rows

One or more rows can be added or existing rows can be modified, using the following methods.

(i) Add rows at the end of the dataframe object

data_frame.**append**(*object, ignore_index*)

object: Dictionary/Series/data_frame, containing the rows to be appended.
ignore_index: Ignores the source object indices when set to True.
Returns a dataframe after appending the rows.

Example

```
pandavas=pd.DataFrame({'Rno':[1,2,3],
   'Names':['Dharma','Bheem','Arjun'], 'Cgp':[8.5, 8.2, 9.2]})
kouravas=pd.DataFrame({'Rno':[1,2],
   'Names':['Duryodhan','Dussasan'], 'Cgp':[6.8, 6.1]})
pandavas=pandavas.append({'Rno':6,
   'Names':'Karna','Cgp':8.99}, ignore_index = True)
print('Pandavas after appending one row :\n', pandavas)
pandavas = pandavas.append(kouravas, ignore_index=True)
print('Pandavas after appending with another dataframe :\n',
   pandavas)
```

Output

Pandavas after appending one row:

	Rno	Names	Cgp
0	1	Dharma	8.50
1	2	Bheem	8.20
2	3	Arjun	9.20
3	6	Karna	8.99

Pandavas after appending with another dataframe:

	Rno	Names	Cgp
0	1	Dharma	8.50
1	2	Bheem	8.20
2	3	Arjun	9.20
3	6	Karna	8.99
4	1	Duryodhan	6.80
5	2	Dussasan	6.10

(ii) *iloc()* method replaces the row at the specified index if the row index exists. Generates an error if the row index does not exist. The row index must be an integer.

data_frame.iloc[row_index] = values_list

(iii) *loc()* method replaces the row at the specified index. Unlike *iloc()* method, no error is generated if the row index does not exist. Row labels can be an integer or non-integer.

data_frame.loc[row_label] = values_list

Example

```
# iloc and loc
pandavas=pd.DataFrame({'Rno':[1,2,3],
```

```
'Names':['Dharma','Bheem','Arjun'], 'Cgp':[8.5, 8.2, 9.2]})
pandavas.iloc[1] = [40, 'Nakul', 7.3]
print('Pandavas after iloc :\n',pandavas)
pandavas.loc[3] = [5, 'Sahadev', 7.4]
print('Pandavas after loc :\n',pandavas)
```

Output

Pandavas after iloc:

	Rno	Names	Cgp
0	1	Dharma	8.5
1	40	Nakul	7.3
2	3	Arjun	9.2

Pandavas after loc:

	Rno	Names	Cgp
0	1	Dharma	8.5
1	40	Nakul	7.3
2	3	Arjun	9.2
3	5	Sahadev	7.4

(iv) Concatenating dataframes

Two or more dataframe objects can be concatenated to generate a new dataframe object.

> pandas.**concat**(*dataframes_list, ignore_index, axis*)

dataframes_list: Rows of the data frame objects in the list are concatenated
axis - 0 to perform vertical concatenation, 1 for horizontal concatenation
ignore_index: ignores the source *dataframes* indices when set to True
Returns a new *dataframe* after concatenation.

Example

```
# concatenating dataframes
pandavas = pd.DataFrame({'Rno': [1,2],
    'Names':['Dharma','Bheem'], 'Quality':['Honesty','Strength']})
kouravas=pd.DataFrame({'Rno':[1,2],
    'Names':['Duryodhan','Dussasan'],
    'Quality':['Arrogance','Antagonist'] })
print('Vertical
    concatenation:\n',pd.concat([pandavas,kouravas],
    ignore_index=True, axis=0))
print('Horizontal
    concatenation:\n',pd.concat([pandavas,kouravas],
    ignore_index=True, axis=1))
```

Output

Vertical concatenation:

	Rno	Names	Quality
0	1	Dharma	Honesty
1	2	Bheem	Strength
2	1	Duryodhan	Arrogance
3	2	Dussasan	Antagonist

Horizontal concatenation:

	0	1	2	3	4	5
0	1	Dharma	Honesty	1	Duryodhan	Arrogance
1	2	Bheem	Strength	2	Dussasan	Antagonist

9.2.6   Deleting Columns

One or more columns of a dataframe can be deleted using the following methods.

(i) **pop()** method deletes the specified column

   *data_frame.***pop(***'col_name'***)**

data_frame gets modified
Returns the deleted column values
Example

```
pandavas = pd.DataFrame({'Rno': [1,2],
    'Names':['Dharma','Bheem'], 'Quality':['Honesty','Strength']})
print('pop() method returns deleted column values :\n',
    pandavas.pop('Rno'))
print('Pandavas after delete :\n ',pandavas)
```

Output

pop() method returns deleted column values:
0   1
1   2
Name: Rno, dtype: int64
Pandavas after delete:

	Names	Quality
0	Dharma	Honesty
1	Bheem	Strength

(ii) **drop()** deletes one or more columns or rows of a dataframe.

   data_frame.**drop**(*col_row_names, axis, inplace*)

col_row_names: List of columns or row labels to be deleted.
axis - specifies the axis, 1 for columns and 0 for rows.
inplace - if set to true, operation is done in the *data_frame* itself.
Returns the modified *data_frame*.
Example: Deleting columns

```
pandavas = pd.DataFrame({'Rno': [1,2],
    'Names':['Dharma','Bheem'], 'Quality':['Honesty','Strength']})
pandavas.drop( [ 'Quality' ] , axis=1, inplace=Ture)
print('Pandavas after delete :\n ',pandavas)
```

Output

   Pandavas after delete:

	Rno	Names
0	1	Dharma
1	2	Bheem

Example: Deleting rows

```
pandavas=pd.DataFrame({'Rno':[1,2,3],
    'Names':['Dharma','Bheem','Arjun']})
pandavas.drop([0,2], axis=0, inplace=True)
print('Pandavas after deleting rows :\n ',pandavas)
```
Output

   Pandavas after deleting rows:

	Rno	Names
0	2	Bheem

9.2.7   Renaming Column Names and Row Labels

Column names or row labels can be renamed using the following methods.

data_frame.**rename**(*dict_obj, axis, inplace*)

dict_obj - dictionary of old and new names as key-value pairs
axis - 0 for rows and 1 for columns
inplace - if set to true, operation is done in the *data_frame* itself

Example

> pandavas = pd.DataFrame({'Rno': [1,2], 'Names':['Dharma','Bheem'],
>   'Quality':['Honesty','Strength']})
> print('Column names : ', pandavas.columns)
> print('Row Labels: ', pandavas.index)
> pandavas.rename({'Rno': 'Position'}, axis=1, inplace=True)
> pandavas.rename({1: 'row2'}, axis=0,inplace=True)
> print('After changing column and row label :\n', pandavas)

Output

> Column names : Index(['Rno', 'Names', 'Quality'], dtype='object')
> Row Labels: RangeIndex(start=0, stop=2, step=1)
> After changing column and row label:

	Position	Names	Quality
0	1	Dharma	Honesty
row2	2	Bheem	Strength

9.2.8   Methods on Dataframes

The following methods give information and summary statistics of the dataframe object.

(i) *data_frame*.**info()**

Displays information about the dataframe like rows labels, column names, and their data types, number of non-null values in each column, memory used by the dataframe etc.

Example

> pandavas=pd.DataFrame({'Names':['Dharma','Bheem','Arjun'],
>   'Cgp':[8.5, 8.2, 9.2], 'Quality':['Honesty','Strength',
>   'Wisdom']})
> print(pandavas.info())

Output

> <class 'pandas.core.frame.DataFrame'>
> RangeIndex: 3 entries, 0 to 2
> Data columns (total 3 columns):

#	Column	Non-Null	Count	Dtype
0	Names	3	non-null	object
1	Cgp	3	non-null	float64
2	Quality	3	non-null	object

dtypes: float64(1), object(2)
memory usage: 200.0+ bytes
None

(ii) **describe()**

Displays statistical information about the dataframe like mean, min, max, count and quartile values of numerical columns.

> *data_frame*.**describe**(*percentile* = None, *include* = None,
> *exclude* = None)

percentile: whether to return percentiles
include: List of data types to be included in the result.
  Default is None. If None, it describes only numerical columns.
exclude: List of data types to be excluded in the result.
  Default is None.
Example

> print(pandavas.describe())

Output

	Cgp
count	3.000000
mean	8.633333
std	0.513160
min	8.200000
25%	8.350000
50%	8.500000
75%	8.850000
max	9.200000

9.2.9 Functions on Columns

Following are the aggregation functions on one or more columns of a
  dataframe like min, max, sum, mean. standard deviation, variance etc.

Example

>   pandavas=pd.DataFrame({'Names':['Dharma','Bheem','Arjun'],
>   'Cgp':[8.5,8.2, 9.2], 'Quality':['Honesty','Strength', 'Wisdom']})
>   print('Max values of Cgp & Quality :
>   \n',pandavas[['Cgp','Quality']].max())
>   print('Min values of Cgp & Quality :
>   \n',pandavas[['Cgp','Quality']].min())
>   print('Sum of Cgp : ',pandavas['Cgp'].sum())print('Average of Cgp :
>   ',round(pandavas['Cgp'].mean(),2))
>   print('Standard Deviation of Cgp : ',round(pandavas['Cgp'].std(),2))
>   print('Variance of Cgp : ',round(pandavas['Cgp'].var(),2))

Output

>   Max values of Cgp & Quality :
>   Cgp   9.2
>   Quality Wisdom
>   dtype: object
>   Min values of Cgp & Quality :
>   Cgp   8.2
>   Quality Honesty
>   dtype: object
>   Sum of Cgp : 25.9
>   Average of Cgp : 8.63
>   Standard Deviation of Cgp : 0.51
>   Variance of Cgp : 0.26

9.2.10   Operators on Dataframes

Vectorization - Arithmetic and relational operators can be applied to the entire columns of the dataframe called vectorization.

(a)

   *data_frame[col_x] **operator** data_frame[col_y]*

operator: is applied on corresponding values of the operand vectors.
Returns a resultant vector.

(b)

   *data_frame[col_x] **operator** constant*

constant is applied on every value of the operand vector *col_x*.
Returns a resultant vector.

Example: Arithmetic operations

```
marks= pd.DataFrame({ 'Maths':[87,65,92,56], 'Python':[76,83,69,88],
  'English':[88,90,79,77] })
marks['Maths'] = marks['Maths'] +3
marks['Total'] = marks['Maths'] + marks['Python'] + marks['English']
print('Result of Arithmetic operations :\n', marks)
```

Output

Result of Arithmetic operations:

	Maths	Python	English	Total
0	90	76	88	254
1	68	83	90	241
2	95	69	79	243
3	59	88	77	224

Example: Relational operation

```
print(marks[marks['Python']>marks['Maths']])
```

Output

	Maths	Python	English	Total
1	68	83	90	241
3	59	88	77	224

9.3 Dataframes and Files

Data can be loaded from a file into a dataframe and vice versa. Common file formats supported are CSV (Comma Separated Values), Excel, and JSON.

(i) Functions to load data from a **file into a dataframe** are

(a) *data_frame = pandas.read_csv('file_path',names,header=None, usecols, nrows, index_col, skiprows, dtypes)*

file_path: Location of the file
names: New column names
header: Which row of the dataframe is to be treated *None* - no header in the file
                 as the header. Default is header=0.
usecols: List of columns to be loaded into the *data_frame*
nrows: Number of rows, from the beginning of the file,
                      to load into *data_frame*
index_col: Column of the file to be used as row index
                      to *data_frame*
skiprows: Number of rows to skip from the beginning
                      of the file
dtypes: Change data types of columns. Specify as dictionary

(b) *pandas.read_excel('file_path', sheet_name, names,header=None, usecols, nrows, index_col, skiprows, dtypes)*

sheet_name: List of sheets to be used. It can be specified either
    as an index or sheet name.
All other arguments have the same meaning as in the read_csv() function.

(c) pandas.**read_json**(*'file_path'*)

(ii) Similarly, functions to save data of a **dataframe into a file** are

(a) *data_frame.to_csv('file_path', columns, header, index, index_label)*

file_path: File into which *data_frame* is to be saved
columns: List of columns to include in the file
header: True - column names to be included
                      in the output
                 False - column names are not included
                      in the output.
                 First row of data is treated as a header.
index: True / False – Skip index column in the output
index_label: Name of row index column

(b) *data_frame.**to_excel**('file_path', sheet_name, header, columns, index, index_label)*

(c) *data_frame.**to_json**('file_path')*

Note: When reading from CSV / Excel files, one additional Unnamed column is created. This can be avoided by reading that as an index column with the following argument.

    index_col=[0]

Example 1:

```
from operator import index
import pandas as pd
import numpy as np
data = pd.read_csv('/content/sample_data/Housing.csv', header=0,
    nrows=5,usecols=['Price','Area','BedRooms'],
    names= ['Price','Area', 'BedRooms'],dtype={'Area': np.int32})
print('Dataframe created from CSV file :\n', data)
print('Data types of columns :\n', data.dtypes)
# dataframe into Excel file
data.to_excel('sample.xlsx', index_label='Row Label')
# read from Excel file
df_new=pd.read_excel('sample.xlsx',index_col=[0],header=0)
print('Dataframe created from Excel file :\n',df_new)
```

Output

Dataframe created from CSV file :

	Price	Area	BedRooms
0	13300000	7420	4
1	12250000	8960	4
2	12250000	9960	3
3	12215000	7500	4
4	11410000	7420	4

Data types of columns:

Price	int64
Area	int32
BedRooms	int64

dtype: object
Dataframe created from Excel file:

Row Label	Price	Area	BedRooms
0	13300000	7420	4
1	12250000	8960	4
2	12250000	9960	3
3	12215000	7500	4
4	11410000	7420	4

Example 2:

```
pandavas=pd.DataFrame({'Names':['Dharma','Bheem','Arjun'],
    'Quality':['Honesty','Strength', 'Wisdom']})
pandavas.to_json('sample.json')      # dataframe into JSON file
df = pd.read_json('sample.json')      # read from JSON file
```

print('Dataframe created from JSON file : \n',df)

Output

Dataframe created from JSON file :

	Names	Quality
0	Dharma	Honesty
1	Bheem	Strength
2	Arjun	Wisdom

9.4   User-Defined Modules

A Python module is a file that contains a Python script of related function definitions and data. Modules provide reusability of code and partition the namespace. Python modules can be of the following types

(i) **Built-in modules** are precoded modules that are built into the Python installation package. For example, datetime, math, random etc.

(ii) **User-defined** modules are the modules defined by the users.

Create user-defined modules: Write the function definitions and data in a file using any text editor and save the file with **.py** suffix. The modules need to be imported to use the functions and data defined in the file. Once the module is imported, it becomes a variable name. Hence, the module names cannot be reserved words. Functions and data defined in the module become attributes of the module.

Example: areas.py file in **Mymodules** directory

```
pi=3.14
def cir_area(radius):
    return pi*radius*radius
def tri_area(base, height):
    return 0.5*base*height
def rect_area(breadth, length):
    return breadth*height
```

(iii) **Using modules:** Once the modules are created, the functions and variables defined in the module can be used by importing them into the scripts. We can import specific or all the functions and data of the module. Following are the different ways of importing modules.

(1) import *module_name*

This does not import the individual functions. To use the function, qualify the function name with the module name.

Example

> import math
> print(math.sqrt(5))

Output

> 2.236

(2) import with renaming

import *module_name* as **alias_name**
Example

> import math as m
> print(m.sqrt(5))

Output

> 2.236

(3) import only specific functions

from *module_name* import fun_name1, fun_name2...
Example

> from math import sqrt, pow
> print(pow(3,5))

Output

> 243.0

(4) import all functions of the module

from *module_name* import *
Example

> from Mymodules.areas import *
> print(cir_area(5))
> print(tri_area(5,6)

Output

> 78.5
> 15.0

(iv) List the functions and data of a module

First import the module, then

> dir(module_name)

Example

dir(Mymodules.areas)

Output

['__builtins__', '__cached__', '__doc__', '__file__', '__loader__',
'__name__', '__package__', '__spec__', 'cir_area', 'pi', 'rect_area',
'square_area', 'tri_area']

To see the descriptions and functions details of a module.

help('Mymodules.areas')

Output

Help on module Mymodules.areas in Mymodules:
NAME
    Mymodules.areas
FUNCTIONS
    cir_area(radius)
    rect_area(breadth, length)
    square_area(side)
    tri_area(base, height)
DATA
    pi = 3.14
FILE
    C:\users\laksh\mymodules\areas.py

List the built-in modules

help('modules')

(v) **Module Search**

Python interpreter searches for the specified module in the following sequence

- Current directory from which the program executes
- If not found in the current directory, it searches in the list of directories specified in the PYTHONPATH environment variable

If not found in PYTHONPATH, it searches in the list of directories configured during Python installation

(vi) **Reloading modules**

If the module is already imported and the module is updated later, to use the newer version, reload the module using

import **importlib**
importlib.reload(*module_name*)

Update the **areas.py** file by adding one more function for calculating the area of square.

```
def square_area(side):
    return side*side
```

Example

```
import importlib
importlib.reload(Mymodules.areas)
from Mymodules.areas import *
print(square_area(5))
print(pi)
```

Output

```
25
3.14
```

9.5   Case Study: Data Manipulation and Analysis

The *mobile* dataset contains sales data of mobiles of different companies. The data includes different features of the mobile, like RAM, internal memory, dual sim, and the price range of the mobile. The objective is to find the relationship between different features of the mobile and its selling price. In this case study, we will use this dataset to do data manipulation using the **pandas** library.

(i) Load the dataset into a dataframe.

```
import pandas as pd
df = pd.read_csv('/content/sample_data/mobile_data.csv')
print('Dataset shape : ', df.shape)
print('No. of rows :',df.shape[0], ' \nNo. of columns :',df.shape[1])
print('Column Names:\n',df.columns)
```

Output

```
Dataset shape : (2000, 21)
No. of rows : 2000
No. of columns : 21
Column Names:
Index(['battery_power', 'blue', 'clock_speed', 'dual_sim', 'fc',
'four_g','int_memory', 'm_dep', 'mobile_wt', 'n_cores', 'pc', 'px_height',
'px_width', 'ram', 'sc_h', 'sc_w', 'talk_time', 'three_g','touch_screen', 'wifi',
'price_range'],dtype='object')
```

(ii) Check the datatypes of the attributes/columns.

```
df.dtypes
```

Output

battery_power	int64
blue	int64
clock_speed	float64
dual_sim	int64
fc	int64
four_g	int64
int_memory	int64

m_dep	float64
mobile_wt	int64
n_cores	int64
pc	int64
px_height	int64
px_width	int64
ram	int64
sc_h	int64
sc_w	int64
talk_time	int64
three_g	int64
touch_screen	int64
wifi	int64
price_range	int64
dtype: object	

Even though the data types are integer & float, some attributes are not continuous. Attributes with few unique values can be considered categorical.

(iii) Let us find the attributes with less than six unique values. These can be considered categorical.

```
import numpy as np
cat_cols = []
print('Columns with less than six unique values:')
for col in df.columns:
    n = len(np.unique(df[col]))
    if n<=5:
        print(' ',col,n)
        cat_cols.append(col)
```

Output

```
Columns with less than six unique values:
 blue 2
 dual_sim 2
 four_g 2
 three_g 2
 touch_screen 2
```

```
wifi 2
price_range 4
```

(iv) The above attributes are binary except, *price_ range*. Let us take only those binary attributes.

```
# Remove price_range from cat_cols
idx = cat_cols.index('price_range')
cat_cols.pop(idx)
print('Binary attributes:\n',cat_cols)
```

Output

```
Binary attributes:
    ['blue', 'dual_sim', 'four_g', 'three_g', 'touch_screen', 'wifi']
```

(v) Let us check the values of these binary attributes.

```
print('Binary attributes values:\n',df[cat_cols].head())
```

Output

Binary attributes values:

	blue	dual_sim	four_g	three_g	touch_screen	wifi
0	0	0	0	0	0	1
1	1	1	1	1	1	0
2	1	1	1	1	1	0
3	1	0	0	1	0	0
4	1	0	1	1	1	0

(vi) It shows that the binary values are numeric 0/1 . Let us convert these binary numeric values 0/1 to No/Yes.

```
for col in cat_cols:
    df[col] = df[col].map(0:'No', 1:'Yes')
print('After conversion :\n',df[cat_cols].head())
```

Output

After conversion :

	blue	dual_sim	four_g	three_g	touch_screen	wifi
0	No	No	No	No	No	Yes
1	Yes	Yes	Yes	Yes	Yes	No
2	Yes	Yes	Yes	Yes	Yes	No
3	Yes	No	No	Yes	No	No
4	Yes	No	Yes	Yes	Yes	No

(vii) After the conversion, the data types of binary attributes are changed to *object* type.

print('Data types of binary attributes:\n',df[cat_cols].dtypes)

Output

Data types of binary attributes:

```
blue            object
dual_sim        object
four_g          object
three_g         object
touch_screen    object
wifi            object
dtype: object
```

(viii) Let us count the unique values in each binary attribute.

```
for col in cat_cols:
    print('Column Name :',col)
    print(df[col].value_counts())
```

Output

```
No  1010
Yes    990
Name: blue, dtype: int64
Yes    1019
No     981
Name: dual_sim, dtype: int64
Yes    1043
No     957
Name: four_g, dtype: int64
Yes    1523
No     477
Name: three_g, dtype: int64
Yes    1006
No     994
Name: touch_screen, dtype: int64
Yes    1014
No     986
Name: wifi, dtype: int64
```

Note: *value_counts()* function returns a series object, which is an integer datatype.

(ix) Let us find the minimum and maximum values of non-binary attributes and create a new dataframe with these values.

```
cols = df.columns
non_cat_cols= [col for col in cols if col not in cat_cols]
# Create a dataframe to contain min & max values
min_max_df = pd.DataFrame()
min_max_df['Min Value'] = df[non_cat_cols].apply(np.min)
min_max_df['Max Value'] = df[non_cat_cols].apply(np.max)
min_max_df.index=non_cat_cols
print(min_max_df)
```

Output

	Min Value	Max Value
battery_power	501.0	1998.0
clock_speed	0.5	3.0
fc	0.0	19.0
int_memory	2.0	64.0
m_dep	0.1	1.0
mobile_wt	80.0	200.0
n_cores	1.0	8.0
pc	0.0	20.0
px_height	0.0	1960.0
px_width	500.0	1998.0
ram	256.0	3998.0
sc_h	5.0	19.0
sc_w	0.0	18.0
talk_time	2.0	20.0
price_range	0.0	3.0

(x) px_width and px_height attributes can be combined into a single attribute, say resolution. First, let us change the data type of these attributes to string. This conversion is done so that the values in the *resolution* column are in a standard format.

```
# change the datatypes to string
df['px_height']=df['px_height'].astype(str)
df['px_width']=df['px_width'].astype(str)
print('After changing the data types:\n',df[['px_height','px_width']].dtypes)
```

Output

```
After changing the data types:
 px_height object
 px_width object
dtype: object
```

(xi) Create a new column called *resolution* and drop *px_width* & *px_height* columns.

```
df['resolution']= df['px_width']+' x '+df['px_height']
# remove 'px_width','px_height' columns
df.drop(['px_width','px_height'], axis=1, inplace=True)
print('Display first five values of "resolution" column
\n',df[['resolution']].head())
```

Output

Display first five values of "resolution" column

```
      resolution
0     756 x 20
1     1988 x 905
2     1716 x 1263
3     1786 x 1216
4     1212 x 1208
```

Exercises

1. Read data from CSV file into a dataframe and perform the following operations

(a) Create a dataframe with all float columns only
(b) Find the mean and standard deviation of each column

2. Create a dataframe of fruits with the columns as Name, Unit price, and Quantity by taking the input from the user. Perform the following operations

(a) Add the 'amount' column by multiplying Unit price with Quantity.
(b) Write the data frame into a JSON file named, Fruits.

3. Read data from excel file containing RNo, Name, and marks in three subjects: Python, Java & Maths, of 10 students. Perform the following operations

(a) Add total marks column with a total of Python, Java, and Maths marks.
(b) Create a CSV file with only those students whose total is more than 200 marks.

4. Create a dataframe with the name and mail Id by taking values from the user. Create two file

(a) Gmails.csv - rows with gmail IDs
(b) Others.csv - remaining rows.

5. A file contains marks in Python, and Java of 10 students. The second file contains Maths, and English marks of the same students. Perform the following operations

(a) Create a dataframe containing all four subject marks
(b) Add a total column with a total of all four subject marks
(c) Create a file where total marks are more than average.

Review Questions

Consider the following data frame named, df, for questions 1 to 5.

	Product	Price
0	Laptop	1200
1	Printer	150
2	Tablet	300
3	Desk	450
4	Chair	200

(1) What is the output of

    df.size

(a) 5
(b) 4
(c) 10
(d) 6

(2) What is the output of

    len(df[df['Price']>400])

(a) 1
(b) 2
(c) 3
(d) Generates Error

(3) What is the output of

    df['Product'].max()

(a) Tablet
(b) Desk
(c) Chair
(d) Printer

(4) What is the output of

    df.loc[2] = ['Desktop', 1300]
    print(df.shape)

(a) (5,2)
(b) (4,2)
(c) (6,2)
(d) (5,3)

(5) What is the output of

print(len(df.columns))

(a) 3
(b) 2
(c) 5
(d) 4

(6) Which of the following is not true about the dataframes

(a) Dataframe can have one column
(b) Dataframe can be empty
(c) Rows of a dataframe have labels
(d) Row labels of dataframe can be only integers

(7) Which of the following method is used to delete a column of a dataframe

(a) del()
(b) delete( )
(c) pop( )
(d) remove( )

(8) Method to display first five rows of a table

(a) head()
(b) head(5)
(c) first(5)
(d) Both a & b

(9) Method to write data from dataframe into CSV file

(a) df.read_csv()
(b) pd.read_csv()
(c) df.to_csv()
(d) pd.to_csv()

(10) Which of the following is not an attribute of a dataframe

(a) Size
(b) len()
(c) ndim
(d) dtypes

Chapter 10
SQLite3

To manage large volumes of data, it has to be stored in an organized and structured fashion so that it is easy to access and manipulate the data. A database management system (DBMS) is a software system for storing, retrieving, and manipulating data in the database. Different types of DBMS are Relational databases, Hierarchical databases, Network databases, etc. Relational database management systems organize data in the form of tables. Each table consists of columns representing attributes (property) and rows representing values of the attributes. Popular relational database systems are Oracle, MySQL, PostgreSQL, IBM DB2, SQLite, etc. SQL is a structured query language used to store, retrieve, and manipulate data stored in relational databases.

Sqlite3 is a file-based relational database management system where data is stored in a flat-file. It is simple to create and use the database. Though it is not a full-featured database, it offers a large set of standard SQL commands and is ideal for beginners. Python provides a Sqlite3 module that implements SQL-based database management systems.

Working with SQLite database requires the following steps:

(1) Import sqlite3 module.

   import sqlite3

(2) Establish connection to the database by opening the database file using **connect** method.

   connection_obj = sqlite3.connect('database_name')

© The Author(s) 2024
A. L. Muddana and S. Vinayakam, *Python for Data Science*,
https://doi.org/10.1007/978-3-031-52473-8_10

The method takes the database name as the parameter and returns the connection object. In case the database name does not exist, a new database file is created.

(3) Create a *cursor* object on the *connection* object. The cursor object acts as an interface between the SQLite database and SQL query.

cursor_object = connection_obj.cursor()

(4) SQL queries are executed using the *execute* method on the cursor object or connection object.

cursor_object.execute(sql_query)
connection_object.execute(sql_query)

*sql*_query is specified as string
Returns the query result as a set of records.
The result set can be accessed using the following fetch methods:

fetchall()—Returns all the remaining records of the result set.
fetchone()—Returns the current record of the result set.
fetchmany(*size*)—Returns the next *size* number of records of the result set.

Note: When the *execute* method is called on a *connection* object, an intermediate *cursor* object is created to execute the query.

10.1   SQL Commands

Commands to interact with SQLite3 databases are similar to standard SQL commands. The commands can be categorized into

10.1.1   Data Definition Language (DDL)

Relational database consists of a set of tables. Each table is defined by columns representing the attributes and records/rows containing values of the attributes.

DDL commands include creating a new table, altering the structure of existing tables by adding/deleting columns, deleting tables, renaming tables and renaming column names, etc.

(i) **Create a new table**

CREATE TABLE table_name (*col1 datatype, col2 datatype...*)

> *col1, col2...*: Names of the columns.
>   Names are case insensitive
> *datatype*:   Data type of the values in the column.

The supported data types are integer, real, text, blob, NULL.

Optional parameters are

> *default:* Default value for each row of the column.
> NOT NULL indicating that the value of the column
>   cannot be null.
> PRIMARY KEY of the table. The values should be
>   unique/distinct.

(ii) **Alter structure of an existing table**

a. Add a new column to the table

> ALTER TABLE table_name ADD COLUMN col_name datatype
> [DEFAULT *value* PRIMARY KEY NOT NULL]

b. Remove a column

> ALTER TABLE table_name DROP COLUMN col_name

c. Rename table name

> ALTER TABLE table_name RENAME TO new_table_name

d. Rename column(after sqlite version 3.25)

> ALTER TABLE table_name RENAME COLUMN col_name TO
> new_col_name

(iii) **Delete the existing table from the database**

DROP TABLE [IF EXISTS] *database_name.table_name*

Generates an error if the table does not exist.
IF EXISTS is optional. When specified in the command, no error is generated
even if the table does not exist.
Only one table can be deleted using the command. To remove multiple tables,
use multiple drop commands.

10.1.2 Data Manipulation Language (DML)

Data manipulation commands include inserting, deleting, or modifying records/rows of the table.

(i) **Insert rows into a table**

    a. Insert single row as per columns order in the table

        INSERT INTO table_name VALUES (column_*values*)

    b. Insert multiple rows as per columns order in the table.

        INSERT INTO table_name VALUES (column_*values*), (column_*values*), (column_*values*). . .

    c. Insert rows as per column list order specified in the command.

        INSERT INTO table1_name (col_list) VALUES (values_list)

(ii) **Update or modify a record of a table**

    a. Update a single column that satisfies the condition.

        UPDATE table_name SET col1= new_value WHERE condition

    b. Update multiple columns that satisfies the condition.

        UPDATE table_name SET col1= new_value, col2= new_value . . . WHERE condition

(iii) **Delete records of a table**

    a. Delete one or more rows satisfying the condition

        DELETE FROM table_name WHERE condition

    b. Delete all rows

        DELETE FROM table_name

All rows are deleted but the table structure exists.

10.1.3   *Data Query Language (DQL)*

select statement retrieves records from one or more tables.

SELECT *column_names* FROM *table_names* WHERE *condition*
    ORDER BY *col_name* ASC/DESC, *col_name* ASC/DESC. . .
    GROUP BY *col_names*

column_names:	Columns in the result set.
table_names:	Table names separated by commas. Records are drawn from multiple tables using join operation.
condition:	selects those rows that satisfy the condition

Sorts the result set as per columns specified in ORDER BY clause in ascending (ASC) or descending (DESC) order.

Records are grouped based on each distinct value of the column specified in the GROUP BY clause. Aggregate functions like min(), max(), avg(), sum(), count(), etc. are applied on each group resulting in a value.

10.1.4   *Examples*

```
con = sqlite3.connect('course.db')
cur = con.cursor()
```

(i) Create a new table named *student*

```
cur.execute('CREATE TABLE student(Rno INTEGER NOT
    NULL, Name TEXT DEFAULT "XYZ")')
cur.execute('CREATE TABLE marks(Rno INTEGER NOT NULL,
    Python INTEGER DEFAULT 0,
    Maths INTEGER DEFAULT 0)')
```

Output

sqlite3.Cursor object at 0x00000299AEADD140>

(ii) Set of tables of the database can be obtained using

```
print(cursor.execute("select name from sqlite_master where
    type='table'").fetchall())
```

Output

[('student',), ('marks',)]

(iii) Table description specifies column number, column names, data types, whether value can be NULL, default value, and whether the column defines the primary key. The following query gives the table description:

```
cur.execute("pragma table_info(student)").fetchall()
```

Output

```
[(0, 'Rno', 'INTEGER', 1, None, 0),
  (1, 'Name', 'TEXT', 0, "'XYZ'", 0)]
```

(iv) Inserting rows into the table

```
# insert single row
cur.execute('INSERT INTO student VALUES(1, "Dharma")')
# insert multiple rows
cur.execute('INSERT INTO student VALUES(1, "Dharma"),
  (2, "Bheem")')
# insert single column value, the other column takes default
# value
cur.execute('INSERT INTO student (Rno) VALUES(3),(4)')
```

(v) Retrieving record from the table using *select* query

```
result = cur.execute('SELECT * FROM student')
print('First record : ',result.fetchone())
print('Next two records : ',result.fetchmany(2))
print('Remaining records ',result.fetchall())
```

Output

```
First record : (1, 'Dharma')
Next two record : [(1, 'Dharma'), (2, 'Bheem')]
Remaining records : [(3, 'XYZ'), (4, 'XYZ')]
```

(vi) Adding new column named *phone*

```
cur.execute("ALTER TABLE student ADD COLUMN phone
  INTEGER DEFAULT 1234")
print('Table description after adding new column- phone : ')
print(cur.execute("pragma table_info(student)").fetchall())
print('Records of the table :')
print(cur.execute("select * from student").fetchall())
```

Output

```
Table description after adding new column- phone :
[(0, 'Rno', 'INTEGER', 1, None, 0), (1, 'Name', 'TEXT', 0,
  "'XYZ'", 0), (2, 'phone', 'INTEGER', 0, '1234', 0)]
```

Records of the table:
(1, 'Dharma', 1234), (1, 'Dharma', 1234), (2, 'Bheem', 1234),
(3, 'XYZ', 1234), (4, 'XYZ', 1234)]

(vii) Rename column *phone* to *Mobile*

```
cur.execute('ALTER TABLE student RENAME COLUMN phone
   TO Mobile')
print(cur.execute('PRAGMA table_info(student)').fetchall())
```

Output

(0, 'Rno', 'INTEGER', 1, None, 0), (1, 'Name', 'TEXT', 0,
'"XYZ"', 0), (2, 'Mobile', 'INTEGER', 0, '1234', 0)]

(viii) Delete the records satisfying the condition

```
# delete rows from table
cur.execute('DELETE FROM student WHERE Name="Dharma"')
print("Records after deleting Dharma :")
print(cur.execute("select * from student").fetchall())
```

Output

Records after deleting Dharma :
(2, 'Bheem', 1234), (3, 'XYZ', 1234), (4, 'XYZ', 1234)]

Note: If *where* clause is not specified, all the records are deleted.

(ix) Update values of Name column

```
nm1, nm2 = input('Enter names of Rno 3 & 4 separated by
   space').split()
cur.execute('UPDATE student SET Name= ?
   WHERE Rno==?', (nm1,3))
cur.execute('UPDATE student SET Name= ?
   WHERE Rno==?', (nm2,4))
print('Records after update :\n',cur.execute('SELECT *
   FROM student').fetchall())
```

Output

Enter names of Rno 3 & 4 separated by space Nakul Sahadev
Records after update :
[(2, 'Bheem', 1234), (3, 'Nakul', 1234), (4, 'Sahadev', 1234)]

(x)   Delete column

```
cur.execute('ALTER TABLE student DROP COLUMN mobile')
print('After deleting mobile column : \n',cur.execute('PRAGMA
    table_info(student)').fetchall())
print('Sorting records by Name :\n')
cur.execute('SELECT * FROM student ORDER BY Name
    DESC').fetchall()
```

Output

```
After deleting mobile column :
[(0, 'Rno', 'INTEGER', 1, None, 0), (1, 'Name', 'TEXT', 0,
    "'XYZ'",0)]
Sorting records by Name :
(4, 'Sahadev'), (3, 'Nakul'), (2, 'Bheem')]
```

(xi)   Change table name to *students_info*

```
cur.execute('ALTER TABLE student RENAME TO
    students_info')
print('List of tables in the database:\n')
cur.execute('SELECT name FROM sqlite_master').fetchall()
```

Output

```
List of tables in the database:
[('students_info',), ('marks',)]
```

(xii)   Delete table from database

```
cur.execute('DROP TABLE students_info')
print("List of tables in the database: ")
cur.execute('SELECT name FROM sqlite_master').fetchall()
```

Output

```
List of tables in the database:
[ ('marks',)]
```

(xiii)   Aggregate functions

```
cur.execute('CREATE TABLE performance(Rno INTEGER,
    Family TEXT, Marks INTEGER)')
# take data from file into dataframe
```

```
df1= pd.read_csv('/content/sample_data/performance.csv')
# records formed from dataframe
records = df1.itertuples(index=False, name=None)
result = list(records)
# insert many records
cur.executemany('insert into performance values(?,?,?)', result)
cur.execute('select * from performance').fetchall()
cur.execute('select round(avg(Marks),2) , sum(Marks),
    Family from performance group by Family').fetchall()
```

Output

```
[(5, 'pandavas', 85),
(1, 'pandavas', 78),
(3, 'pandavas', 91),
(2, 'pandavas', 82),
(4, 'pandavas', 79),
(6, 'kouravas', 93),
(8, 'kouravas', 67),
(7, 'kouravas', 69)]
[(76.33, 229, 'kouravas'), (83.0, 415, 'pandavas')]
```

(xiv) Accessing records from multiple tables

```
df1 = pd.read_csv('/content/sample_data/samp1.csv')
df1.to_sql('samp1', con, index=False)
df2= pd.read_csv('/content/sample_data/samp2.csv')
df2.to_sql('samp2', con, index=False)
print(cur.execute('select * from samp1').fetchall())
print(cur.execute('select * from samp2').fetchall())
# join on Rno and extract Name from samp1 & Marks from
# samp2
print(cur.execute('select samp1.Name, samp2.Marks from
    samp1 inner join samp2 on
    samp1.Rno=samp2.Rno').fetchall())
```

Output

```
[(1, 'Ram'), (2, 'Bheem'), (3, 'Shyam'), (4, 'Tom')]
[(3, 78), (2, 87), (1, 98), (4, 76)]
[('Ram', 98), ('Bheem', 87), ('Shyam', 78), ('Tom', 76)]
```

(xv) To obtain the number of rows inserted, deleted, or modified since the connection was open, use the following method:

```
con.total_changes()
```

Output: 9

(xvi) The transactions should be committed. Otherwise, the changes are not saved in the database and not visible to other database connections.

    con.commit()

(xvii) Once done with the operations on the database, close the connection using

    con.close()

10.2   Case Study: Database Creation and Operations

Consider the following files containing information about the students.

details.csv: The file contains student details like Roll No., Name, and Mail_id of students.

sem1.csv, sem2.csv, sem3.csv: Each file contains Roll No. and grade points obtained by the student in the corresponding semester.

Create a database of tables, one table for each file. Apply the following sqlite3 functions, like creating a new table by joining the existing tables and data analysis queries, etc.

(i) Read the contents of each file into a dataframe.

```
import pandas as pd
df_details =
    pd.read_csv('/content/sample_data/Marks/details.csv')
df_sem1 =
    pd.read_csv('/content/sample_data/Marks/sem1.csv')
df_sem2 =
    pd.read_csv('/content/sample_data/Marks/sem2.csv')
df_sem3 =
    pd.read_csv('/content/sample_data/Marks/sem3.csv')
```

(ii) Open the database and create a cursor to execute the queries.

```
#import the module
import sqlite3
con = sqlite3.connect('performance.db')
cur = con.cursor()
```

New database with name, *performance.db*, is created, if it does not exist.

(iii) Display the tables of the database.

```
print(cur.execute("select name from sqlite_master where
type='table'").fetchall())
```

Output

[ ]

As a new database is created, it contains no tables.

(iv) Create tables from the data frames.

```
df_details.to_sql('details', con, index=False)
df_sem1.to_sql('sem1', con, index=False)
df_sem2.to_sql('sem2', con, index=False)
df_sem3.to_sql('sem3', con, index=False)
```

(v) After creating the tables, display the tables in the database.

```
print(cur.execute("select name from sqlite_master where
    type='table'").fetchall())
```

Output

[('details',), ('sem1',), ('sem2',), ('sem3',)]

(vi) Display table descriptions.

```
print('Description of the table- details:')
print(cur.execute("pragma table_info(details)").fetchall())
print('Description of the table- sem1:')
print(cur.execute("pragma table_info(sem1)").fetchall())
print('Description of the table- sem2:')
print(cur.execute("pragma table_info(sem2)").fetchall())
print('Description of the table- sem3:')
print(cur.execute("pragma table_info(sem3)").fetchall())
```

Output

```
Description of the table- details:
[(0,'Rno', 'INTEGER', 0, None,0),(1, 'Name', 'TEXT',0, None,0),
    (2, 'Mail_id', 'TEXT', 0, None, 0)]
Description of the table- sem1:
[(0, 'Rno', 'INTEGER', 0, None, 0),
    (1,'sem1_gp', 'REAL', 0, None, 0)]
Description of the table- sem2:
[(0,'Rno', 'INTEGER',0, None, 0),
    (1, 'sem2_gp', 'REAL',0, None, 0)]
Description of the table- sem3:
[(0,'Rno', 'INTEGER', 0, None, 0),
    (1, 'sem3_gp', 'REAL', 0, None, 0)]
```

(vii) Create a new table, *marks*, by joining the four tables on the *Rno* column.

> cur.execute('CREATE TABLE marks AS select a.Rno,a.Name,
> b.Sem1_gp, c.Sem2_gp, d.Sem3_gp from details a INNER JOIN
> sem1 b on a.Rno=b.Rno INNER JOIN sem2 c on a.Rno=c.Rno
> INNER JOIN sem3 d on a.Rno=d.Rno')

Output

> <sqlite3.Cursor at 0x7f55a6a59ce0>

(viii) Display the tables of the database after creating the *marks* table.

> print('Tables of the database')
> print(cur.execute("select name from sqlite_master where
> type='table'").fetchall())

Output

> Tables of the database
> [('details',), ('sem1',), ('sem2',), ('sem3',), ('marks',)]

(ix) Fetch first record of the *marks* table.

> cur.execute('select * from marks').fetchone()

Output

> (222010401002, 'Boyapalli Sreenath Reddy', 8.59, 8.66, 8.77)

(x) Extract and display the toppers of each semester.

> sem1_topper = cur.execute('select Name, max(Sem1_gp)
> from marks').fetchall()
> print('Sem1 Topper : ',sem1_topper)
> sem2_topper = cur.execute('select Name, max(Sem2_gp)
> from marks').fetchall()
> print('Sem2 Topper : ',sem2_topper)
> sem3_topper = cur.execute('select Name, max(Sem3_gp)
> from marks').fetchall()
> print('Sem3 Topper : ',sem3_topper)

Output

> Sem1 Topper : [('Vijay Paul Reddy Nakkala', 9.68)]
> Sem2 Topper : [('Kaila Kavya', 9.2)]
> Sem3 Topper : [('Chittimalla Aravind', 9.6)]

(xi) Extract the students who scored more than 9 grade points in all three semesters.

```
all_above9 = cur.execute('select Rno, Name, Sem1_gp, Sem2_gp,
    Sem3_gp from marks where (Sem1_gp>=9 and Sem2_gp>=9
    and Sem3_gp>=9)').fetchall()
print('Students who scored more 9 grade point in all
    three semesters:')
for student in all_above9:
    print(' ',student)
```

Output

Students who scored more 9 grade point in all three semesters:
(222010401004, 'Kaila Kavya', 9.43, 9.2, 9.33)
(222010401031, 'Chittimalla Aravind', 9.14, 9.11, 9.6)

(xii) Extract students who got zero grade points in any of the semesters.

```
gp_0 = cur.execute('select * from marks where (Sem1_gp=0
    or Sem2_gp=0 or Sem3_gp=0 )').fetchall()
print('Students who scored 0 grade point in any of the
    3 semesters:')
for student in gp_0:
    print(' ', student)
```

Output

Students who scored 0 grade point in any of the 3 semesters:
(222010401030, 'Vadde Shirisha', 8.35, 8.14, 0.0)
(222010401032, 'Rishi Kanth Reddy', 8.46, 7.82, 0.0)
(222010401037, 'Nallama Veena Anusha', 7.0, 0.0, 0.0)
(222010401047, 'Rakesh Daddali', 7.43, 0.0, 7.7

(xiii) Create a new column, *Average_gp*, in the marks table containing an average of three-semester grade points.

(a) Calculate the average grade point for the three semesters.

```
avg_gp = cur.execute('select Rno,
    round(( Sem1_gp+Sem2_gp + Sem3_gp)/3,2)
    from marks ').fetchall()
```

(b) Add the new column.

```
cur.execute('ALTER TABLE marks ADD COLUMN
    Average_gp REAL').fetchall()
cur.execute("pragma table_info(marks)").fetchall()
```

Output

>[(0, 'Rno', 'INT', 0, None, 0),
> (1, 'Name', 'TEXT', 0, None, 0),
> (2, 'sem1_gp', 'REAL', 0, None, 0),
> (3, 'sem2_gp', 'REAL', 0, None, 0),
> (4, 'sem3_gp', 'REAL', 0, None, 0),
> (5, 'Average_gp', 'REAL', 0, None, 0)]

(c) Update the column with the calculated average grade point.

>for val in avg_gp:
>   cur.execute('UPDATE marks SET Average_gp=? where
>Rno=?',[val[1],val[0]])

(d) Display the first three records after updating the *Average_gp* column.

>results = cur.execute('select * from marks').fetchmany(3)
>for record in results:
>   print(record)

Output

>(222010401002, 'Boyapalli Sreenath Reddy', 8.59, 8.66,
>   8.77, 8.67)
>(222010401003, 'Adnan Yacoob Mohammed', 7.84, 7.93,
>   7.98, 7.92)
>(222010401004, 'Kaila Kavya', 9.43, 9.2, 9.33, 9.32)

Exercises

1. Create a database named branch with the following tables:

   >Student table with Rno, Name, e_mail
   >Marks table with Rno, Python_marks, Maths_marks (max 100)

2. Perform the following operations:

   1. Insert 10 rows in Student table by taking values from the user.
   2. Insert 10 rows in Marks table from the .CSV file.
   3. Add a column Total that sum up Python and maths marks.
   4. Display the students whose total is more than 150 out of 200.
   5. Find the student with highest total and display his name and e_mail.
   6. Add a grace mark of 5 to the students who scored less than 50 in each subject.

Review Questions

(1) sqlite3 is a .... based database management system.

    (a) File
    (b) Object
    (c) Relational object
    (d) Hierarchical

(2) .... method is used to create a database in sqlite3.

    (a) Create()
    (b) Connect()
    (c) Open()
    (d) execute()

(3) Identify the correct statement about importing sqlite3 module.

    (a) import sqlite3
    (b) import Sqlite
    (c) import SQLite3
    (d) import SQLITE3

(4) .... object acts as an interface between sqlite3 database and SQL query.

    (a) Execute
    (b) Cursor
    (c) Connect
    (d) Sqlite

(5) .... method of sqlite3 is used to access the result of a SQL query.

    (a) fetchall()
    (b) select()
    (c) fetch()
    (d) get()

(6) Find out a DDL command from the following.

    (a) INSERT
    (b) UPDATE
    (c) ALTER
    (d) SET

(7) Identify the correct syntax of connecting databases in sqlite3.

    (a) sqlite.connect()
    (b) sqlite.connect.'database'
    (c) sqlite3.connect('database')
    (d) sqlite('database')

(8) The .... command is used to alter the structure of an existing table.

    (a) CREATE
    (b) DELETE
    (c) UPDATE
    (d) ALTER

(9) To retrieve one or more records from database table .... statement is used.

    (a) RETRIEVE
    (b) EXECUTE
    (c) SELECT
    (d) RUN

(10) .... statement is used to change a column value based on condition.

    (a) SELECT
    (b) UPDATE
    (c) ALTER
    (d) DROP

Chapter 11
Regular Expressions

Regular expression is a sequence of characters that defines a search pattern in the given text. These are used in pattern matching, pattern finding, and replacing in the given text. Regular expressions may contain meta characters and special sequences that have special meaning in defining a pattern. Regular expressions are commonly used in natural language processing tasks like data validations, data filtering and cleaning, web scraping, etc.

Python provides **re** module to work with regular expressions. The **re** module provides the following functions:

(i) search()
(ii) sub()
(iii) subn()
(iv) findall()
(v) split()

First, import the **re** module to use the functions

        import re

In addition to the characters, regular expressions may include meta characters and special sequences to define the pattern.

11.1 Meta Characters and Special Sequences

(i) • matches any single character except new line (\n) in that position

  e.g., **.ock** matches lock, mock, rock, sock. . .
(ii) * matches zero or more occurrences of the character preceding it

  e.g., **a*z** matches z, az, aaz, aaaz. . .

© The Author(s) 2024
A. L. Muddana and S. Vinayakam, *Python for Data Science*,
https://doi.org/10.1007/978-3-031-52473-8_11

(iii) + matches one or more occurrences of the character preceding it

e.g., **a+z** matches az, aaz, aaaz. . .

(iv) ? matches zero or one occurrences of character preceding it

e.g., **a?z** matches z, az

(v) {**n**} to repeat the left character n times

e.g., **a{2}z** matches aaz

(vi) {**n1,n2**} to repeat the character left to it- at least n1 times and atmost n2 times

e.g., **a{3,5}z** matches aaaz, aaaaz, aaaaaz

(vii) [   ] matches any characters specified in square brackets. Set of characters can be specified either as individual characters or as a range.

e.g., **[crmpb]**at matches cat, rat, mat, pat, bat

[b-h]at matches any character from b to h
bat, cat, dat, eat, fat, gat, hat

(viii) ^ can be used inside [   ] to match characters other than those specified.

(ix) \d Matches any single decimal digit. It is same as [0-9].

e.g., **9\d** matches 90,91,92,. . .99

(x) \D Matches any single character other than the decimal digit. It is same as [^0-9].

(xi) \s Matches any single white space like space, tab, carriage return, form feed, new line character.

(xii) \S Matches any single non-white space character.

e.g., **A\s\d** matches A followed by any white space followed by a digit.

(xiii) \w Matches any single alphanumeric characters, i.e., alphabets, digits, and underscore.

e.g., **A\w** matches A followed by any alphabet or digit or underscore

(xiv) \W Matches any non-alphanumeric character.

(xv) $ Checks if the string ends with the pattern preceding dollar symbol.

(xvi) ^ Checks if the string starts with the pattern following caret symbol.

Example

greet = "Python is a high level language"
print(re.search('language$', greet))
print(re.search('^Python', greet))

Output

<re.Match object; span=(23, 31), match='language'>
<re.Match object; span=(0, 6), match='Python'>

(xvii) | The operator matches either of the operands.

Example

> fruits = "Banana Rs40, Apples $10, Oranges Rs55 Mango $11"
> print(re.findall("Rs\d+|\$\d+",fruits))

Output

> ['Rs40', '$10', 'Rs55', '$11']

(xviii) ( ) Group the patterns by enclosing each pattern in ( ).
 (xix) \ Is an escape character. The character followed by \ has no special meaning.

Special sequences

 (i) \A Returns a match if the sequence following it is, at the beginning of the string.
 (ii) \Z Returns a match if the sequence preceding it, is at the end of the string.
 (iii) \B Returns a match if the sequence following it, is at the end of the word.

11.2 Functions on Regular Expressions

re module of Python provides the following functions to work with regular expressions.

 (i) **split()** function splits the input string wherever the pattern occurs in the string.

> **Syntax**

> ***re.split***(*pattern*, input_*string, max_split*)

pattern	Regular expression that defines the separator for the split.
input_string	Input string to be split.
max_split	Maximum number of splits that can occur.

> It is optional and default is all possible splits.
> Returns list of substrings.

Example

```
# make two splits by space
feature = "Python is a dynamically typed language"
words = re.split('\s',feature,2)
print("Two splits by space :\n", words)
# split by pattern
fruits = "Banana 40Rs.Apples 65Rs.Oranges 55"
print("Split by a pattern : ", re.split("Rs.", fruits))
```

Output

```
Two splits by space :
    ['Python', 'is', 'a dynamically typed language']
Split by a pattern : ['Banana 40', 'Apples 65', 'Oranges 55']
```

(ii) **Pattern Substitution:** Searches for pattern matching in the input string and substitutes with a new string. This can be done with the following two functions:

(a) **sub()** function substitutes the matched pattern with new string

| Syntax |

> *re.sub(pattern, new_substring, input_string)*

pattern	Regular expression to be matched.
input_string	Input string to be searched.
new_substring	String to be substituted for the matched occurrences.

In case the match is found, it returns a new string after substitution. Otherwise the original input string is returned.

(b) **subn()** function is the same as **sub()** except that it returns a tuple containing a new string and number of substitutions done.

Example

```
fruits = "Banana Rs.40 Apples Rs.65 Oranges Rs.55"
fruits_new = re.sub('Rs.', '$',fruits)
print("Result of sub() : ", fruits_new)
print("Result of sub()– only first two matches
    :\n",re.sub('Rs.', '$',fruits,2))
print("Result of subn()– substitute digits
    :\n",re.subn('\d', '?', fruits))
print("Result of subn()– substitute non-alphanumeric: \n",
    re.subn('\W', '?', fruits))
print('Input string is unchanged :\n', fruits)
```

Output

>   Result of sub(): Banana $40 Apples $65 Oranges $55
>   Result of sub()– only first two matches :
>   Banana $40 Apples $65 Oranges Rs.55
>   Result of subn()– substitute digits :
>   ('Banana Rs.?? Apples Rs.?? Oranges Rs.??', 6)
>   Result of subn()– substitute non-alphanumeric:
>   ('Banana?Rs?40??Apples?Rs?65?Oranges?Rs?55', 9)
>   Input string is unchanged :
>   Banana Rs.40 Apples Rs.65 Oranges Rs.55

(iii) **search()** function searches for the pattern in the input string.

| **Syntax** |

>   *search(pattern, input_string)*

In case the pattern is found, it returns the match object containing

>   span - First match index range
>   match - The first matched pattern

Otherwise **None** is returned.

Example

>   in_str = 'Banna Rs.40 Apples Rs.65 Oranges Rs.055 Total 160 '
>   print('"es" at end of the word: \n',re.search('\Bes', in_str))
>   print('"Ba" at beginning of the string :\n',re.search('\ABa', in_str))
>   res = re.search('(\d\d).+(\w{5}\s)', in_str)
>   print('Grouping patterns : ',res.groups())
>   print('Matched pattern :', res.group(0))
>   print('First group :',res.group(1),'\t Second Group :', res.group(2))

Output

>   "es" at end of the word:
>   <re.Match object; span=(16, 18), match='es'>
>   "Ba" at beginning of the string :
>   <re.Match object; span=(0, 2), match='Ba'>
>   Grouping patterns : ('40', 'Total ')
>   Matched pattern : 40 Apples Rs.65 Oranges Rs.055 Total
>   First group : 40   Second Group : Total

Example

features = "Is Python object oriented language? Does it require
   variable declarations?."
print("Match result : ",re.search('\s[a-zA-Z]+\?\s', features))
print("Word starting with lowercase
   vowel:",re.search('\s[aeiou][a-z]+',features))
print("'script' in the string : ",re.search("script", features))
res = re.search("^[A-Z].*\.$", features)
print("Does the string starts with uppercase and ends with dot :
   ", res!=None)

Output

Match result : <re.Match object; span=(25, 36),
   match=' language? '>
Word starting with small vowel: <re.Match object; span=(9, 16),
   match=' object'>
'script' in the string : None
Does the string starts with uppercase and ends with dot : True

(iv) **findall()** function finds all the occurrences of the pattern.

| Syntax |

findall(*pattern, input_string*)

Finds all the *pattern* matches in the *input_string*. In case the pattern is found,
it returns a list of all occurrences of the pattern and **None** otherwise.

Example

in_str = 'Banna Rs.40 Apples Rs.65 Oranges Rs.055 Total 160 '
print(re.findall('\d+\s', in_str))
print(re.findall('Rs.\d?\s', in_str))
print(re.findall('Rs.\d*\s', in_str))
print(re.findall('Rs.\d+ | \d+', in_str))

Output

['40 ', '65 ', '055 ', '160']
[]
['Rs.40', 'Rs.65', 'Rs.055']
['Rs.40', 'Rs.65', 'Rs.055', '160']

Example

```
result = "Arjun scored 90 marks in Python 85 marks in Maths"
print("Marks obtained:", re.findall('\d+ marks ',result))
print("Five letter words:", re.findall('\s[a-zA-Z]{5}\s', result))
print("2 to 6 letter Words starting with uppercase : ")
print(re.findall('\s[A-Z][a-z]2,6\s',result))
```

Output

```
Marks obtained: ['90 marks', '85 marks']
Five letter words : ['Arjun', 'marks', 'marks', 'Maths']
2 to 6 letter Words starting with uppercase :
['Arjun', 'Python', 'Maths']
```

11.3   Case Study: Regular Expressions

Perform data analysis on a text file containing information about the Olympic games.

(i) Read the contents of the file.

```
fp = open('/content/sample_data/Olympics_new.txt','r')
text = fp.read()
```

(ii) Import the module for handling regular expressions and count the number of times *Olympic* appeared in the text.

```
import re
olympic_count = re.findall('\s[oO]lympic[s]*\s',text)
print('No. of times Olympic or Olympics appeared :
   ',len(olympic_count))
```

Output

No. of times Olympic or Olympics appeared : 38

(iii) Substitute 'olympic' or 'olympics' with 'Olympic Games'.

subn() function returns a tuple containing the new text after substitution and the number of times the substitution was done.

```
result = re.subn('\s[oO]lympic[s]*\s', 'Olympic Games', text )
print('Type of value returned : ',type(result))
print('No. of times substituted: ',result[1])
```

Output

> Type of value returned : <class 'tuple'>
> No. of times substituted: 38

(iv) Find the number of words with at least three characters and at least ten occurrences.

```
# words of atleast 3 more characters
words = re.findall('\s[\w\d][\w\d][\w\d]+[\s\.\n]',text)
print('No. of words with atleast 3 letters : ', len(words))
words_set = set(words)
print('No. of unique words with atleast 3 letters :
  ',len(words_set))
print('words with more than 10 frequency :')
for word in words_set:
    freq= words.count(word)
    if freq>10:
      print(' ',word, freq)
```

Output

> No. of words with atleast 3 letters: 1019
> No. of unique words with atleast 3 letters: 526
> words with more than 10 frequency:
>   The 21
>   and 47
>   Greek 11
>   Games 15
>   Olympic 21
>   was 15
>   the 124
>   were 17
>   that 13
>   for 11

(v) Find the abbreviations with at least two characters long.

```
caps = re.findall('\s[A-Z][A-Z]+\s',text)
print('Abbreviations: ',set(caps))
```

Output

> Abbreviations: {' CE ', 'IOC', 'BCE'}

(vi) Count the number of paragraphs, number of sentences, and number of sentences ending with ! mark.

```
paras = re.findall('[\w\d\s]+\.\n',text)
print('No. of paragraphs : ',len(paras))
sentenses = re.findall('[\w\d\s]+\.',text)
print('No. of sentenses : ',len(sentenses))
exclam = re.findall('[\w\d\s]+!',text)
print('No. of sentenses ending with ! mark : ',len(exclam))
```

Output

No. of paragraphs : 25
No. of sentenses : 107
No. of sentenses ending with ! mark : 1

(vii) Count the number of punctuations and articles present.

```
punc = re.findall('[,.:;]',text)
print('No. of punctuations : ',len(punc))
articles = re.findall('\s[aA]\s|\s[Aa]n\s|\s[Tt]he\s',text)
print('No. of articles : ', len(articles))
```

Output

No. of punctuations : 268
No. of articles : 255

(viii) Count the number of numeric values present and display the first five of them.

```
numbers = re.findall('\s\d+\w+\s',text)
print('No. of Numbers : ',len(numbers))
print('First five numbers : ', numbers[:5])
```

Output

No. of Numbers : 34
First five numbers : ['19th', '1970s', '1980s', '32', '1924']

(ix) Find the *throw* games present.

```
throws = re.findall('\w+\s[tT]hrow[s]*',text)
print(throws)
```

Output

['javelin throw', 'discus throw']

(x) Find the number of occurrences of text enclosed in parenthesis and display the first three of them.

```
brackets = re.findall('\([a-zA-Z0-9\s]+\)',text)
print('No. of times text enclosed in ( ) : ',len(brackets))
print('First three: ',brackets[:3])
```

Output

> No. of times text enclosed in ( ) : 13
> First three: ['(soccer)', '(210 yards)', '(from Greek pankration)']

Exercises

1. Take a paragraph from any Wikipedia webpage. Write a function that returns: (a) number of words, (b) number of articles (a, an, the).
2. Write a function that replaces comma, semicolon, dot, and space with a colon.
3. Write a function that returns a string with words of length less than five in the input string.
4. Write a function that returns a list of two digit numbers in the input string.
5. Write a function that finds the words ending with a vowel, in the input string.
6. Write a function that returns a string after replacing 1 with True and 0 with False, in the input string.
7. Write a function that returns number of special characters ($, %, ?, #, !) in the input string.
8. Write a function that returns a string after capitalizing the first character of each word, in the input string.
9. Read the text from a file. Count the number of numeric values present in the text.
10. Take text from a Wikipedia webpage and count the number of unique words.

Review Questions

(1) What is the output of the following code?

```
in_str = 'Welcome to Python'
print(re.subn('[aeiou]', '*',in_str))
```

(a) ('W*lc*m* t* Pyth*n', 5)
(b) 'W*lc*m* t* Pyth*n'
(c) ('W*lc*m* t* Pyth*n')
(d) 5

(2) What is the output of the following code?

```
in_str= 'Is it ver 3.7?'
print(re.sub('\W', '*',in_str))
```

(a) ('Is*it*ver*3*7*', 5)
(b) ** ** *** *.*?
(c) Is*it*ver*3*7*
(d) ('** ** *** *.*?', 9)

(3) What is the output of the following code?

    in_str = 'Python is an interpreted language'
    print(re.split('\s', in_str,2))

    (a) ['Python', 'is', 'an', 'interpretted', 'language']
    (b) ['Python', 'is', 'an interpretted language']
    (c) ['Python', 'is an interpretted language']
    (d) Error is generated

(4) What is the output of the following code?

    in_str= 'Python version 3.7'
    print(re.split('[0-5]',in_str))

    (a) ['Python version', ' ']
    (b) ['Python version', '.']
    (c) ['Python version', '.','']
    (d) ['Python version ', '.7']

(5) Which of the following is False about meta characters?

    (a) "*" means zero or more occurrences
    (b) "?" means zero or one occurrence
    (c) "-" means one or more occurrences
    (d) [ ] matches any characters in the given range

(6) Which symbol is used to match other than the specified characters in the range [ ]?

    (a) ^
    (b) $
    (c) *
    (d) +

(7) What is the output of the following code?

    in_str = 'Banna Rs.40 Apples Rs.65 Oranges Rs.055 total 160'
    print(re.findall('\s\w{5}\s', in_str))

    (a) 1
    (b) [' Banna', 'total']
    (c) 2
    (d) ['total']

(8) What is the output of the following code?

    in_str='python- No variable declarations in python'
    print(re.search('python$', in_str))

    (a) <re.Match object; span=(36, 42), match='python'>
    (b) <re.Match object; span=(0, 6), match='python'>

   (c) <re.Match object; span=(1, 6), match='python'>
   (d) <re.Match object; span=(35, 42), match='python'>

 (9) Which of the following functions return the match object?

   (a) split()
   (b) Sub()
   (c) search()
   (d) findall()

 (10) What is the output of the following code?

   in_str= 'Python is simple, obj-oriented language'
   print(re.findall('Age', in_str))

   (a) None
   (b) [ ]
   (c) 0
   (d) ['age']

Chapter 12
Data Visualizations

Visualizations present the data in the form of graphs and charts. It reveals the patterns, trends, and correlations that might not be observed otherwise. Data visualization is an important step in data analytics to visualize complex data relationships that help in data-driven decisions.

Python provides multiple packages for data visualizations. Popular packages are

- matplotlib
- seaborn
- ggplot
- plotly

Matplotlib and seaborn are widely used visualization libraries, as the graphs can be produced easily and quickly.

12.1 Matplotlib

Matplotlib is the visualization library for two-dimensional plots and charts. John Hunter introduced it in 2002. It provides lots of features to produce elegant graphs. The Pyplot module of matplotlib provides an interface for graphs. It offers low-level libraries with an interface similar to MATLAB. It can be used in Python, IPython, and Jupyter notebooks.

First, install the package using

> pip install matplotlib

Then, import the package before using the library functions.

> import matplotlib.pyplot as plt

In the above plt is the shortcut name for maptplotlib.pyplot.

© The Author(s) 2024
A. L. Muddana and S. Vinayakam, *Python for Data Science*,
https://doi.org/10.1007/978-3-031-52473-8_12

12.2 Seaborn

Seaborn is a Python data visualization library developed on top of matplotlib. It provides high-level interfaces for building statistical graphs with default matplotlib parameters like styles and color palettes to make the plots attractive and informative. It is a dataset-oriented library and integrated with data frames and numPy arrays.

Both matplotlib and seaborn offer a number of library functions for basic graphs like scatter, line, bar, box plot, *etc.*. The type of plot to choose depends on the type of data, target audience, context, and the question we are trying to answer.

First, import the seaborn module to start using its library functions

> import seaborn as sns.

12.3 General Functions in Plotting

(i) Graph **title**

> plt.*title*(*label, loc* = 'center'*,fontdict*=None)

label: Actual title text
loc: Alignment of the label in the graph. The value can be center (default), left, right.
fontdict: Dictionary that controls the appearance of the label font like color, size, style, *etc.*

(ii) Label for the **x-axis**

> plt.*xlabel*(label_text)

(iii) Label for the **y-axis**

> plt.*ylabel*(label_text)

(iv) Display **grid lines** in the graph

> plt.*grid*()

(v) Display the plots

> plt.*show*()

(vi) Display tick locations and labels for x-axis and y-axis

> plt.**xticks**(*ticks*=None, *labels*=None)
> plt.**yticks**(*ticks*=None, *labels*=None)

ticks: List of tick locations
labels: List of labels at tick locations

(vii) Set the **limits** for **x-axis** and **y-axis** values

> plt.*xlim*(left_value , right_value)
> plt.*ylim*(bottom_value , top_value)

(viii) Describe the elements of the graph.

> plt.*legend*(*loc*=None)

> *loc:* where to place the legend like upper left, upper right, center, lower left, lower right *etc.*. Default is 'best'.

12.4   Basic Graphs and Plots

Following are the widely used basic graphs and plots provided by matplotlib and seaborn.

(i) **Scatter plot** exhibits the relationship between a dependent and an independent variable. It shows the correlation between the two variables, which may be a positive relation, negative relation, or no correlation at all. It is also useful in identifying the outliers in the dataset. This plot is used to see the correlation, before building the regression model. The scatter plot displays one dot for each data point.

(a) **Scatter plot using matplotlib**

> plt.*scatter*(*x,y*, size =None, color=None, marker=None, alpha=None)

x, y:	Array of values for x & y-axis
	Both the arrays should be of the same size
color or *c:*	Color of the data points. The argument can be specified as a single value, in which case each data point takes the same color or array of colors for each data point
	The color array should be of the same size as the x and y array sizes
marker:	Specify the shape of each data point
	Different markers are dot (default), circle (o), star (*), plus (+), *etc.*
size:	The size of each data point
	The argument value can be a single or array of sizes
alpha:	Transparency of each data point
	The value ranges from 0 (transparent) to 1 (opaque).

Example

```
import pandas as pd
# load the dataset into dataframe- data
data = pd.read_csv('/content/sample_data/Housing.csv')
x = data['area']
y = data['price']
```

```
plt.scatter(x, y, c = 'green', marker='o', s=30 )
plt.title( 'Area vs Price of house', fontdict={ 'color': 'blue',
    'size':20, 'style': 'italic' } )
plt.xlabel('Area of the House')      # name to x-axis
plt.ylabel('Price of the house')      # name to y-axis
plt.show()      # to display the graph
```

Output

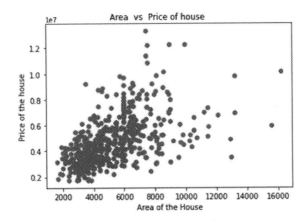

(b) **Regression plot using seaborn**

The plot is a combination of scatter plot and fitting the regression line.

seaborn.***regplot***(x=None, y=None, data, scatter=True,
    fit_reg=True)

data:	Dataframe
x, y:	Columns of the dataframe
scatter:	Boolean value indicating whether to draw a scatter plot or not. Default is True
fit_reg:	Boolean value indicating whether to fit a regression line or not. Default is True

Example

```
import pandas as pd
data = pd.read_csv('/content/sample_data/Housing.csv')
sns.regplot(x= 'area', y= 'price', data=data)
plt.title('Area vs Price of house')
plt.show()
```

Output

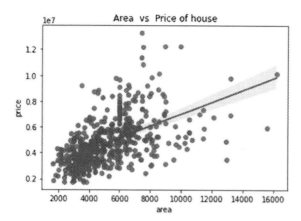

Note: In the above seaborn plot, even though x-axis and y-axis labels are not specified, they are taken as column names, i.e., **area** and **price**.

(ii) **Line graph** draws line by connecting the data points. The graph represents the trends, patterns, and fluctuations in the values of continuous variables over time. It helps in making projections beyond the given data.

(a) **Using matplotlib**

    *plt.*__plot__*(x,y,color=None,linewidth=None,marker=None,*
        linestyle=None,markersize=None,markerfacecolor=None,
        markeredgecolor=None)

x, y :	Array of values for x & y-axis
color or c:	Line color
linestyle or ls:	solid(-), dotted(.), dashed(–), dashed-dotted(-.)
linewidth or lw:	Float value representing the width of the line
marker or m:	Data point marker like a circle(o), cross(x), star(*), plus(+)
markersize or ms:	Size of the data point
markerfacecolor:	Color for the marker
markeredgecolor:	Edge color for the marker.

Example

```
x = list(range(10))
y1 = [ i *i for i in x]
plt.plot(x,y1,c='red',linewidth=5,linestyle='-',marker='*',
markersize=20,markerfacecolor='green',markeredgecolor='orange')
plt.title('Squares of x')
plt.xlabel('X-axis')
plt.ylabel('Squares')
plt.grid()     # shows grid lines for x, y values
plt.show()
```

Output

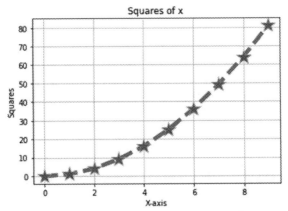

Multiple line graphs can be displayed in the same plot

Example

```
x = list(range(10))
y1 = [ i *i for i in x]
y2 = [ i**3 for i in x]
# Line graph of Square values
plt.plot(x, y1, label='Square', ls='dashed', marker='x')
# Second Line graph of Cube values
plt.plot(x, y2, label='Cube', marker ='o')
plt.title('Multiple line graphs: X vs Square and
   Cube values')
# Legend labels for each line graph
plt.legend()
plt.show()
```

Output

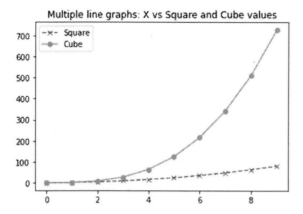

(b) **Using seaborn**

seaborn.**lineplot**(*x, y, data*)

data: Dataframe
x, y: Columns of the dataframe

Example

```
import pandas as pd
x = list(range(10))
y1 = [ i *i for i in x]
y2 = [ i**3 for i in x]
df=pd.DataFrame('X' : x, 'Y1': y1, 'Y2' : y2 )
# Draw line graph
sns.lineplot(x='X',y='Y1',data=df,linestyle='–',
    markersize=2,marker='*')
sns.lineplot(x='X',y='Y2',data=df, linewidth=5,marker='+')
plt.legend(['Squares','Cubes'])
plt.ylabel('Squares & Cubes of X')
plt.show()
```

Output

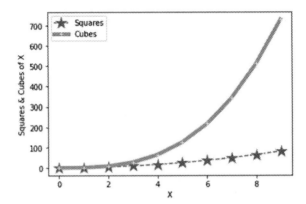

(iii) **Histogram** shows how the values of a continuous variable are distributed. Data is divided into discrete consecutive intervals. Each interval is called a bin. The bin is represented by a bar and the graph consists of a sequence of bars. The number of values in each interval determines the height of the bar. The width of the bars can be specified as an argument to the function.

(a) **Using matplotlib**

*plt.***hist***(x, bins=None, edgecolor=None, orientation=None) x:* Array of values of a continuous variable
bins: Number of bins in the range of x.*min*() to x.*max*()
orientation: whether the bars are oriented vertically (default) or horizontally
edgecolor: Color of bin edges

Example

```
import pandas as pd
titanic=pd.read_csv('/content/sample_data/
   Titanic_train.csv')
age = titanic['Age'].fillna(titanic['Age'].mean())
# Specify bin edges
bin_edges= [0,10,20,30,40,50,60,70,80]
plt.hist(age,bins=bin_edges,color='orange',
   edgecolor='black', width=10)
plt.title('Distribution of passengers Age')
plt.xlabel('Passengers Age')
plt.ylabel('Count of values in each bin')
# X-axis values
plt.xticks(bin_edges)
plt.show()
```

Output

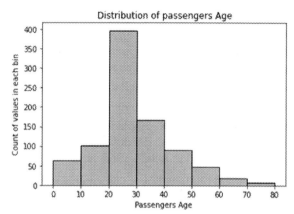

Note: In the above example, the variable, *bin_edges*, represents the interval ranges, i.e., the first bin is [0, 10) where 10 is not inclusive, [10, 20), [20,30), and so on. But in the last bin, [70, 80], the last value 80 is also inclusive.

(b) **Using Seaborn**

   *sns.***histplot***(x, bins, fill, binwidth, kde, alpha)*

Following are the most used arguments

x: List of numeric values
bins: Integer that specifies the number of bins
      or vector of values that specify bin edges
   fill: whether to fill the histogram bins
binwidth: Width of bins as integer
kde: when set to true, displays the distribution as curve
alpha: opacity of bars. The value ranges from 0 to 1.

Example

```
import pandas as pd
titanic = pd.read_csv('/content/sample_data/Titanic.csv')
age = titanic['Age'].fillna(titanic['Age'].mean())
bin_edges= [0,10,20,30,40,50,60,70,80]
sns.histplot(x=age,bins=bin_edges,fill = True,
    color='orange', binwidth=8, kde = True, alpha=0.7)
plt.show()
```

Output

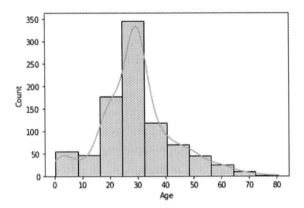

(iv) **Pie chart** is a circular graph representing the proportions of different components in the given whole. Each proportion or piece of the pie chart is called a
wedge. Each wedge indicates a parts-of-whole relationship. Each value of the
component is specified as the percentage and sum of all segments totaling to
100%. Pie charts are preferable when there are few components in the data. It
is widely used in business applications to show the contribution of each item in
the data.

(a) **Using matplotlib**

*plt.**pie**(x,colors=None,explode=None,*
labels=None,autopct=None,shadow=False)

x:	Array of values
colors:	List of colors for each wedge
explode:	List of values representing how far the wedge is from the center
labels:	Array of labels for each wedge
autopct:	Label of the wedges indicating the proportion of the wedge as the percentage
shadow:	Boolean value indicating whether to add shadow to the pie chart

Example

```
results = [10, 15, 18, 8, 5]
grades = ['O','A','B','C','F']
expl = [0, 0, 0, 0, 0.2]
cols = ['green','yellow', 'purple', 'orange', 'red' ]
plt.figure(figsize=(5,5))
```

```
plt.pie(results, autopct='%1.1f%%', explode=expl,
    colors=cols, shadow=True, labels=grades)
plt.show()
```

Output

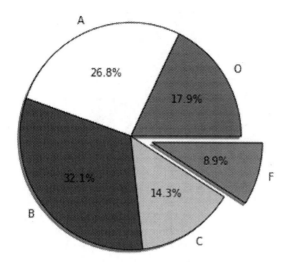

(b) **Seaborn** does not have built-in library function for the pie chart. Use pie( ) function of matplotlib and make use of seaborn color palette for wedges.

Example

```
results = [10, 15, 18, 8, 5]
grades = ['O','A','B','C','F']
# To highlight the weg
expl = [0, 0, 0, 0, 0.2]
cols= sns.color_palette('bright')
plt.pie(results, autopct='%1.1f%%', explode=expl,
    colors=cols, labels=grades)
plt.title('Distribution of grades among 60 students
    of a class')
plt.show()
```

Output

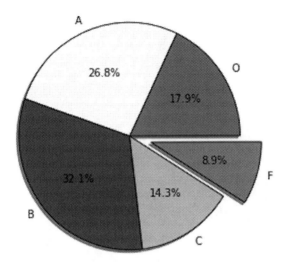

(v) **Bar chart** represents the relationship between categorical and corresponding numeric values. One axis represents the category and the other represents the numeric value. Each category is represented by a rectangular bar. The height of bars is proportional to corresponding numeric values. Same chart can also be used to compare two or more values in the same category. This graph is preferable and effective when data contains few categories. Bars can be laid either vertically or horizontally.

(a) **Using matplotlib**

   plt.bar(x, height, width, align, color, edgecolor, linewidth)

x: List of x-axis values or categories
height: Height of bar indicating y-axis values
width: Bars width
align: Alignment of bars to x coordinates. Default is center.
color: Color of bar faces
edgecolor: Color of bar edges

Example

```
maths = [10, 15, 18, 8, 5]
grades = ['O','A','B','C','F']
plt.bar(x=grades, height=maths, linewidth=5,
    edgecolor='red')
plt.xlabel('Grades')
plt.ylabel('No. of students in each grade')
plt.title('Students Grades in Maths')
plt.show()
```

Output

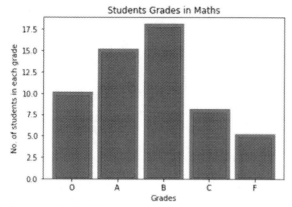

Multiple bar graphs in the same chart.

Example

```
idx1 = list(range(len(grades)))
idx2 = [i+0.2 for i in idx1]
python = [15, 13, 19, 10,3]
maths = [10, 15, 18, 8, 5]
grades = ['O','A','B','C','F']
plt.bar(grades, maths, width=0.2, label='Maths')
plt.bar(idx2, python, width=0.2, label='Python')
plt.title('Students Grades in Maths & Python')
plt.xlabel('Grades')
plt.ylabel('Number of students in each grade')
plt.legend()
plt.xticks(grades)
plt.show()
```

Output

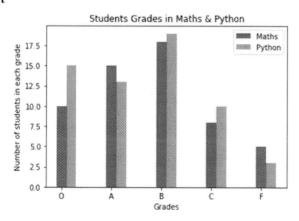

(b) **Using seaborn**

    sns.***barplot***(*x, y, data, palette*)

x, y: Values along x and y axis
data: Data frame
palette: Color variations

Example

```
maths = [10, 15, 18, 8, 5]
grades = ['O','A','B','C','F']
g = sns.barplot(x = grades, y=maths, palette='pastel')
g.set_title('Students Grades in Maths')
g.set_ylabel('No. of Students')
g.set_xlabel('Grades')
plt.show()
```

Output

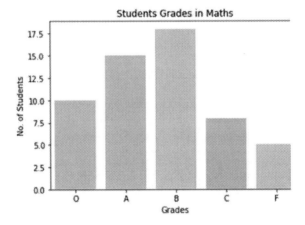

(vi) **Box Plot** is used to visualize data distribution based on five number summaries namely, minimum, first quartile, median, third quartile, and maximum values in the data. It is also called the whisker plot. It is a rectangular plot with lines extending from bottom to top. The box in the graph extends from quartile1 (Q1) to quartile3 (Q3) with a line indicating quartile2 (Q2) or median. It also shows the outliers.

*plt.***box***(data, notch=None, vert=None, patch_artist=None) data:* List of values.
vert: Whether to display the plot vertically or not.
notch: Whether a clear indication of median required.
patch_artist: Whether to fill the quartiles.

Example

```
import pandas as pd
titanic = pd.read_csv('/content/sample_data/Titanic_train.csv')
# Drop rows with null values
titanic = titanic.dropna()
plt.boxplot(titanic['Age'],vert=True, notch=True,
    patch_artist=True)
plt.xlabel('Age')
plt.ylabel('Frequency distribution of Age')
plt.title('Summary statistics of Age')
plt.show()
```

Output

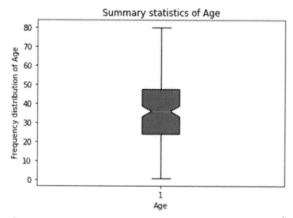

Using seaborn

*sns.**boxplot***(x, y, data)

data: Dataframe
x: Column of the dataframe on x-axis
y: Column of the dataframe on y-axis

Example

```
import pandas as pd
titanic = pd.read_csv('/content/sample_data/Titanic.csv')
# Drop rows with null values
titanic = titanic.dropna()
sns.set(style='whitegrid')
g=sns.boxplot(x = 'Sex', y = 'Age', data=titanic)
g.set_title('Distribution of Age across Male and Female')
plt.show()
```

Output

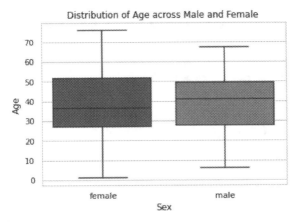

(vii) **Heatmap of seaborn**

Heatmap is a two-dimensional graphical representation of values in the matrix. The values are represented using different shades of color based on the magnitude of the value. Darker shades indicate higher data values.

*seaborn.***heatmap***(data, annot, fmt, cmap, cbar)*

data:	Two-dimensional array of data
annot:	Boolean value. When set to True data values are written in the cells of the heat map. The default value is False
fmt:	String format to be used to specify the number of decimal places for the values. Default is two decimal places
cmap:	Map data values to color space
cbar:	Boolean value indicating whether to draw a color bar in the graph. Default value is True.

Example

```
import pandas as pd
df = pd.read_csv('/content/sample_data/Housing.csv')
df_new = df[['area','price','stories']]
# correlation among the attributes
cr = df_new.corr()
sns.heatmap(data= cr, annot=True, fmt='0.3f', cmap='Blues')
plt.show()
```

Output

(viii) **Facetgrid**

Facetgrid maps multiple axes into grid cells that show the distribution of a variable and relationship between multiple variables. It takes dataframe as input and categorical columns as row and column arguments to the functions. Data is split into subsets based on the categorical values. Each graph in the grid is the visualization of a subset of data.

seaborn.*facetgrid(data, row, col, hue)*

data: Dataframe
row, col: Define subsets of dataframe based on categorical values.
hue: Different categories are plotted with different colors

Example

```
import pandas as pd
df = pd.read_csv('/content/sample_data/Titanic.csv')
gr = sns.FacetGrid(df, row='Pclass', col='Sex', hue='Sex')
gr.map(plt.hist, 'Age', bins=20)
```

Output

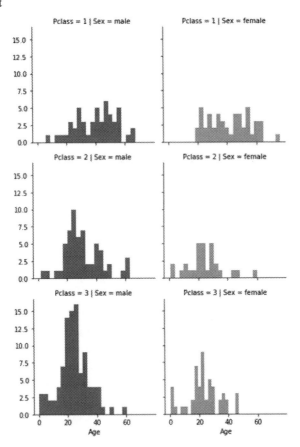

12.5   Subplots

Multiple plots can be drawn in one canvas, creating a grid of plots. Each plot is called a subplot.

figure_object, axis_objects = plt.*subplot(nrows, ncols, sharex, sharey)*

nrows, ncols:	Integers indicating the number of rows and columns in the grid. Default value is 1
sharex, sharey:	Controls sharing of x-axis or y-axis among the subplots

nrows, ncols: Integers indicating the number of rows and columns
                    in the grid. Default value is 1
sharex, sharey: Controls sharing of x-axis or y-axis among the subplots
                    True or 'all' :- share x-axis/y-axis for all subplots
                    False :- each subplot x-axis/y-axis is independent
                    'row' :- x-axis/y-axis is shared along the row of subplots
                    'col' :- x-axis/y-axis is shared along the column
                    of subplots.

Returns tuple containing figure_object and array of axis_objects.

We can set properties of each subplot like title, xlabel, ylabel using

  set_title(), set_xlabel(), set_ylabel()

Set the title for the entire figure using

  figure_object.*suptitle*(text)

Unused grid cell in the figure can be made empty using

  *axis_object.***axis**(*'off'*)

Example

```
results = [10, 15, 18, 8, 5]
grades = ['O','A','B','C','F']
fig, ax = plt.subplots(2,2, figsize=(8,8))
fig.suptitle("Demo of subplots")
# Draw bar graph
ax[0,0].bar(grades,results)
ax[0,0].set_title("this is bar chart")
ax[0,0].set_xlabel('Grades')
ax[0,0].set_ylabel('No. of Students')

x = list(range(10))
y1 = [ i *i for i in x]
# Draw line graph
ax[1,1].plot(x, y1, color='red', lw = 2.0, ls = 'solid', marker = 'o',
  markersize = 10)
ax[1,1].set_title("X vs square of X")
ax[1,1].set_xlabel('X values')
ax[1,1].set_ylabel('Square of X')

# Hiding the subplot at 0,1 index
ax[0,1].axis('off')
plt.show()
```

Output

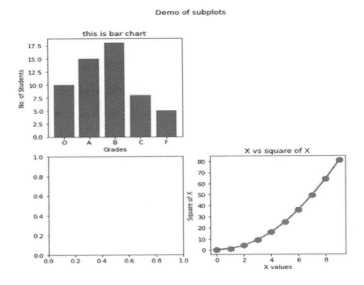

12.6   Case Study: Data Visualizations

Perform data visualizations on the mobile dataset consisting of 21 attributes and 2000 instances. The attributes include continuous and categorical data types. Library functions of **Matplotlib** and **Seaborn** modules are used to draw the graphs.

(i) Load the dataset into a dataframe.

```
import pandas as pd
df = pd.read_csv('/content/sample_data/mobile_data.csv')
print('Dataset shape : ',df.shape)
print('Columns : ',df.columns)
```

Output

```
Dataset shape : (2000, 21)
Columns : Index(['battery_power', 'blue', 'clock_speed', 'dual_sim', 'fc',
'four_g','int_memory', 'm_dep', 'mobile_wt', 'n_cores', 'pc',
'px_height','px_width', 'ram', 'sc_h', 'sc_w', 'talk_time',
'three_g','touch_screen', 'wifi', 'price_range'],
  dtype='object')
```

(ii) Import the visualization libraries—*matplotlib* and *seaborn*.

import matplotlib.pyplot as plt
import seaborn as sb

(iii) Visualize the correlation between *pixel_width* and *pixel_height* using a *scatter* plot of matplotlib. pyplot.

plt.scatter(x=df['px_width'], y=df['px_height'])
plt.xlabel('Pixel Width')
plt.ylabel('Pixel Height')
plt.title('Pixel Width Vs Pixel Height')
plt.show()

Output

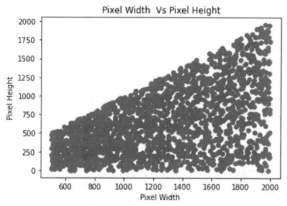

The plot shows a positive correlation between px_width & px_height.

(iv) Count the number of records for each value of the *n_cores* attribute using *countplot( )* function of *seaborn*.

sb.countplot(df['n_cores'])
plt.title('Count of records for each value of n_cores')
plt.show()

Output

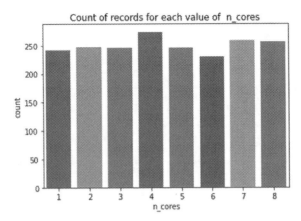

(v) Let us draw a grid of histogram plots on *battery_power* over different values of *dual_sim & touch_screen*.

```
fg = sb.FacetGrid(df, row='dual_sim', col='touch_screen' )
fg.map(sb.histplot, 'battery_power')
plt.show()
```

Output

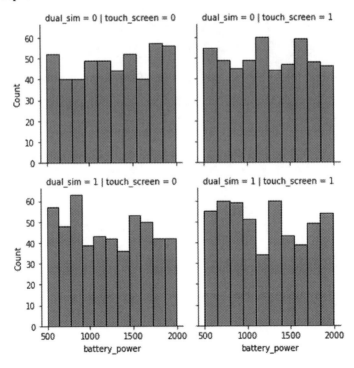

(vi) Let us check the correlation among *price_range*, *battery_power*, *n_cores*, *ram* attributes using *corr()* function on dataframe. Then visualize the correlation using the *heatmap()* function of *seaborn*.

```
cols= ['battery_power','n_cores','ram', 'price_range' ]
cm = df[cols].corr()
print(cm)
sb.heatmap(cm)
plt.show()
```

Output

	battery_power	n_cores	ram	price_range
battery_power	1.000000	−0.029727	−0.000653	0.200723
n_cores	−0.029727	1.000000	0.004868	0.004399
ram	−0.000653	0.004868	1.000000	0.917046
price_range	0.200723	0.004399	0.917046	1.000000

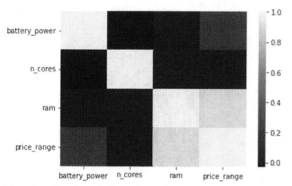

The visualization shows a high positive correlation between *ram* and *price_range*.

(vii) Visualize the proportion of instances on each value of *n_cores* using a *pie* chart of *matplotlib*.

```
cores= df['n_cores'].value_counts()
lab = cores.index
plt.pie(cores.values, autopct='%1.1f%%',labels=lab)
plt.title('Number of Cores')
plt.show()
```

Output

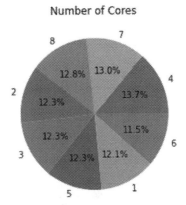

(viii) Plot the data distribution summary on *four_g* and *price_range* attributes using *boxplot()* of *seaborn*.

sb.boxplot(x= 'four_g', y='price_range', data=df)
plt.show()

Output

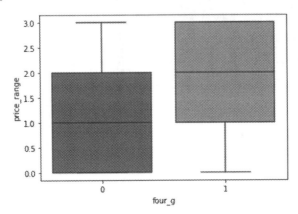

Exercises

1. Take a public dataset, identify dependent and independent variables, and draw an attractive scatter plot by taking appropriate arguments.
2. Take COVID-19 data of total confirmed and deceased cases of the top five countries. Draw pie charts (one for confirmed and one for deceased) and highlight the country with maximum cases. Give appropriate title and percentage in the wedges.

3. Take a public dataset containing both categorical and continuous variables. Draw a facetgrid chart.
4. Take a public dataset and draw box plot, line graph, pie chart, and bar graph in the same canvas using subplots. Give appropriate title and labels for each graph.
5. Take COVID-19 data of total confirmed and deceased cases of the top ten countries. Draw a bar graph of confirmed and deceased cases in the same chart. Use appropriate arguments to make the graph attractive.

Review Questions

(1) What is the default location for **legend** in a given plot?

(a) Upper left
(b) Upper right
(c) Center
(d) best

(2) The built-in function for generating a **scatter plot** using matplotlib is

(a) regplot()
(b) reg()
(c) scatter()
(d) scatterplot()

(3) The ————— argument of the **hist()** function represents the number of bars for given data x.

(a) bins()
(b) x.min()
(c) x.max()
(d) bars()

(4) The middle horizontal line in a box plot represents —————.

(a) Quartile 1
(b) Quartile 2
(c) Quartile 3
(d) Mean

(5) The ————— attribute of **heatmap()** represents the data values to be written in each cell.

(a) cmap
(b) annot
(c) cbar
(d) fmt

(6) Which plot among the following represents the relationship between dependent variable and independent variable?

(a) Bar
(b) Scatter
(c) Line
(d) MultiLine

(7) What does the **is explode** argument in a Pie Chart mean?

(a) Proportions of Different Component
(b) Color of Wedge
(c) Distance of wedge from the center
(d) Size of Wedge

(8) Which of the following graphs is used to visualize changes in data over time?

(a) Line
(b) Pie
(c) Histogram
(d) Box

(9) Which of the following is false about Searborn built-in functions?

(a) Seaborn has built-in pie chart()
(b) Seaborn has lineplot()
(c) Seaborn is built on top of Matplotlib
(d) Seaborn has histplot()

(10) The histplot() built-in function in seaborn has an argument **kde** that accepts ——————— value to display distribution as curve.

(a) Integer
(b) Float
(c) Boolean
(d) String

Chapter 13
Python for Machine Learning

Introduction

Machine learning is a sub-field of artificial intelligence capable of giving intelligent solutions to real-world problems. It is data-driven technology that enables computers to learn from data with little programming. A mathematical model is built through the process of training on the data by finding hidden patterns and extracting useful information. This model can then be used for predictions on the new data.

Machine learning solutions are used in every field to solve complex problems. Popular applications include autonomous vehicles, intelligent home solutions, precision agriculture, personalized treatment, machine translation, speech recognition, product recommendations, mail filtering, etc.

Machine learning methods can be broadly classified into:

- *Supervised learning* uses labeled data that contains example inputs and the desired output. The learning process builds a model that finds the relationship between the inputs and the output.
- *Unsupervised learning* learns without any supervision. It uses unlabeled data that contains only inputs and no output variable. It is used to find structures, patterns, and groups in the data.
- *Semi-supervised learning* is a combination of supervised and unsupervised learning approaches. A vast portion of real-world data is unlabeled. Labeling data is expensive as it requires human expertise and is time-consuming. Semi-supervised learning addresses the challenges of supervised learning by using partially labeled data. Initially, the model is trained on the available labeled data and then iteratively apply it on the unlabeled data.
- *Reinforcement learning* is a feedback-based learning system. The learning agent interacts with a dynamic environment to take action and learn by trial and error. Agent gets a reward for the right action and punishment for the wrong action. The agent strives to maximize the rewards to complete the task. Popular applications are self-driving cars, chatbots, gaming, robotics, etc.

© The Author(s) 2024
A. L. Muddana and S. Vinayakam, *Python for Data Science*,
https://doi.org/10.1007/978-3-031-52473-8_13

The machine learning process involves the following significant steps:

1. Data loading.
2. Data preprocessing and preparation.
3. Training the model.
4. Measure the model performance. Repeat training with different hyperparameter values if the performance is below the desired level.
5. Make predictions on the new data.

Sklearn is an open-source Python library for Machine Learning. It provides several library functions for supervised and unsupervised algorithms, ensemble methods, preprocessing, cross-validation, hyperparameter tuning, etc. It also contains in-built datasets that help beginners understand the learning algorithms and build basic models. The focus of *sklearn* is on the model building but not on data loading, data manipulations, and data visualization. For these tasks, better tools are available, like *pandas, numpy,* and *matplotlib*. Sklearn integrates well with *numpy* arrays for vectorization, *pandas* for data manipulation, and *matplotlib* for visualizations.

13.1   Data Loading

(i) *Loading in-built datasets:* sklearn package provides a few clean datasets to build the models.

- *load_bostan:* Contains information about different features and prices of houses in Boston. It is used for regression problems.
- *load_breast_cancer:* Binary classification dataset to predict the tumor as benign or malignant.
- *load_wine:* Multi-class classification dataset to classify the wine based on different parameters for wine.
- *load_iris:* Multi-variate flower dataset for multi-class classification.
- *load_diabetes:* Contains diabetic patients' information used to predict the disease progression in the patients. Used for regression task.
- *load_digits:* Multi-class classification image dataset to classify the handwritten digits.

These datasets are available in *sklearn.datasets* module.

Example:

To load the dataset

    dataset = load_boston()

Returns a dictionary with the following objects:

> *data*—Feature matrix as NumPy array.
> *target*—Target variable as NumPy array.
> *feature_names*—Names of feature columns.
> *target_names*—Target labels.
> *DESCR*—Brief description of the dataset.

Example

```
from sklearn.datasets import load_wine
data = load_wine()
print('Objects of data : ', data.keys())
x = data.data
print('Feature data : first row \n', x[:1])
print('Feature names:\n',data.feature_names)
y = data.target
print('First four target values :\n', y[:4])
print('Target Names: ', data.target_names)
#print('Dataset description', data.DESCR)
```

Output

```
Objects of data: dict_keys(['data', 'target', 'frame',
   'target_names', 'DESCR', 'feature_names'])
Feature data : first row
   [[1.423e+01 1.710e+00 2.430e+00 1.560e+01 1.270e+02
      2.800e+00 3.060e+00 2.800e-01 2.290e+00 5.640e+00
      1.040e+00 3.920e+00 1.065e+03]]
Feature names :
   ['alcohol', 'malic_acid', 'ash', 'alcalinity_of_ash', 'magnesium',
      'total_phenols', 'flavanoids', 'nonflavanoid_phenols',
      'proanthocyanins', 'color_intensity', 'hue',
      'od280/od315_of_diluted_wines', 'proline']
First four target values:
   [0 0 0 0]
Target Names: ['class_0' 'class_1' 'class_2']
```

(ii) *Loading other datasets:* Datasets are commonly available in **csv**, **txt**, **xlsx**, and **json** formats. The Pandas package of Python provides the following library functions to read data from the file into a dataframe, which can then be processed efficiently.

   (i) pandas.**read_csv()**
   (ii) pandas.**read_table()**
   (iii) pandas.**read_excel()**
   (iv) pandas.**read_json()**

Note: Detailed description of these functions is discussed in Chap. 9 on Pandas.

13.2   Data Preparation and Preprocessing

Real-world data come from many sources. It often contains noise, missing values, and unusual values. Also, data may not be in a format that can be used directly by machine learning algorithms. Hence, data must be processed before feeding to the learning algorithm called preprocessing. Data preprocessing includes the following processes:

a. Data cleaning by identifying and handling missing values and removing duplicate and extreme values.
b. Normalizing the data to bring the values to similar scales.
c. Transforming the data into a format suitable for the learning algorithms.

Preprocessing is a crucial step in machine learning, as clean and formatted data improves model performance, resulting in more accurate data interpretations and predictions.

13.2.1   Data Cleaning

The data cleaning step includes identifying and handling the missing values, removing duplicates and outliers.

A. **Identifying missing values**

Missing values are identified by NaN, Null? or the cell being empty. Most learning algorithms like SVM and LDA generate errors if the dataset contains missing values. Whereas algorithms like KNN, decision tree can be applied even when some values are missing. Consider the following .csv file with missing values.

Rno	Name	Marks	Pass
1	Arjun	876	Yes
2	Ram	765	
3	Shyam	?	No
4	Bheem	563	Yes
5		653	NA
6	Ravan		na

Pandas represent missing values, also called null values, as **NaN**. It can detect blanks, NA, and replace them with NaN automatically when the data is loaded into the dataframe.

Example

```
import pandas as pd
df = pd.read_csv("/content/sample_data/Marks sample.csv")
print(df)
```

Output

	Rno	Name	Marks	Pass
0	1	Arjun	876	Yes
1	2	Ram	765	NaN
2	3	Shyam	?	No
3	4	Bheem	563	Yes
4	5	NaN	653	NaN
5	6	Ravan	NaN	na

But special symbols like *na, ?, n/a, n.a* cannot be detected automatically. Such values can be put in a list and pass it to the *na_values* parameter of the *read_csv()* function when loading the file into a dataframe. Such values are replaced with *NaN* by pandas.

Example

```
data_frame = pd.read_csv("/content/sample_data/Marks
    sample.csv", na_values = ['?','na'])
print(df)
```

Output

Rno	Name	Marks	Pass
0	1	Arjun	876.0	Yes
1	2	Ram	765.0	NaN
2	3	Shyam	NaN	No
3	4	Bheem	563.0	Yes
4	5	NaN	653.0	NaN
5	6	Ravan	NaN	NaN

Now ?, na are also replaced with NaN.

Pandas provide the following functions to identify the missing values:

(i) *data_frame*.isnull()
Returns a dataframe of Boolean values with True for NaN values and False otherwise.

(ii) *data_frame*.notnull()
Returns a dataframe of Boolean values with True for not NaN values and False otherwise.

(iii) *data_frame*.info()
Returns information about the dataframe, including the number of non-null values for each column.

B. **Handling missing values**
Missing values can be handled as follows:

- Ignore the missing values: But some algorithms do not process the data with missing values.
- Remove the rows/columns having missing values.
- Fill the missing values with some meaningful data.

The extent of the missingness influences the strategy to be used.

(i) **Removing missing observations**
The row or column of the dataframe having the missing values is deleted. This strategy is appropriate when many values are missing in a row or column. But this is not advisable as it reduces the dataset size and may result in losing important information.

Pandas provide **dropna()** library function to delete rows/columns with missing values.

Syntax

data_frame.**dropna**(*axis, how, thresh, inplace*)

axis:	0 indicates row & 1 indicates column.
how:	string, with the following values
	any - drop rows/columns if one or more values are missing.
	all - drop rows/columns when all the values are missing.
thresh:	Threshold that specifies the proportion of null values required to remove the row/column.
inplace:	Changes are reflected in the same dataframe.

(ii) **Imputation or filling in the missing values**

Compute the missing values from the available data in the dataset. Sensible values may be inferred in the following ways:

- Replace the missing value with a meaningful, constant value in that domain.
- Replace with a value from any other randomly selected record.
- Use statistical methods like mean, median, and mode.
- Use another predictive model like regression to estimate the value.

Pandas provide the following functions for filling in the missing values.

(a) Syntax

data_frame.**fillna**(*value, method, axis, inplace*)

value	used to fill in missing values.
method	used for filling. The method can be
	ffill/pad—fill with the previous valid value in that column.
	bfill—fill with the next valid value in that column.
	Any computed value like constant, mean, median, or mode of the column.
	The default is None.
axis & inplace	parameters have the same meaning as in dropna() function.

(b) | Syntax |

    data_frame.**replace**(*to_replace, value, inplace*)

                to_replace: Value to be replaced
                value: Substitute value

inplace parameter has same meaning as in *dropna()* function.

This function is a more generic form of fillna().

(c) | **Syntax** |

    data_frame.**interpolate**(*method, axis, inplace*)

        method: string, Interpolation technique to be used.
                                   Values are *linear, time, index*, and *pad*.
                                   The default is *linear*.
        axis & inplace   parameters have the same
                                   meaning as in *dropna()* function.

Sklearn provides the *Imputer()* library function to fill in missing values.

    from sklearn.impute import SimpleImputer

| **Syntax** |

  SimpleImputer(*missing_values, strategy, fill_value*)

  missing_values: The placeholders for the missing values.
                                   Values are numpy.nan, pandas.NA, None.
  strategy: string, the method used for imputation.
                                     Values are
                                     mean (default) - Replace with column mean.
                                     Applicable to numerical data.
                                     median - Replace with median along each
                                     column. Applicable to numerical data.
                                     most_frequent - Replace with the most
                                     frequent value along each column.
                                     Applicable to both string and numeric data.
                                     constant - Replace with fill_value.
                                     Applicable to both string and numeric data.
  fill_value: string or numeric, Relevant only when the
                                     strategy is constant. Default is 0 for numeric
                                     data and 'missing_value' for strings.

13.2.2   *Data Transformations*

Data should be transformed into a form suitable for the learning algorithms. Following are the data transformation techniques:

(i) **Dimensionality reduction** is a preprocessing step that reduces the number of dimensions of the feature matrix. It reduces the data representation to a lesser volume but still has similar analytics quality.
Sklearn provides PCA algorithm to perform dimensionality reduction.

   from sklearn.decomposition import PCA

> **Syntax**

   PCA(*n_components* **)**

   n_components: Number of principal components to keep.

(ii) **Feature scaling:** Real-world datasets contain feature values of varying ranges and units. Hence the feature matrix must be scaled to bring the feature values to similar ranges.
SKlearn has the following library functions for feature scaling.

   • *MinMaxScaler:* Transforms each feature by scaling to the specified range.
   • *StandardScaler:* Transforms each feature by bringing the mean value to zero and variance to 1.

   from sklearn.preprocessing import MinMaxScaler,
            StandardScaler

> **Syntax**

   MinMaxScaler(*feature_range, copy* **)**

   feature_range: Tuple that specifies minimum & maximum values.
                Default is (0,1).
   copy: Boolean, If False, avoid creating a copy and do
                in-place scaling.

| Syntax |

StandardScaler(*with_mean, with_std*)

with_mean: Boolean, if True, centers the data before scaling.
with_std: Boolean, if True, scales the data to unit variance.
copy: Boolean, If False, avoid creating a copy and do
             in-place scaling

(iii) ***Encoding categorical data:*** Machine learning algorithms require the data to be numeric. Categorical features must be transformed into numeric values before training the model.
Common techniques to convert categorical variables are

- *Using map() function on the pandas dataframe.*

| Syntax |

   *data_frame[col] = data_frame[col].***map***(dict_value_mapping*)

Example

   df['sex']= df['sex'].map({ 'male': 1, 'female' : 2})

- *Label Encoder:* Encode target labels with numeric values between 0 and n_classes-1. It is applied to the target variable but not to features.

   from sklearn.preprocessing import LabelEncoder

| Syntax |

   LabelEncoder( )

- *get_dummies()* transforms categorical variables into dummy or indicator variables. A new column is created for each categorical value. The name of the new column is the column name appended by categorical value.

| Syntax |

   pandas.**get_dummies**(*data, prefix, prefix_sep, columns,*
       sparse, dtype)

data:	Data to be transformed.
prefix:	String, to append to column names. Default is None.
prefix_sep:	String, the separator between prefix and column name. Default is underscore.
columns:	Columns of the dataframe to be transformed.
sparse:	Boolean, if True, dummy encoded columns are backed by SparseArray else by Numpy Array.
dtype:	Data type of new columns. Only a single data type is allowed. Default is numpy.uint8.

Returns a dataframe of dummy coded data.

- *One-hot encoding*—Transforms categorical variables into a binary vector. It creates a new column for each unique value of the categorical variable. 1 if the value is present and 0 otherwise. If the unique values are high, the encoding will result in a dataset with a large number of columns leading to a high-dimensional dataset.

> from sklearn.preprocessing import OneHotEncoding

Syntax	**OneHotEncoding**(*n_values,dtype,sparse,categorical_features*)

n_values:	Number of values per feature. *auto* - value range is determined from the data. *int* - max value for all features. *array* - max value per feature.
dtype:	Desired data type of output. Default is numpy. float.
sparse:	Boolean, return sparse matrix if set to True otherwise, return numpy array
categorical_features:	What features are treated as categorical? *all(Default)* - All features are treated as categorical. An array of indices of categorical features. *mask* - Array of n_features with Boolean values.

Example: Apply the encoding methods on a dataframe.
- **Create dataframe**

```
import pandas as pd
data={'Rno':[1,2,3,4,5],
    'Gender':['Male','Female','Female','Male','Female'],
    'Grade':['A','B','A','C','A']}
df = pd.DataFrame(data)
print(df)
```

Output

	Rno	Gender	Grade
0	1	Male	A
1	2	Female	B
2	3	Female	A
3	4	Male	C
4	5	Female	A

- **Apply label encoder on the 'Grade' column.**
  ```
  from sklearn.preprocessing import LabelEncoder
  le = LabelEncoder()
  df['Grade'] = le.fit_transform(df['Grade'])
  print(df)
  ```

Output

	Rno	Gender	Grade
0	1	Male	0
1	2	Female	1
2	3	Female	0
3	4	Male	2
4	5	Female	0

- **Apply get_dummies() method on categorical columns.**
  ```
  df_dum = pd.get_dummies(df,
      columns=['Gender','Grade'])
  print(df_dum)
  ```

Output

	Rno	Gender_Female	Gender_Male	Grade_A	Grade_B	Grade_C
0	1	0	1	1	0	0
1	2	1	0	0	1	0
2	3	1	0	1	0	0
3	4	0	1	0	0	1
4	5	1	0	1	0	0

- **Apply one-hot encoder on categorical columns.**

```
import numpy as np
from sklearn.preprocessing import OneHotEncoder
cols= ['Gender','Grade']
names = np.append(df['Gender'].unique(),
    df['Grade'].unique())
ohe = OneHotEncoder(sparse=False)
ohe_df=pd.DataFrame(ohe.fit_transform(df[cols]),
    dtype=int, columns=vals )
new_df = df.join(ohe_df)
new_df.drop(cols, axis=1, inplace=True)
print(new_df)
```

Output

	Rno	Male	Female	A	B	C
0	1	0	1	1	0	0
1	2	1	0	0	1	0
2	3	1	0	1	0	0
3	4	0	1	0	0	1
4	5	1	0	1	0	0

13.2.3   Splitting the Dataset

Before training the model, the dataset is split into train and test sets. The train dataset is used to train the model, and the test dataset evaluates the model's performance. Typical split ratios are 70:30 and 80:20. This is a hyperparameter that can be tuned. Sklearn provides the following library function for the dataset split.

from sklearn.model_selection import train_test_split

Syntax

train_test_split(*x, y, test_size, random_state* **)**

x, y: Feature matrix & Target vector.

test_size: Proportion of test set size.

random_state: Integer, The seed value for the random generator so that the split is consistent over multiple runs.

The function returns four subsets:

> train & test subsets of x.
>
> train & test subsets of y.

13.3   Case Study: Preprocessing on the Titanic Dataset

The Titanic dataset contains information about the passengers who traveled on the RMS Titanic, which sank after colliding with an iceberg that resulted in many deaths. This dataset can best be used to demonstrate many preprocessing methods.

- **Load Dataset**

```
import pandas as pd
titanic = pd.read_csv('/content/sample_data/titanic.csv')
print('Shape of Dataset :',titanic.shape)
print('Columns :\n',titanic.columns)
```

  Output

```
Shape of Dataset : (1310, 14)
Columns: Index(['pclass', 'survived', 'name', 'sex', 'age', 'sibsp',
   'parch', 'ticket','fare', 'cabin', 'embarked', 'boat', 'body',
   'home.dest'],dtype='object')
```

- **Identify and handle missing values**

  (i) Identify the missing values

```
print('Null values :\n',titanic.isnull().sum())
```

Output

Null values:

pclass	1
survived	1
name	1
sex	1
age	264
sibsp	1
parch	1
ticket	1
fare	2
cabin	1015
embarked	3
boat	824
body	1189
home.dest	565

dtype: int64

(ii) Find rows with all null values.

```
print('Indices of rows with all null values:',
    titanic[titanic.isnull().all(axis=1)].index)
```

Output

Indices of rows with all null values: Int64Index([1309],
    dtype='int64')

Note: Row number 1309 has all null values.

(iii) Drop the row with all null values.

```
titanic.dropna(axis=0, how='all', inplace=True)
print('Shape after deleting row with all null values:
    ',titanic.shape)
```

Output

Shape after deleting row with all null values: (1309, 14)

(iv) As there are columns with many null values, delete those columns with more than 30% null values.

```
# delete the columns with less than 70% non-null values
titanic.dropna(axis=1,thresh = int(len(titanic)*0.7),
    inplace=True)
print('Dataset shape : ', titanic.shape)
print('Columns :\n',titanic.columns)
```

Output

Dataset shape : (1309, 10)
Columns:
Index(['pclass', 'survived', 'name', 'sex', 'age', 'sibsp',
'parch', 'ticket','fare', 'embarked'], dtype='object'

The columns, *boat, body, home.dest, cabin*, are deleted as they have more than 30% null values. Now let us display the null values of all the columns.

print('Null values after deleting some rows and columns :\n',
titanic.isnull().sum())

Output

Null values after deleting some rows and columns:

pclass	0
survived	0
name	0
sex	0
age	263
sibsp	0
parch	0
ticket	0
fare	1
embarked	2

dtype: int64

(v) *Filling the null values*

Age and fare columns are continuous data types. Let us fill the null values with the corresponding column mean.

titanic['age'].fillna(value=titanic['age'].mean(), inplace=True)
titanic['fare'].fillna(value=titanic['fare'].mean(), inplace=True)
print('Null values:\n',titanic.isnull().sum())

Output

Null values:

pclass	0
survived	0
name	0
sex	0
age	0
sibsp	0
parch	0
ticket	0
fare	0
embarked	2

dtype: int64

Embarked column is a categorical data type. Let us see its categorical values.

```
print('Unique values of embarked_column:',
      titanic['embarked'].unique())
```

Output

Unique values of embarked_column : ['S' 'C' nan 'Q']

Let us fill the null values with its most frequent value (mode).

```
titanic['embarked'].fillna(value=titanic['embarked'].
      mode().iloc[0], inplace=True)
print('Total Null values in the dataset:\n',
      titanic.isnull().sum().sum() )
```

Output

Total Null values in the dataset: 0

- **Data transformations:** Encoding the categorical features
  Let us first find the categorical columns with at most 5 unique values.

```
cat_cols = []
for col in titanic.columns:
  num_vals = len(titanic[col].unique())
  if num_vals<=5:
    cat_cols.append(col)
print('Categorical columns :',cat_cols)
```

Output

Categorical columns : ['pclass', 'survived', 'sex', 'embarked']

- Let us find the unique values of each categorical column

```
print('sex column values :',titanic['sex'].unique())
print('embarked column values :',titanic['embarked'].unique())
```

Output

```
sex column values : ['female' 'male']
embarked column values : ['S' 'C' 'Q']
```

This is a nominal feature of type string. Apply *get_dummies* method of pandas for data transformation.

```
sex_embarked__du = pd.get_dummies(titanic[['sex','embarked']])
print('Dummy columns:\n',sex_embarked__dum.head())
```

Output

Dummy columns:

	sex_ female	sex_ male	embarked_C	embarked_Q	embarked_S
0	1	0	0	0	1
1	0	1	0	0	1
2	1	0	0	0	1
3	0	1	0	0	1
4	1	0	0	0	1

Now that dummy columns are created for sex and embarked, let us add the dummy columns to the Titanic dataframe and drop the sex and embarked columns

```
titanic = pd.concat([titanic,sex_embarked__dum], axis=1)
titanic = titanic.drop(['embarked','sex'], axis=1)
print('Columns :\n',titanic.columns)
```

Output

```
Columns :
   Index(['pclass', 'survived', 'name', 'age', 'sibsp', 'parch', 'ticket',
      'fare','sex_female', 'sex_male', 'embarked_C', 'embarked_Q',
      'embarked_S'],dtype='object')
```

Let us take the other two categorical columns, *pclass and survived* and apply *OneHotEncoder*.

```
print(titanic['survived'].unique())
print(titanic['pclass'].unique())
```

Output

[1. 0.]
[1. 2. 3.]

from sklearn.preprocessing import OneHotEncoder

cat_cols = ['pclass','survived']
ohe = OneHotEncoder(sparse=False)
oh_cols = ohe.fit_transform(titanic[cat_cols])
print(oh_cols)

Output

array([[1., 0., 0., 0., 1.],
       [1., 0., 0., 0., 1.],
       [1., 0., 0., 1., 0.],
       ...,
       [0., 0., 1., 1., 0.],
       [0., 0., 1., 1., 0.],
       [0., 0., 1., 1., 0.]])

13.4 Supervised Learning

13.4.1 Regression

Regression is a machine learning technique to find the relationship between the dependent variable and one or more independent variables. The dependent variable is called the target, which is a continuous data type. It is usually represented by y. Independent variables are called features. Feature values are represented as a matrix called a feature matrix. It is usually represented by X.

Regression is used as a predictive model to forecast the values of the target variable given the feature matrix. It explains the correlation between the target and the features.

Typical regression applications are predicting house prices, stock values, customer trends in e-commerce, forecasting sales of products, etc.

The regression model is a function between X and y.

$$y = f(X)$$

$$y = w_0 + w_1 x_1 + w_2 x_2 + \cdots + w_N x_N$$

where $x_1, x_2, \ldots, x_N$ are the N features or independent variables. $w_1, w_2 \ldots$, and w_N are coefficients or weights of the features in fitting the regression function. w_0 is the intercept term.

Building a regression model involves the following steps:

(i) Training the model on the train dataset. This step determines the regression function coefficients.
(ii) Evaluate the model performance using the test dataset.

13.4.1.1 Model Evaluation Metrics

The following evaluation metrics are commonly used for linear regression.

- R^2—Square of the correlation coefficient. It is the proportion of variance of the dependent variable (y) that can be explained by independent variables (X). The value is between 0 and 1.

  0 indicates that y cannot be explained by X
  1 indicates that y can be perfectly explained by X

  A higher value indicates a better fit of the model.
- *MSE (Mean Squared Error)*—It is the average of error squares. Error is the difference between the actual and predicted values of y. It measures how far the predicted values are from the true values of the target variable. The lower the value, the better the fit. Zero value indicates a perfect fit.
  Challenges of this metric are: (i) This value can be very big as the errors are squared. (ii) High error values are made even larger. (iii) The value is not on the same scale as the data. (iv) It is sensitive to outliers. (v) It is hard to interpret whether the model performs well based on this value.
- *MSLE (Mean squared log error)* is a variation of mean squared error. It is the mean squared error of log-transformed predicted and log-transformed true values. It adds 1 to actual and predicted values before applying log to avoid logarithm on zero values. This metric cannot be used if the predicted or true values are negative.
- *MAE (Mean Absolute Error)*—Average of the absolute difference between actual and predicted values of y. The closer the value to 0, the better the model is. Zero value indicates a perfect fit.

Sklearn provides **LinearRegression()** library function to build a regression model. This function is available in the *linear_model* module.

    from sklearn.linear_model import LinearRegression

| Syntax |

LinearRegression(*fit_intercept, normalize, copy_X, n_jobs, positive***)**

Commonly used parameters are

fit_intercept: boolean, Whether to calculate the intercept value for the
function. If set to False, no intercept is used for
calculations. Default is True.

normalize: boolean, If true, feature matrix X is normalized before
training by subtracting the mean and dividing
by the L2 norm.
Ignored when fit_intercept is set to false.

copy_X: boolean, If true, X is copied otherwise, X is overwritten.
Default is true.

n_jobs: integer, Number of jobs used in the computation.

positive: boolean, When set to true, it forces the coefficients to be
positive. Default is false.

13.4.1.2 Case Study

Regression model on Housing dataset to predict the price of the house given its features.

- Load the dataset

```
import pandas as pd
data = pd.read_csv('/content/sample_data/
    kc_house_data.csv')
print('Dataset Shape : ',data.shape)
print('Columns : \',data.columns)
```

Output

```
Dataset Shape : (21613, 21)
Columns : Index(['id', 'date', 'price', 'bedrooms', 'bathrooms',
    'sqft_living','sqft_lot', 'floors', 'waterfront', 'view',
    'condition', 'grade', 'sqft_above', 'sqft_basement',
    'yr_built', 'yr_renovated', 'zipcode','lat', 'long',
    'sqft_living15', 'sqft_lot15'], dtype='object')
```

- Data Preprocessing

  (i) As the '*id*' feature is irrelevant, remove it using the *drop()* function.

```
data.drop('id',axis=1, inplace=True)
print('Number of Columns after removing id column:\n',
    len(data.columns))
```

Output

Number of Columns after removing id column: 20

(ii) Identify the Null values using *info()* method on the dataframe.

data.info()

Output

```
<class 'pandas.core.frame.DataFrame'>
RangeIndex: 21613 entries, 0 to 21612
Data columns (total 20 columns):
```

#	Column	Non-null count	Dtype
0	date	21613 non-null	object
1	price	21613 non-null	float64
2	bedrooms	21613 non-null	int64
3	bathrooms	21613 non-null	float64
4	sqft_living	21613 non-null	int64
5	sqft_lot	21613 non-null	int64
6	floors	21613 non-null	float64
7	waterfront	21613 non-null	int64
8	view	21613 non-null	int64
9	condition	21613 non-null	int64
10	grade	21613 non-null	int64
11	sqft_above	21611 non-null	float64
12	sqft_basement	21613 non-null	int64
13	yr_built	21613 non-null	int64
14	yr_renovated	21613 non-null	int64
15	zipcode	21613 non-null	int64
16	lat	21613 non-null	float64
17	long	21613 non-null	float64
18	sqft_living15	21613 non-null	int64
19	sqft_lot15	21613 non-null	int64

```
dtypes: float64(6), int64(13), object(1)
memory usage: 3.3+ MB
```

(iii) There are two null values in the *sqft_above* feature. Drop the rows with null values using *dropna()* function.

```
data.dropna(axis=0, inplace=True)
print('Dataset dimensions after dropping null values: ',
     data.shape)
```

Output

Dataset dimensions after dropping null values: (21611, 20)

(iv) *Visualize the data:* Draw a scatter plot between *sqft_living* and *price* using *scatter()* function of *matplotlib.pyplot.*

```
import matplotlib.pyplot as plt
plt.xlabel('Squarefoot Living')
plt.ylabel('Price of the House')
plt.title('Sqft_living vs Price')
plt.scatter(data['sqft_living'],data['price'])
plt.show()
```

Output

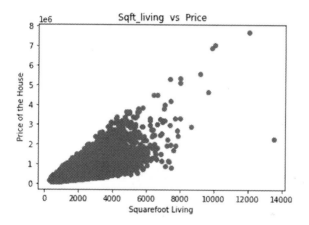

(v) Let us remove the outliers

```
# get the idices of the outliers
idx = data[data['sqft_living']>10000].index
print('Indices of outliers : ',idx)
data = data.drop(idx)
print('Dataset dimensions after removing outliers: ',
        data.shape)
```

Output

Indices of outliers : Int64Index([3914, 7252, 12777],
        dtype='int64')
Dataset dimensions after removing outliers: (21608, 20)

(vi) Visualize the data after removing outliers.

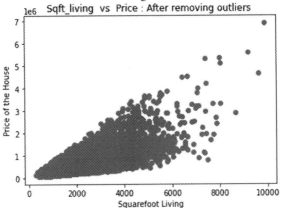

(vii) Find the contributing features by determining the correlation matrix and selecting those features whose correlation is more than 0.4. Also, remove '*price*' from the feature set as it is the target variable.

```
temp = data.corr()['price']
features= temp[temp>0.4].index
features= features.drop('price')
print(features)
```

Output

Index(['bathrooms', 'sqft_living', 'grade', 'sqft_above', 'sqft_living15'], dtype='object')

(viii) Prepare feature matrix x, and target vector, y.

```
x = data[features]
y = data['price']
```

(ix) Find the ranges of feature values.

```
print('Min and Max values of features:\n')
for feat in features:
   print(feat,': ', min(x[feat]),' ', max(x[feat]) )
```

Output

Min and Max values of features:

bathrooms:	0.0	7.75
sqft_living:	290	9890
grade:	1	13
sqft_above:	290.0	8860.0
sqft_living15:	399	6210

(x) As feature ranges are different, normalize the data.

```
from sklearn.preprocessing import MinMaxScaler
scaler = MinMaxScaler()
x_scaled = scaler.fit_transform(x)
# now x_scaled is a numpy array
print('After Normalization :\n', x_scaled[:4])
```

Output

```
After Normalization :
 [[0.12903226  0.09270833   0.5    0.10385064
     0.16193426]
 [0.29032258  0.2375   0.5    0.21936989   0.22216486]
 [0.12903226  0.05   0.4   1666667   0.05600933
     0.3994149 ]
 [0.38709677   0.17395833   0.5    0.08868145
     0.16537601]]
```

- Split the dataset into a train set and a test set.

```
from sklearn.model_selection import train_test_split
x_train,x_test, y_train, y_test= train_test_split(x_scaled,y,
        test_size=0.3, random_state=40)
print('Dimensions of Train and Test sets : ',x_train.shape,
        x_test.shape, y_train.shape, y_test.shape)
```

Output

```
Dimensions of Train and Test sets : (15125, 5) (6483, 5)
        (15125,) (6483,)
```

- Build the Regression model

```
from sklearn.linear_model import LinearRegression
lr=LinearRegression()
lr.fit(x_train, y_train)
y_preds = lr.predict(x_test)
```

- Evaluate the model

```
from sklearn.metrics import r2_score, mean_squared_error,
        mean_absolute_error, mean_squared_log_error
print('R2 : ',r2_score(y_test,y_preds))
print('MAE : ', mean_absolute_error(y_test,y_preds))
print('MSE : ',mean_squared_error(y_test,y_preds))
```

Output

R2: 0.547363994385045
MAE: 163352.7986832477
MSE: 68809985836.71199

mean_squared_log_error is not applied because the predicted values are negative as shown below.

print(y_preds[y_preds<0])

Output

[−113573.68269179   −81638.31689536   −248.67633989
    −179101.70244725   −36561.40819972   −6628.10284697
−6703.89769234   −215772.83445319   −11539.90843627
    −14269.87426284   −116717.06425597]
    −97674.12542794]

- Display model parameters: Intercept and feature coefficients.

print('Intercept : ', lr.intercept_)
print('Coefficients : ',lr.coef_)

Output

Intercept: -488880.066750332
Coefficients: [−238201.92580502   2114513.48240623
    1377740.92680231   −723748.61008129   217984.4423223]

13.4.2   Classification

Classification is a supervised learning technique that categorizes data points into different classes or categories. The dataset contains features and the target variable. The target variable is of categorical data type. The classification model determines the decision boundary that separates the data points into different classes. The model is then used to predict the class label for the given new data point.

Following are the use cases of classification:

- Classifying the emails into spam and non-spam.
- Categorizing news articles into education, political, business, sports, etc.
- Classifying images into objects of different categories.
- Sentiment classification, where the reviews are classified into positive, negative, and neutral.
- Speech recognition, etc.

Based on the number of classes, the classification task is categorized into

(i) *Binary classification* categorizes the data points into two classes.
(ii) *Multi-class classification:* The number of classes is more than two.
(iii) *Multi-label classification:* A given data point can be assigned to more than one class.

13.4.2.1 Evaluation Metrics

Commonly used performance metrics for classification model are

- *Accuracy score:* This shows the fraction of correct predictions out of the total number of predictions.
- *Confusion matrix/Error matrix:* A two-dimensional matrix of N x N, where N is the number of classes. It represents the performance of the classification model that compares the actual and predicted labels. Columns represent actual labels and rows represent predicted labels. Diagonal values represent the number of correctly classified data points, and others are the misclassifications.
- *Classification Report:* Measures the quality of the prediction model using the number of true positives (TP), true negatives (TN), false positives (FP), and false negatives (FN).
  The classification report shows precision, recall, and F1 score, for each class based on TP, TN, FP, and FN values.

Precision: Ratio of true positives to total positives predicted.
Recall: Ratio of true positives to the total number of positive samples.
F1 score: Precision and recall are combined into a single metric which is their harmonic mean. Increasing precision value results in a reduction of recall value. A high value for the F1 score indicates similar values for precision and recall.

These performance metrics are available in *metrics* module of sklearn.

```
from sklearn.metrics import accuracy_score, confusion_matrix,
    classification_report
```

13.4.2.2 Classification Algorithms

Widely used classification algorithms are

1. *Logistic regression* is a basic classification method similar to linear regression but applied to classification tasks. It uses the logit function to output a binary value. It works well when the relationship between features and target is not too complex.

   from sklearn.linear_model import LogisticRegression

Syntax

> **LogisticRegression(** *solver, fit_intercept, C, tol, penalty, multi_class, max_iter, random_state* **)**

solver:	string, Algorithm used in optimizing the cost function. Different solvers are liblinear, lbfgs, newton_cg, sag, and saga
	liblinear—fast for small datasets. Uses one vs rest method to solve multi-class problems.
	lbfgs—Used for multi-class problems and handles L2 penalty. Not fast for large datasets.
	newton_cg—is slow for large datasets as it computes second derivatives. It is a good choice for small datasets. It also handles the L1 penalty.
	sag - suitable for large datasets.
	saga - An extension of sag that allows L1 regularization. It works faster than sag and is suitable for large datasets.
fit_intercept:	boolean, Indicates whether a constant is to be added to the decision function.
C:	float, It is the inverse of regularization strength. Default is 1.0.
	The smaller the value stronger the regularization.
	Commonly used values are [0.001, 0.01, 0.1, 1, 10, 100, 1000].
tol:	float, Represents the tolerance for stopping criteria.
penalty:	string, Specifies the type of regularization.
	Values are l1, l2 (default), elasticnet, and None.
multi_class:	string, for handling multi-classes. The values are ovr, multinomial, auto.

max_iter: integer, The maximum number of iterations the
                  solver uses during model fitting.
random_state: integer, It is a seed of the pseudo-random number
                  generator used while shuffling the data.

2. *Decision Tree* is a tree structure where internal nodes represent features, edges represent decision rules, and leaf nodes represent outcomes or labels. The tree structure is built during the training process. To predict the class of a new data point, the tree is parsed from the root till the leaf node that gives the class label. A decision tree can be used for both classification and regression problems but is preferred for classification. It can take features of both numerical and categorical data types.

   The model is simple to understand and interpret. It requires minimal data cleaning and no need to scale the data. But the model training is time-consuming, and a higher depth tree makes the problem more complex, which may lead to overfitting.

   from sklearn.tree import DecisionTreeClassifier

Syntax

DecisionTreeClassifier(*criterion, max_depth, splitter,*
    min_samples_split, min_samples_leaf, max_features,
    max_leaf_nodes, random_state)

Commonly used parameters are

criterion: Measures the quality of the node split. Values
                      are Gini, entropy, and log_loss. Default is gini.
max_depth: integer, the maximum depth of the tree.
splitter: string, used to split at each node.
                      Values are best, random
min_samples_split: integer, Indicates the minimum number of
                      samples required in each split. Default is 2.
min_samples_leaf: integer, Minimum number of samples required
                      in each leaf node. Default is 1.
max_features: float, Number of features to consider for the best
                      split. Values are int, auto, sqrt, and log2.
                      Default is none.
max_leaf_nodes: The tree will grow up to the maximum number
                      of leaf nodes in the best-first fashion.

random_state parameter has same meaning as in *LogisticRegression()* function.

3. *K-Nearest Neighbors (KNN)* is a distance-based algorithm that classifies the new data point based on the majority class of its K-nearest neighbors. It uses Euclidean distance to determine the neighbors. It is an instance-based learning algorithm that does not require a training phase. It can be used for both regression and classification problems.

The algorithm is simple, easy to understand and implement. Data scaling is required as Euclidean distance is used. The algorithm is slow as the dataset grows and unsuitable for high-dimensional datasets. Also, it requires large memory as the entire dataset is used for prediction.

from sklearn.neighbors import KNeighborsClassifier

Syntax

KneighborsClassifier(*n_neighbors, algorithm, metric, p, n*)

Commonly used parameters are

n_neighbors	integer, k value in KNN is the number of neighbors. Default is 5.
algorithm	to compute nearest neighbors. Values are ball_tree, kd_tree, brute, and auto. The 'auto' will decide the most appropriate algorithm based on the data passed to the fit method.
metric	used to compute the distance between the data points. Values are cosine, Euclidean, Manhattan, etc. Default is 'minkowski'.
p	integer value for Minkowski metric. Default is 2, which is Euclidean distance.
n	integer to parallelize the processing on multiprocessors.

4. *Support Vector Machine (SVM):* A popular machine learning algorithm that can be used for classification and regression but is primarily used for classification tasks. The model determines the hyperplane in n-dimensional space that separates different classes. The data points closest to the hyperplane are called support vectors. The algorithm aims at maximizing the margin between the hyperplane and support vectors to classify the data points distinctly.

SVM classifies non-linearly separable data points using a kernel trick. A kernel converts a non-linear problem into a linear problem by transforming low-dimensional input space into high-dimensional space. Popular kennel functions are *linear, polynomial, rbf* (radial basis function).

from sklearn.svm import SVC

Syntax

SVC(*C, kernel, degree, gamma, tolerance, verbose,max_iter*)

C:	float, Inverse of regularization strength. Smaller values specify stronger regularization. The default is 1.0.
kernel:	string, Values are linear, poly, rbf, sigmoid. The default is rbf.
degree:	integer, Degree of the polynomial kernel function. Other kernels ignore this. The default is 3.
gamma:	kernel coefficient for rbf, poly and sigmoid. Values are scale, auto, or float. The default is scale.
tolerance:	float, the threshold value for stopping the iterations of the solver. Default is 1e-3.
verbose:	boolean, enables output during training.
max_iter:	integer, a limit on the number of iterations of the solver. Default is -1 indicating no limit.

5. *Naive Bayes* is a probabilistic classifier based on the Bayes theorem. A simple and effective algorithm for building models quickly. It can work on continuous and discrete data. It is particularly used for large datasets like text data. Naive Bayes is based on the assumption that all the features are independent and contribute equally to the outcome. But the real-world features are dependent, and this assumption hinders the model performance.

```
from sklearn.naive_bayes import GaussianNB
```

13.4.2.3 Case Study

Apply different classification algorithms on the glass dataset with six classes defined based on oxide content.

- Loading the Dataset

```
import pandas as pd
data = pd.read_csv('/content/sample_data/glass.csv')
print('Shape of Dataset: ',data.shape)
print('Columns : \n', data.columns)
```

Output

```
Shape of Dataset: (214, 10)
Columns :
    Index(['RI', 'Na', 'Mg', 'Al', 'Si', 'K', 'Ca', 'Ba', 'Fe', 'Type'],
          dtype='object')
```

- Data Preprocessing

    (i) Check the null values

```
print('Total number of null values : ',
      data.isnull().sum().sum())
```

Output

Total number of null values : 0

(ii) Divide the dataset into feature matrix & target vector

```
x = data.drop('Type',axis=1)
y = data['Type']
print(x.shape, y.shape)
```

Output

(214, 9) (214,)

(iii) Display the first five rows of the feature matrix to check the range of values.

```
from tabulate import tabulate
print(tabulate(x.head(), headers = 'keys', tablefmt = 'psql') )
```

Output

	RI	Na	Mg	Al	Si	K	Ca	Ba	Fe
0	1.52101	13.64	4.49	1.1	71.78	0.06	8.75	0	0
1	1.51761	13.89	3.6	1.36	72.73	0.48	7.83	0	0
2	1.51618	13.53	3.55	1.54	72.99	0.39	7.78	0	0
3	1.51766	13.21	3.69	1.29	72.61	0.57	8.22	0	0
4	1.51742	13.27	3.62	1.24	73.08	0.55	8.07	0	0

(iv) *Normalization:* Feature matrix is normalized as values are in different ranges

```
from sklearn.preprocessing import MinMaxScaler
scaler = MinMaxScaler()
x_scaled = scaler.fit_transform(x)
```

(v) *Split the dataset* into train and test sets.

```
from sklearn.model_selection import train_test_split
xtrain, xtest, ytrain, ytest = train_test_split(x_scaled, y,
        test_size=0.2, random_state=40)
print(xtrain.shape, xtest.shape, ytrain.shape, ytest.shape)
```

Output

(171, 9) (43, 9) (171,) (43,)

Build the model using different classification algorithms.

1. *Build a Logistic Regression model* and its performance with the Confusion matrix.

```
from sklearn.linear_model import LogisticRegression
from sklearn.metrics import confusion_matrix
lr = LogisticRegression(random_state=2, solver='saga')
lr.fit(xtrain, ytrain)
lr_ypred = lr.predict(xtest)
print('Counts of each lebel in ytest: \n',ytest.value_counts())
print('\n Confusion Matrix :\n',
        confusion_matrix(ytest,lr_ypred))
```

Output

```
Counts of each lebel in ytest:
2    17
1    13
7    4
3    4
5    3
6    2
Name: Type, dtype: int64

Confusion Matrix:

[[10 3 0 0 0 0]
 [10 7 0 0 0 0]
 [ 2 2 0 0 0 0]
 [ 0 3 0 0 0 0]
 [ 0 2 0 0 0 0]
 [ 0 1 0 0 0 3]]
```

Out of 13 samples of label 1, only 10 are correctly predicted and remaining are predicted as class 2.

Out of 17 in class 2, 7 are correctly predicted and the remaining 10 are predicted as class 1.

None of the data points of class 3, 5, 6 are correctly predicted.

Out of 4 data points in class 7, only 3 are correctly predicted, and the other one is predicted as class 2.

2. *K-Nearest Neighbors model:* KNN model for different values of K and accuracy tabulated below.

```
from sklearn.neighbors import KneighborsClassifier
from sklearn.metrics import accuracy_score
acc=[]
for n in range(3,10,2):
    knn = KNeighborsClassifier(n_neighbors=n)
```

```
knn.fit(xtrain, ytrain)
ypred = knn.predict(xtest)
acc.append(accuracy_score(ytest,ypred)*100)
accuracy = pd.DataFrame({'No. Neighbors': range(3,10,2),
    'Accuracy': acc})
print('KNN Accuracy for different values of K:\n', accuracy)
```

Output

KNN Accuracy for different values of K:

No.	Neighbors	Accuracy
0	3	67.441860
1	5	62.790698
2	7	62.790698
3	9	62.790698

3. Decision Tree classifier

```
from sklearn.tree import DecisionTreeClassifier
from sklearn.metrics import classification_report
dt = DecisionTreeClassifier(max_depth=2, random_state=0)
dt.fit(xtrain, ytrain)
ypred= dt.predict(xtest)
print('Classification Report of Decision Tree \n',
    classification_report(ytest,ypred))
```

Output

Classification Report of Decision Tree

	Precision	Recall	F1 score	Support
1	0.55	0.85	0.67	13
2	0.60	0.71	0.65	17
3	0.00	0.00	0.00	4
5	0.00	0.00	0.00	3
6	0.00	0.00	0.00	2
7	1.00	0.75	0.86	4
accuracy			0.60	43
macro avg	0.36	0.38	0.36	43
weighted avg	0.50	0.60	0.54	43

Let us visualize the tree.

```
from sklearn import tree
# convert numeric labels into strings
cn = str(y.unique())
fn= x.columns
print('Class Labels : ',cn)
print('Feature Names : ', fn)
_=tree.plot_tree(dt, class_names= cn,
        feature_names=fn, filled=True )
```

Output

Class Labels : [1 2 3 5 6 7]
Feature Names : Index(['RI', 'Na', 'Mg', 'Al', 'Si', 'K', 'Ca',
    'Ba', 'Fe'], dtype='object')

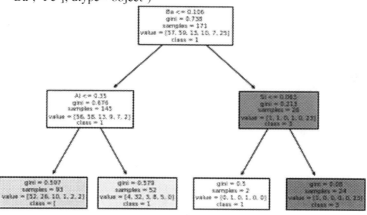

4. Support Vector Machine (SVM) with different kernels

```
from sklearn.svm import SVC
kern=['rbf', 'poly', 'linear', 'sigmoid']
acc=[]
for k in kern:
    svm = SVC(kernel = k)
    svm.fit(xtrain, ytrain)
    ypred = svm.predict(xtest)
    acc.append(accuracy_score(ytest,ypred)*100)
accuracy = pd.DataFrame(acc,columns=['Accuracy'],
        index=kern)
print('SVM model accuracy for different kernel values \n',
        accuracy)
```

Output

SVM model accuracy for different kernel values

	Accuracy
rbf	67.441860
poly	65.116279
linear	48.837209
sigmoid	44.186047

5. Naive Bayes Classifier

```
from sklearn.naive_bayes import GaussianNB
from sklearn.metrics import accuracy_score
nb = GaussianNB()
nb.fit(xtrain, ytrain)
ypred= nb.predict(xtest)
print('Accuracy Score of Naive Bayes: ',
    accuracy_score(ytest,ypred)*100)
```

Output

Accuracy Score of Naive Bayes: 48.837209302325576

13.5   Model Selection

Model parameters are the weights learned from the data during the model's training process. These parameters map the feature variables to the target variable. Parameters are initialized with 0s or some random values before starting the training process. As the training progresses, these values are updated using optimization algorithms like gradient descent, Adam, RMSProp, etc. At the end of the training process, the updated parameter values constitute the model. These values are used to make predictions.

Examples of model parameters are coefficients of the linear regression function, the values that constitute hyperplane in classification, cluster centroids in clustering, etc.

Hyperparameters are the values used to control the training process. These values are set before the training begins. They are external to the model and do not change during training. The choice of hyperparameter values affects the model parameters determined by the training process. Choosing the best values is very important in building good models.

Examples of hyperparameters are the regularization parameter, optimization algorithm in model training, learning rate, kernel, etc.

13.5.1 Hyperparameter Tuning

The process of choosing the best hyperparameter values is called hyperparameter tuning. Hyperparameter tuning can be done in two ways:

1. *Manual tuning:* Hyperparameters values are set to some recommended values and then searched through a range of values by trial and error. This process is tedious and time-consuming. This approach is not practical when there are many hyperparameters. To get default values used by the model.

Syntax
---

    model_name.*get_params()*

2. *Automated tuning:* It uses an algorithm to search for optimal values. Sklearn provides the following algorithms for automated tuning.

    (a) **Grid search:** Creates a grid of discrete values for the hyperparameters. The model is trained on each possible combination of the values and evaluated. The values for which the model performs best are the best hyperparameter values. This approach is an exhaustive sampling of hyperparameter space. As the model is trained on all possible combinations of values, it requires more computational power and is time-consuming.

    Limitations of this approach are: (i) Search is on the values specified in the hyperparameter grid. But, other hyperparameter combinations may further improve the performance. (ii) Performing an exhaustive search is time-consuming.

      from sklearn.model_selection import GridSearchCV

Syntax

    GridSearchCV(*estimator, param_grid, scoring. cv, n_jobs, refit,*
      return_train_score, verbose)

estimator:	Estimator object for which hyperparameters are determined.
param_grid:	A dictionary of hyperparameter names and their values.
scoring:	Evaluation metrics used in model evaluation.
cv:	Number of folds used in cross-validation. Default is 5.
n_jobs:	Number of processes created to execute the job. Default is None
refit:	boolean, whether to refit the estimator on the best hyperparameter values on the whole dataset.
return_train_score:	Returns the training score of different hyperparameter settings. This helps in determining the overfit or underfit.
verbose:	Gives detailed output while training.

To get the best hyperparameters values and corresponding accuracy, apply the fit method on the grid search object and access the values from the result as follows.

> *results* = **gs.fit**(x_train, y_train)
> *results.***best_params_**
> *results.***best_score_**

(b) **Randomized search** takes random combinations from grid space to train and evaluate the model. This is repeated for the specified number of iterations. Statistical distributions can also be specified for each hyperparameter from which values are randomly sampled.

As it is not an exhaustive search, there is no guarantee of the best result but it is very effective in practice. Computational time is significantly less compared to grid search. This approach is appropriate when the number of hyperparameters is more.

> from sklearn.model_selection import
> RandomizedSearchCV

Syntax

> RandamizedSearchCV(estimator, n_iter, param_grid,
> scoring, cv, refit, return_train_score, verbose)

n_iter: integer, Number of parameter settings that are sampled. Default 10.

Other parameters like *estimator, param_grid, scoring. cv, refit, return_train_score*, and *verbose* are the same as in the GridSearch( ) function.

13.5.2 Case Study

Apply hyperparameter tuning techniques on **Pima Indian Diabetes** dataset. The dataset consists of patients' diagnostic measurements, and the outcome of whether the patient is diabetic. A predictive model is built with the best hyperparameter values after tuning.

- Load the dataset

```
import pandas as pd
data = pd.read_csv('/content/sample_data/pima_indian_
    diabetis.csv')
print('Dataset shape :',data.shape)
print('Columns :\n',data.columns)
```

Output

```
Dataset shape : (768, 9)
Columns: Index(['Pregnancies', 'Glucose', 'BloodPressure',
    'SkinThickness', 'Insulin', 'BMI', 'DiabetesPedigreeFunction',
    'Age', 'Outcome'],dtype='object')
```

- Identify the total number of null values in the dataset

```
print('Total number of null values: ',data.isnull().sum().sum())
```

Output

```
Total number of null values: 0
```

- Prepare feature matrix and target vector.

```
x = data.drop('Outcome', axis=1)
y = data['Outcome']
print('Shape of x :',x.shape, ' Shape of y :',y.shape)
```

Output

```
Shape of x : (768, 8)
Shape of y : (768,)
```

- Count number of observations in each label

```
import numpy as np
print('Count of Labels :\n',y.value_counts())
```

Output

```
Count of Labels :
0    500
1    268
Name: Outcome, dtype: int64
```

- Normalize the feature matrix

```
from sklearn.preprocessing import MinMaxScaler
scaler = MinMaxScaler()
x_scaled = scaler.fit_transform(x)
```

- Split the dataset into train set and test set

```
from sklearn.model_selection import train_test_split
xtrain, xtest, ytrain, ytest = train_test_split(x_scaled,y,test_size=0.2,
    random_state=1)
print(xtrain.shape, xtest.shape, ytrain.shape, ytest.shape)
```

Output

(614, 8) (154, 8) (614,) (154,)

Hyperparameter tuning

(i) Grid search for SVM

```
hyper_param_grid={'kernel':['rbf','linear','poly'],'degree':
    [3,4,5], 'C' : [0.1, 1,10,100], 'gamma':[0.1,0.01, 0.001]}
from sklearn.svm import SVC

%%time
from sklearn.model_selection import GridSearchCV
grid = GridSearchCV(estimator= SVC(), param_grid=
    hyper_param_grid, verbose=1)
print("Grid Search : \n")
grid.fit(xtrain, ytrain)
print('Best hyperparameter values:\n',grid.best_params_)
print('Best Score : ',grid.best_score_ * 100)
```

Output

Grid Search :

Fitting 5 folds for each of 108 candidates, totaling 540 fits

Best hyperparameter values:
{'C': 10, 'degree': 3, 'gamma': 0.1, 'kernel': 'rbf'}
Best Score : 77.52499000399841
CPU times: user 6.09 s, sys: 6.3 ms, total: 6.1 s
Wall time: 6.1 s

(ii) Randomized grid search

```
%%time
from sklearn.model_selection import RandomizedSearchCV
grid = RandomizedSearchCV(estimator= SVC(), param_
    distributions= hyper_param_grid, n_iter=5, verbose = 1)
print("Randomized Search : \n")
grid.fit(xtrain, ytrain)
print('Best Hyperparameter values:\n',grid.best_params_)
print('Best Score : ',grid.best_score_ * 100)
```

Output

Randomized Search :

Fitting 5 folds for each of 5 candidates, totaling 25 fits
Best Hyperparameter values:
{'kernel': 'poly', 'gamma': 0.1, 'degree': 3, 'C': 100}
Best Score : 77.35972277755565
CPU times: user 363 ms, sys: 1.98 ms, total: 365 ms
Wall time: 366 ms

Randomized grid search achieves almost the same score as grid search with only 5 hyperparameter settings instead of 108 taken by grid search.

13.6 Ensemble Methods

Ensembling is a process of combining predictions of multiple models. Each model is called a base model, which is a weak learner. These weak learners are combined to form stronger learner. This technique helps in improving the model performance and overcomes bias and variance problems. Ensembling can be used for both regression and classification tasks.

13.6.1 Basic Ensembling Techniques

(i) *Max voting:* For a given data point, each model's prediction is considered a vote. The final prediction is the class that wins the majority votes. This applies to classification tasks.

Example: Take a datapoint P

      Model-1   predicted   Class A
      Model-2   predicted   Class B
      Model-3   predicted   Class A

The final prediction for the datapoint P is Class A.

(ii) *Averaging:* The final prediction, for the given datapoint P, is the average of all the model's predictions.

$$\text{Final\_prediction} = (\ \text{model1\_prediction} + \text{model2\_prediction} + \cdots + \text{modelN\_prediction}\ ) / N$$

(iii) *Weighted averaging:* Each model prediction is given a weight. A model with higher predictive power is given more weight. All weights of the models sum up to 1. The final prediction is a weighted average of all models.

$$\text{Final\_prediction} = (\text{prediction\_1} * w1 + \text{prediction\_2} * w2 + \cdots + \text{prediction\_N} * wN\ ) / N$$

Averaging and weighted averaging methods are used for regression tasks.

13.6.2 Advanced Ensembling Techniques

In addition to the basic methods, there are advanced ensembling methods. Widely used advanced ensembling approaches are Bagging, Boosting, and Stacking.

1. *Bagging:* Subsets of the training data are sampled using the bootstrap sampling method with replacement. Then each subset is trained independently and in parallel using the same base model, forming weak learners. Predictions of these weak learners are then combined to form the final prediction. In the case of regression tasks, the average of all the individual models is taken as the final prediction and majority voting for classification tasks.

   The bagging method is used when weak learners show high variance and low bias. The decision tree is commonly used as a base model algorithm. As the number of subsamples increases, the bagging process takes more time.

   Random forests is a bagging method that uses a decision tree as the base model. Instances as well as features are sampled to form subsamples. Decision tree algorithm is applied to each of these subsamples. Predictions of the individual decision trees are then combined to form the final prediction. Random forests can be used for both classification and regression tasks.

2. *Boosting:* The objective of boosting is to convert weak learners to the strong learner. A sequence of models is developed by correcting the errors made in the prior model by giving more weightage in the next model. The first model gives all the data points the same weightage. In the subsequent model, wrongly classified data points are given more weight, and the weights of correctly classified data points are reduced. Normalize the weights and repeat the steps until the required accuracy is reached. Each subsequent model is influenced by the performance of the previous model. Boosting method is used when weak learners show low variance and high bias. It aims at decreasing the bias. Popularly used boosting algorithms are *Adaboost, Gradient Boost, XGBoost,* etc.

3. *Stacking:* Train a set of models on the given training dataset. Predictions of these models form a new train dataset. Another model is trained on this new train dataset and evaluate this new model on the test data. Sklearn provides the following library functions for the ensemble algorithms.

(i)

from sklearn.ensemble import BaggingClassifier

| Syntax |

BaggingClassifier(*base_estimator, n_estimators, max_samples, max_features, random_state*)

base_estimator:	The base model used for fitting on subsets of the dataset. The default is a decision tree.
n_estimators:	Number of base estimators.
max_samples:	Number of samples to draw from the dataset.
max_features:	Number of features included in each sample subset.
random_state:	Method of the random split. When this value is the same for models, random selection is also the same.

(ii)

from sklearn.ensemble import RandomForestClassifier

| Syntax |

RandomForestClassifier(*n_estimators, criterion, max_features, max_depth, min_samples_split, min_samples_leaf, max_leaf_nodes, random_state*)

n_estimators:	Number of decision trees in the random forest.
criterion:	Function used for splitting tree nodes.
max_features:	Maximum number of features allowed for the split in each decision tree.
max_depth:	Maximum depth of each decision tree.
min_samples_split:	Minimum number of samples required in leaf node before attempting to split.
min_samples_leaf:	Minimum number of samples required in the leaf node.
max_leaf_nodes:	Maximum number of leaf nodes for each decision tree.
random_state:	Specifies random split method. When this value is the same for different models, random selection is also the same.

(iii)

from sklearn.ensemble import AdaBoostClassifier

Syntax

AdaBoostClassifier(*base_estimator, n_estimators, learning_rate, max_depth, random_state* **)**

base_estimator:	Type of base estimator.
n_estimators:	Number of base estimators. The default is 10.
learning_rate:	Controls the contribution of base estimators in the final combination.
max_depth:	Maximum depth of each estimator.
random_state:	Integer that indicates random split.

(iv)

from sklearn.ensemble import GradientBoostingClassifier

Syntax

GradientBoostingClassifier(*min_samples_split, min_samples_leaf, min_weight_fraction_leaf, max_depth, max_leaf_nodes, max_features* **)**

min_samples_split:	Minimum number of samples required to split the node.
min_samples_leaf:	Minimum samples required in a leaf node.
min_weight_fraction_leaf:	same as above, except that it is specified as a fraction of total number of samples.
max_depth:	Maximum depth of a tree.
max_leaf_nodes:	Maximum number of leaf nodes in a tree.
max_features:	Number of features considered for best split.

(v) import xgboost as xgb

Syntax

xgb.XGBClassifier(*n_estimators, eta, gamma, min_child_weight, max_depth, max_features*)

n_estimators:	number of boosting strategies. 100(default).
eta:	Same as learning_rate.
gamma:	Minimum loss reduction to make a split. Values are deviance, and exponential (for 2 classes). Default Loss - log_loss.
min_child_weight:	Minimum sum of weights of samples required in a child.
max_depth:	Maximum depth of a tree.
max_features:	auto, sqrt, log2. Default None.

(vi)

from sklearn.ensemble import StackingClassifier

Syntax

StackingClassifier(*estimators, final_estimator*)

| *estimators:* | List of base estimators. |
| *final_estimator:* | Classifier that combines the base estimators. Default is logistic regression. |

13.6.3   Case Study

Apply different ensemble algorithms on *Pima Indian Diabetes* dataset that contains features describing patient's medical indicators and the target indicates whether a patient is diabetic.

- Load dataset

```
import pandas as pd
data = pd.read_csv('/content/sample_data/pima_
    indian_diabetis.csv')
print('Shape of Dataset: ',data.shape)
print('Columns : \n', data.columns)
```

Output

```
Shape of Dataset: (768, 9)
Columns :
    Index(['Pregnancies', 'Glucose', 'BloodPressure', 'SkinThickness',
        'Insulin', 'BMI', 'DiabetesPedigreeFunction', 'Age',
        'Outcome'], dtype='object')
```

- Identify the null values

```
print('Total number of null values : ', data.isnull().sum().sum())
```

Output

```
Total number of null values : 0
```

- Prepare Feature Matrix and Target Vector

```
x = data.drop('Outcome',axis=1)
y = data['Outcome']
print('Dimensions of Feature matrix and Target Vector: ',
    x.shape, y.shape)
```

Output

```
Dimensions of Feature matrix and Target Vector: (768, 8) (768,)
```

- Normalize the feature matrix

Check the value ranges of features

```
print('Feature value ranges :\n')
for col in x.columns:
    print(col,' : ', min(x[col]),' to ', max(x[col]))
```

Output

Feature value ranges :

Pregnancies: 0 to 17
Glucose: 0 to 199
BloodPressure: 0 to 122
SkinThickness: 0 to 99
Insulin: 0 to 846
BMI: 0.0 to 67.1
DiabetesPedigreeFunction: 0.078 to 2.42
Age: 21 to 81

As feature value ranges are different, let us normalize the feature matrix.

```
sklearn.preprocessing import MinMaxScaler
scaler = MinMaxScaler()
x_scaled = scaler.fit_transform(x)
```

- Create train and test datasets using scaled feature matrix

```
from sklearn.model_selection import train_test_split
xtrain, xtest, ytrain, ytest = train_test_split(x_scaled, y,
    test_size=0.2, random_state=40)
print('Dimensions of train & test sets: ',xtrain.shape, xtest.shape,
    ytrain.shape, ytest.shape)
```

Output

Dimensions of train & test sets: (614, 8) (154, 8) (614,) (154,)

- Apply different ensemble methods

  1. Bagging ensemble method using support vector machine as the base estimator.

```
from sklearn.ensemble import BaggingClassifier
from sklearn.svm import SVC
bc_svm=BaggingClassifier(base_estimator=SVC(),
    n_estimators=50)
bc_svm.fit(xtrain, ytrain)
print('Auuracy Score using Bagging classifier : ',
    bc_svm.score(xtest, ytest)*100)
```

Output

Auuracy Score using Bagging classifier : 75.32467532467533

2. Random Forest

```
from sklearn.ensemble import RandomForestClassifier
from sklearn.model_selection import KFold, cross_val_score
rf = RandomForestClassifier(n_estimators= 30, max_features=5)
rf.fit(xtrain,ytrain)
print('Accuracy Score using Random Forest : ',
    rf.score(xtest, ytest)*100)
```

Output

Accuracy Score using Random Forest : 76.62337662337663

3. Adaboost Algorithm

```
from sklearn.ensemble import AdaBoostClassifier
ada_boost = AdaBoostClassifier(n_estimators=30)
ada_boost.fit(xtrain,ytrain)
print('Accuracy Score using AdaBoost: ',
    ada_boost.score(xtest, ytest)*100)
```

Output

Accuracy Score using AdaBoost: 72.07792207792207

4. Gradient Boost Algorithm

```
from sklearn.ensemble import GradientBoostingClassifier
gbc = GradientBoostingClassifier(n_estimators=30)
gbc.fit(xtrain,ytrain)
print('Accuracy Score using Gradient Boost: ',
    gbc.score(xtest, ytest)*100)
```

Output

Accuracy Score using Gradient Boost: 75.32467532467533

5. XGBoost Algorithm

```
import xgboost as xgb
model = xgb.XGBClassifier(n_estimators=30)
model.fit(xtrain,ytrain)
print('Accuracy Score using XGBoost: ',
    model.score(xtest, ytest)*100)
```

Output

Accuracy Score using XGBoost: 78.57142857142857

6. *Stacking Method* using Support Vector Machine, Decision Tree, and K-Nearest Neighbor classifiers.

```
from sklearn.ensemble import StackingClassifier
from sklearn.svm import SVC
from sklearn.tree import DecisionTreeClassifier
from sklearn.neighbors import KneighborsClassifier
from sklearn.linear_model import LogisticRegression
lr = LogisticRegression()
svm = SVC()
dt = DecisionTreeClassifier()
knn = KNeighborsClassifier()
sc = StackingClassifier(estimators=[('svm', svm), ('Dec Tree',dt),
    ('knn',knn)], final_estimator=lr )
sc.fit(xtrain,ytrain)
print('Accuracy Score of Stacking Classifier : ',
    sc.score(xtest, ytest)*100)
```

Output

Accuracy Score of Stacking Classifier : 75.9740259740259

13.7   Unsupervised Learning

Unsupervised learning is a machine learning approach that learns from unlabeled data. The dataset contains feature values but no target variable. It is mainly used to uncover the hidden patterns, and groups present in the data. Generally used as a pre-processing step to understand the data and the relationships in the data. Unsupervised learning tasks include Clustering, Association, and Dimensionality reduction.

Popular applications of unsupervised learning are product recommendations, detecting social media groups, data exploration, and fraud detection.

13.7.1   Unsupervised Learning Techniques

1. **Dimensionality reduction**
   Each feature of a dataset is called a dimension. When a dataset has many features, it is considered a high-dimensional dataset. Building a predictive model on a high-dimensional dataset faces challenges called the curse of dimensionality. The challenges are

(i) A model built on a high-dimensional dataset becomes more complex and is likely to overfit. Such models do not generalize well, resulting in less accurate predictions on new data.

(ii) Model building requires more computational time and storage space as the data has many values.

Dimensionality reduction is a technique that reduces the number of features in the dataset. This can be done in the following ways:

- *Feature selection:* Select which features to keep and which features to discard. This can be done using two methods.
  - (i) *Wrapper method* fits and evaluates the model with different subsets of input features and selects the subset with the best model performance.
  - (ii) *Filter method* finds the correlation between features and the target variable. Select the more predictive features.
- *Feature extraction:* Data in high-dimensional space is reduced to lower dimensional space. New features are obtained from the existing features by capturing the essential information in the data. Popular algorithms are Principal Component Analysis (PCA), Linear Discriminant Analysis (LDA), and Singular Value Decomposition (SVD).
- *Autoencoders* is a deep neural network that performs a complex non-linear function to reduce the dimensions. Whereas PCA performs linear transformations.

Dimensionality reduction has the following benefits:

(i) Less computational time and storage space.
(ii) When dimensions are reduced to 2 or 3, the dataset can be visualized using graphs.
(iii) Redundant features are removed.

Sklearn provides PCA() library functions to perform dimensionality reduction. **PCA** performs a linear transformation on the data to create new features that capture the most variance in the data. These new features are called principal components.

> from sklearn.decompose import PCA

| Syntax |

PCA(*n_components* **)**

n_components: Number of principal components to keep or a float value indicating the variance in the data to be retained. If the argument is not set, all components are retained.

2. **Clustering**

Clustering is an unsupervised machine learning technique to group the data points based on the attribute values present in the data. These groups are called clusters. The clusters reveal associations present in the data. It helps in exploring and understanding the data that is useful in other machine learning tasks.

Clustering is similar to classification task, but clustering is an unsupervised method that does not require labels. Clustering is widely used in social network analysis, grouping news articles, identifying customer segments, and grouping patients for personalized treatment.

Clustering can be broadly classified as soft clustering and hard clustering. In hard clustering, each data point belongs to only one cluster. Whereas, in soft clustering, a data point may belong to multiple clusters with some probability.

13.7.2 Clustering Methods

Major types of clustering methods are partitioning clustering, density-based clustering, distribution model-based clustering, hierarchical clustering, and fuzzy clustering.

1. **Density-based clustering:** Data points are grouped by identifying the areas of high concentration. The threshold value determines how close the point must be to consider it as a cluster member. This method does not require the user to specify the number of clusters. Clusters can be of arbitrary shapes, and also ignores the outliers. This approach is not suitable for high-dimensional space. Some of the algorithms that fall in this category are DBSCAN, OPTICS.
2. **Distribution-based clustering:** Data points are assigned to a cluster based on the probability that it belongs to the cluster. Probability is based on the distance from the point to the cluster center. This approach is suitable when you know the distribution of the data, e.g., Gaussian mixture model.
3. **Centroid-based/Partition clustering:** This algorithm divides the datapoints into non-overlapping clusters. Datapoint is assigned to the cluster that has a minimum squared distance to the cluster centroid. Distance measures are Euclidean, Manhattan, and Minkowski. This is a simple and widely used clustering approach but is suitable when clusters are of spherical shapes. For example, K-means, K-medoids, and meanshift algorithms.
4. **Hierarchical-based clustering:** A hierarchy of clusters is formed by grouping similar data points. The tree can be built either using a top-down or bottom-up approach.

   Agglomerative clustering is a bottom-up approach. Initially, each data point is considered a cluster. Then similar clusters are merged to form next-level clusters. This process continues until all the data points are merged or the desired number of clusters are formed.

Divisive clustering is a top-down approach. Initially, the entire dataset is considered as a single cluster. It performs the split recursively until clusters with a single datapoint are formed or the desired number of clusters is reached.

This method is computationally expensive for huge datasets and is sensitive to noise and outliers. Hierarchical clustering is typically used for hierarchical data like company databases, and social network analysis to identify the groups.

Sklearn provides a set of clustering algorithms that use different approaches. These are available in *cluster* module of *sklearn*.

1. K-means, a widely used centroid-based hard clustering method.

   from sklearn.cluster import KMeans

Syntax

Kmeans(*n_clusters, init, random_state, max_iter* **)**

n_clusters:	*integer*, Number of clusters to be formed. Default is 8.
init:	*string*, Method to select the initial centroids. Different values are *k-means++, random.* Default is *k-means++.*
random_state:	*integer*, Random seed used to reproduce the exact clusters over multiple runs. Default is None.
max_iter:	*integer*, Maximum number of iterations of the algorithm for a single run. The default is 300.

The *inertia* metric measures the performance of the clustering model. It is the sum of squared distances from the points to their respective centroids.

2. **MiniBatchKMeans:** A variation of K-means in which cluster centroids are updated based on mini-batches of samples. Whereas K-means works on the entire dataset. This is faster for large datasets and robust to noise.

   from sklearn.cluster import MiniBatchKmeans

Syntax

MiniBatchKMeans(*n_clusters, init, max_iter, batch_size, random_state* **)**

batch_size:	integer, Number of datapoints in a mini-batch. Default is 1024.

Other parameters are same as in K-means except for the default value of 100 for *max_iter*.

3. *DBSCAN* is a density-based algorithm where data points with many nearby neighbors are grouped together. The algorithm does not require the number of clusters to be specified as a parameter. It can identify outliers as noise and is good at forming arbitrarily shaped and sized clusters. But it cannot detect clusters of varying density. Finding the distance threshold is a challenging task for high-dimensional datasets.

   from sklearn.cluster import DBSCAN

| Syntax |

   DBSCAN(eps, min_samples, metric)

eps:	float, How close the data points to each other to consider as part of the cluster. Default value is 0.5.
min_samples:	integer, Minimum number of datapoints (threshold) to construct a cluster. Default is 5.
metric:	string, Distance measure used. Default is Euclidean.

4. *OPTICS:* A modified version of DBSCAN that works well when data points have density drops between clusters.

   from sklearn.cluster import OPTICS

| Syntax |

   OPTICS(*eps, min_samples, metric*)

eps : float	How close the data points to each other to consider as part of the cluster. Default value is None.
min_samples: integer	The minimum number of data points (threshold) to construct a cluster. Default is 5
metric: string	Distance measure used. Default is minkowski.

5. *Affinity Propagation:* Datapoints are grouped by passing messages to each other until cluster representatives are formed. These representatives are called exemplars. The algorithm does not require the number of clusters to be specified in advance.

   from sklearn.cluster import AffinityPropagation

| **Syntax** |

AffinityPropagation(*damping, preference, max_iter* **)**

damping: *float*, Extend to which current value is maintained
relative to incoming values. The value is between
0.5 & 1.0. Default is 0.5.

preference: *float*, Controls the number of exemplars used.
Default is None.

max_iter: *integer*, Maximum number of iterations. Default is 200.

6. *Agglomerative clustering* is a hierarchical clustering method where data points
are merged into clusters until the desired number of clusters is formed.

   from sklearn.cluster import AgglomerativeClustering

| **Syntax** |

AgglomerativeClustering(*n_clusters,affinity,compute_full_tree,*
linkage,distance_threshold **)**

n_clusters: *int*, Number of clusters to be formed.
Default is 2.

affinity: *string*, Metric used to compute linkage.
Default is Euclidean.

compute_full_tree: *Boolean or auto*, Stop the construction of the tree
at n_clusters.

linkage: Linkage criteria that determine the distance
between pairs of clusters. Default is ward.
ward minimizes the variance of the clusters
being merged.
average is the average distance of each
observation in the clusters being merged.
complete or maximum is the maximum distance of
all the observations in the clusters being
merged.
single is the minimum distance of all the
observations in the clusters being merged.

distance_threshold: *float*, Clusters will not be merged if the linkage
distance is more than this value.
Default is None.

7. **BIRCH**—This algorithm is used for large datasets with limited memory and
CPU cycles. It generates a summary of a large dataset into smaller regions called
clustering feature entries (CF) that retain as much information as possible. These
are then used for clustering instead of the original large dataset.

   from sklearn.cluster import Birch

Syntax

Birch(n_clusters, threshold, branching_factor)

n_clusters:	number of clusters to be formed after the final clustering step. When set to None, final clustering is not performed, and intermediate clusters are returned. Default is 3.

threshold:	Maximum number of data points in a sub-cluster in the leaf node of the CF tree.
branching_factor:	*integer*, Maximum number of CF sub-clusters in each node. Default is 50.

8. **Gaussian Mixture Model:** Real-life data is modeled by Gaussian distribution. So a dataset can be modeled as a mixture of several Gaussian distributions. The model is built by estimating the Gaussian parameters for each cluster. After the parameters are estimated, calculate each data point's probability of belonging to a cluster.

   from sklearn.mixture import GaussianMixture

Syntax

GaussianMixture(*n_components, n_init, random_state* **)**

n_components:	*integer*, Number of clusters.
n_init:	*integer*, Number of times the algorithm is initialized to decrease the chance of forming bad clusters.
random_state:	*integer*, Random seed used to reproduce the exact clusters over multiple runs. Default is None.

13.7.3   Case Study

Perform dimensionality reduction and then apply different clustering algorithms on the Breast Cancer dataset that contains 30 useful features.

- Data loading

```
import pandas as pd
data = pd.read_csv('/content/sample_data/Breast_cancer.csv')
print(data.shape)
print(data.columns)
```

Output

(569, 33)
Index(['id', 'diagnosis', 'radius_mean', 'texture_mean',
  'perimeter_mean', 'area_mean', 'smoothness_mean',
  'compactness_mean', 'concavity_mean',
  'concave points_mean', 'symmetry_mean',
  'fractal_dimension_mean', 'radius_se', 'texture_se',
  'perimeter_se', 'area_se', 'smoothness_se',
  'compactness_se', 'concavity_se', 'concave points_se',
  'symmetry_se', 'fractal_dimension_se', 'radius_worst',
  'texture_worst', 'perimeter_worst', 'area_worst',
  'smoothness_worst', 'compactness_worst', 'concavity_worst',
  'concave points_worst', 'symmetry_worst',
  'fractal_dimension_worst', 'Unnamed: 32'],
dtype='object')

- Data preprocessing

  (i) Delete non-useful columns like *id, Unnamed: 3* and also target column, *diagnosis*, as we are using unsupervised learning. This results in dataset with 30 columns.

    ```
    x = data.drop(['id','Unnamed: 32', 'diagnosis'], axis=1)
    print(x.shape)
    ```

Output

(569, 30)

  (ii) Check the null values

    ```
    print('Null values: \n',x.isnull().sum().sum())
    ```

Output

Null values: 0

  (iii) Check the range of values of first five columns

    ```
    for col in x.columns[:5]:
        print(col, min(x[col]), max(x[col]))
    ```

Output

```
radius_mean 6.981 28.11
texture_mean 9.71 39.28
perimeter_mean 43.79 188.5
area_mean 143.5 2501.0
smoothness_mean 0.05263 0.1634
```

As the ranges are varying, the dataset need to be normalized.

(iv) Data normalization

```
from sklearn.preprocessing import MinMaxScaler
scaler = MinMaxScaler()
x_scaled= scaler.fit_transform(x)
print('Normalized data : \n',x_scaled[:1])
```

Output

Normalized data :

```
[[0.52103744 0.0226581 0.54598853 0.36373277 0.59375282
  0.7920373 0.70313964 0.73111332 0.68636364 0.60551811
  0.35614702 0.12046941 0.3690336 0.27381126 0.15929565
  0.35139844 0.13568182 0.30062512 0.31164518 0.18304244
  0.62077552 0.14152452 0.66831017 0.45069799 0.60113584
  0.61929156 0.56861022 0.91202749 0.59846245 0.41886396]]
```

(v) Dimensionality Reduction: Reduce the dimensions to retain 90% variance using PCA.

```
from sklearn.decomposition import PCA
pca_var = PCA(0.9)
x_decomposed = pca_var.fit_transform(x_scaled)
n_comp =pca_var.n_components_
print('No. of principal components : ',n_comp)
print('Variance retained by the Principal Components : \n',
    pca_var.explained_variance_ratio_)
```

Output

No. of principal components : 6
Variance retained by the Principal Components :

```
[0.53097689 0.1728349 0.07114442 0.06411259 0.04086072
 0.03071494]
```

For the purpose of visualization, perform dimensionality reduction to have two principal components.

```
from sklearn.decomposition import PCA
pca = PCA(n_components=2)
x_decomposed = pca.fit_transform(x_scaled)
print('Variance retained by the principal components:',
    pca.explained_variance_ratio_)
# create a dataframe with the principal components
x_new = pd.DataFrame(x_decomposed, columns=
    ['pc1', 'pc2'])
print(x_new.head())
```

Output

Variance retained by the principal components :
[0.53097689 0.1728349]

	pc1	pc2
0	1.387021	0.426895
1	0.462308	−0.556947
2	0.954621	−0.109701
3	1.000816	1.525089
4	0.626828	−0.302471

About 70% of the variance is retained by the two components.

(vi) *Visualize the data* after dimensionality reduction.

```
import matplotlib.pyplot as plt
plt.tick_params(labelbottom=False, bottom=False)
plt.tick_params(labelleft=False, left=False)
plt.scatter(x_new['pc1'], x_new['pc2'])
plt.title('Dataset with first two principal components')
plt.show()
```

Output

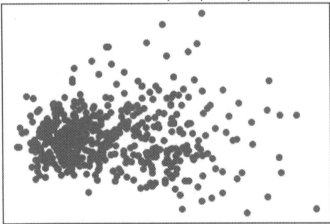

- *Clustering algorithms:* Apply different clustering algorithms on the decomposed data.

  (i) *K-means clustering*

    Let us first determine the optimal value of k, the number of clusters, using the Elbow method.

    ```
    from sklearn.cluster import Kmeans
    sum_sq=[]
    for i in range(2,9):
        km= KMeans(n_clusters=i, init='k-means++',
            random_state=40)
        km.fit(x_new)
        sum_sq.append(km.inertia_)
    plt.plot(range(2,9), sum_sq)
    plt.title('No. of clusters vs Inertia ')
    plt.show()
    ```

Output

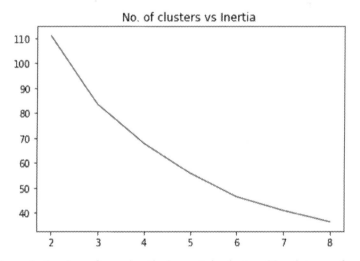

As shown in the above figure, inertia drops at six clusters. Now let us perform K-means clustering with six clusters.

```
# apply k-means clustering for 6 clusters
km = KMeans(n_clusters=6,
    init='k-means++',random_state=40)
clusters = km.fit_predict(x_decomposed)
cluster_labels = np.unique(clusters)
print('Cluster Labels : ',cluster_labels)
```

Output

Cluster Labels : [0 1 2 3 4 5]

Visualize the clusters

```
import numpy as np
markers=['*','+','>','o','v','^']
print('No. of clusters',len(cluster_labels))
plt.title('KMeans Clustering')
plt.tick_params(labelbottom=False, bottom=False)
plt.tick_params(labelleft=False, left=False)
for i in cluster_labels:
    idx = np.where(clusters==i)
    plt.scatter(x_decomposed[idx,0], x_decomposed[idx,1],
        marker=markers[i] )
```

Output

No. of clusters 6

KMeans Clustering

(ii) *DBSCAN Algorithm:* Outliers can be identified using DBSCAN.

```
from sklearn.cluster import DBSCAN
model=DBSCAN(min_samples=15)
clusters = model.fit_predict(x_decomposed)
cluster_labels = np.unique(clusters)
print('Cluster Labels : ',cluster_labels)
```

Output

Cluster Labels : [-1 0]
No. of clusters: 2

DBSCAN Clustering

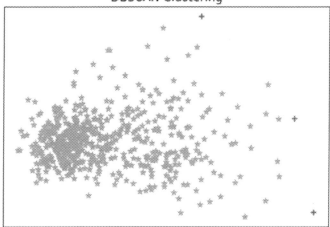

(iii) Gaussian Mixtures

```
from sklearn.mixture import GaussianMixture
model = GaussianMixture(n_components=4, n_init=10,
random_state=40)
clusters = model.fit_predict(x_decomposed)
cluster_labels = np.unique(clusters)
print('Cluster Labels : ',cluster_labels)
```

Output

Cluster Labels : [0 1 2 3]

Gaussian Mixtures Clustering

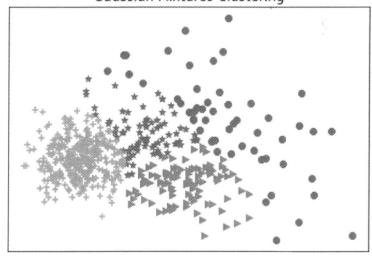

(iv) Optics

```
from sklearn.cluster import OPTICS
model=OPTICS(min_samples=15)
clusters = model.fit_predict(x_decomposed)
cluster_labels= np.unique(clusters)
print('Cluster Labels: ',cluster_labels)
```

Output

Cluster Labels: [-1 0 1 2]

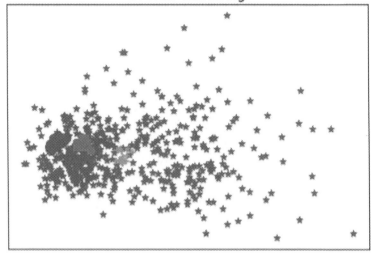

OPTICS Clustering

(v) BIRCH

```
from sklearn.cluster import Birch
model = Birch(n_clusters=4, threshold = 0.03)
clusters = model.fit_predict(x_decomposed)
cluster_labels = np.unique(clusters)
print('Cluster Labels: ',cluster_labels)
```

Output

Cluster Labels: [0 1 2 3]

Birch Clustering

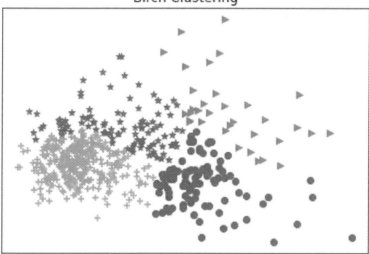

(vi) Meanshift

```
from sklearn.cluster import MeanShift
model =MeanShift()
clusters = model.fit_predict(x_decomposed)
cluster_labels = np.unique(clusters)
print('Cluster Labels: ', cluster_labels)
```

Output

Cluster Labels: [0 1]

Meanshift Clustering

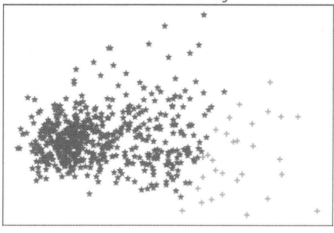

(vii) Agglomerative clustering

```
from sklearn.cluster import AgglomerativeClustering
model = AgglomerativeClustering(n_clusters=4)
clusters = model.fit_predict(x_decomposed)
cluster_labels = np.unique(clusters)
print('Cluster Labels: ',cluster_labels)
```

Output

Cluster Labels: [0 1 2 3]

Agglomerative   Clustering

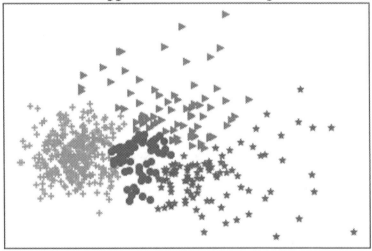

(viii) Affinity clustering

```
from sklearn.cluster import AffinityPropagation
model = AffinityPropagation(damping=0.7)
clusters = model.fit_predict(x_decomposed)
cluster_labels = np.unique(clusters)
print('Cluster Labels: ',cluster_labels)
```

Output

Cluster Labels: [0 1 2 3 4 5 6 7 8 9 10 11 12 13 14 15 16 17 18 19
    20 21 22 23 24]

Affinity   Clustering

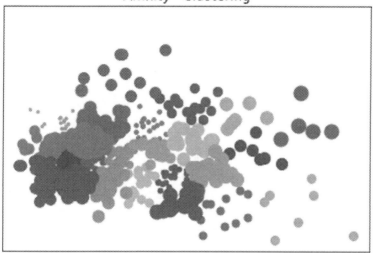

Chapter 14
Python for Deep Learning

14.1 Introduction

Deep learning is a subset of machine learning for developing intelligent applications. It uses a neural network that simulates the human brain. Artificial neural networks consist of layers. Each layer contains a number of nodes. Nodes take the previous layer outputs as inputs and apply a non-linear function to produce the output. Neural networks are popularly used for building classification models.

Deep learning techniques differ from traditional machine learning methods in the following ways:

(i) Deep learning networks have complex multilayer structures that mimic the human brain. The neural network can capture non-linear correlations in the data for solving complex problems.
(ii) Neural networks require large datasets with millions of data points. Hence, it requires more computing power and training time but produces more accurate results.
(iii) Neural networks perform automatic feature extraction by self-learning.
(iv) Deep learning models can analyze structured and unstructured data like images, videos, and text, which machine learning techniques cannot do easily.

Deep learning techniques are used for building smart applications. Popular use cases are

- Self-driving cars.
- Personalized healthcare applications like personalized treatment, predicting upcoming health risks based on the real-time data collected from connected devices, drug discovery, predictive analytics to identify people for clinical trials, etc.
- Precision agriculture, including soil and moisture monitoring, crop disease detection, and crop yield estimation.

© The Author(s) 2024
A. L. Muddana and S. Vinayakam, *Python for Data Science*,
https://doi.org/10.1007/978-3-031-52473-8_14

- Identifying trends and patterns in sales, product recommendations, and customer churn in e-commerce.
- Virtual assistants and chatbots for customer support, enhanced security to prevent illegal transactions and detecting money laundering in Banking and Finance.
- News aggregation and fake news detection.

Following are the widely used open-source frameworks for building deep learning models.

TensorFlow is an end-to-end open-source deep learning framework developed by Google. It uses Python for the front end and optimized C++ to run efficiently. All computations involve the use of tensors which is a multidimensional array. It is available on Windows, Linux, macOS, and mobile computing platforms, including Android and iOS.

Keras is a popular Python library for deep learning, developed by Francois Chollet. A simple and user-friendly high-level library that runs on top of TensorFlow. It supports easy and fast experimentation and deployment. Keras works best when working with small datasets. It is supported by multiple backends. TensorFlow and Theano are commonly used backend supports that handle low-level computations.

Users require knowledge of Python to work with Keras and TensorFlow. Other deep learning frameworks are Pytorch, Caffe, Theano, Deeplearning4j, etc.

14.2   Data Loading

Data loading is the first step in the model-building process. Data may be in the form of numeric, image, or text. It needs to be converted into a form suitable for the deep learning model. For example, image and text data have to be converted to numeric before training the model.

14.2.1   In-built Datasets

Many machine learning and deep learning frameworks provide in-built datasets for experimentation. Keras has a few in-built datasets that are cleaned and vectorized to build simple deep learning models.

- *MNIST* is a handwritten digits image dataset with 28 × 28 pixel images of 70000 samples for image classification tasks.
- *CIFAR10* is a color image dataset of 10 different objects. Each image is 32 × 32 pixels, with 6000 images per class.
- *CIFAR100* dataset consists of 32 × 32 different color images of 100 classes with 600 images per class.

- *IMDB* is a movie review dataset of 50000 reviews for binary text classification.
- *FashionMNIST* is a dataset of 28 × 28 Zalando's article images of 70000 samples with ten classes.
- *Boston* housing price regression dataset consisting of 13 attributes of houses around Boston City.
- *Reuters*, a classification dataset with 11228 newswires on 46 topics.

Example: Loading *mnist* dataset

```
from keras.datasets import mnist
(x_train, y_train), (x_test, y_test ) = mnist.load_data()
```

The function returns two tuples—one for train data and the other for test data.

14.2.2 Loading csv Dataset

Comma Separated Values (csv) dataset can be loaded into a dataframe and then split into feature matrix, x, and target vector, y. This x, y can then be passed to the model for training.

Example

```
import pandas as pd
data = pd.read_csv('/content/sample/pima_indian_diabetis.csv')
x = data.drop('Outcome', axis=1)
y = data['Outcome']
```

14.3 Image Data Loading and Preparation

Keras provides the following functions for image data.

(i) Load an image into PIL object

```
from tensorflow.keras.preprocessing .image import load_img
```

| Syntax |

load_img(*path, color_mode,target_size, interpolation*)

path:	Path of the image file.
color_mode:	The desired image format. Values are *"grayscale"*, *"rgb"*, *"rgba"*. Default: *"rgb"*.
target_size:	Tuple of (img_height, img_width). The default is None which is the original size.
interpolation:	Method used when target size is different from the loaded image size. Supported methods are *"nearest"*, *"bilinear"*, and *"bicubic"*.

The function returns PIL object.

(ii) Convert PIL image to NumPy array

> from tensorflow.keras.preprocessing.image
>   import image_to_array

Syntax

img_to_array(*img, data_format, dtype*)

img:	Input PIL Image instance.
data_format:	Image data format as either *channels_first* or *channels_last*. Default is channels_last.
dtype:	Data type to use. Default is float32.

The function returns 3D NumPy array.

(iii) Convert NumPy array to image

> from tensorflow.keras.preprocessing.image import array_to_img

Syntax

array_to_img(*x, scale, data_format, dtype*)

x:	Input data in any form that can is converted to numpy array.
scale:	whether to rescale the image so that minimum & maximum values are 0 & 255. Default is True.
data_format, dtype	parameters are the same as in *img_to_array()* function.

(iv) Loading image data from the local directory

To load the image dataset from the directory, store the image files as per the following directory structure:

- Create folders for train, test, and validation sets.
- Under each folder, create subdirectories for each of the classes.
- Under each class folder, store the corresponding image files.

Supported image formats are *jpeg, png, bmp, gif.*
Keras provides the following functions:

(a) *image_dataset_from_directory ()* is a preprocessing function of keras to load the image dataset from the directory structure.

from keras.preprocessing import image_dataset_from_directory

Syntax

image_dataset_from_directory(*directory,labels, label_mode,
    class_names, color_mode,batch_size, image_size, shuffle,
    seed, validation_split*)

directory:	Directory where images are located.
labels:	Specifies class labels. Values are
	inferred - labels are inferred from the directory structure.
	None - No labels are generated.
	tuple or list of integer labels.
label_mode:	*int* - labels are encoded as integers.
	categorical - labels are encoded as categorical.
	binary - labels are encoded as 0 or 1.
	None - no labels.
class_names:	List of class names. Must match with subdirectory names. This is valid when labels are inferred.

color_mode:	Image can be converted to grayscale or rgb.
batch_size:	Number of images in a batch for progressive loading. Default is 32.
image_size:	Resize the images after loading from the directory. Default is (256, 256).
shuffle:	Boolean. True-shuffles the data. False-sorts the data in alphabetical order.
seed:	Random seed value for shuffling and transformations.
validation_split:	Fraction of data to be used for validation.

Returns an image dataset that yields batches of images from the directory structure together with labels.

(b) *ImageDataGenerator:* Image data generator function is an easy way to load the image data progressively, together with labels. In addition to loading batches of images, transformations can also be applied on the original images to produce new images with the same class. This not only increases the dataset size but also incorporates variations in the dataset so that the model is generalized better. Transformations like scaling, shifts, rotations, brightness change, etc. can be done on the fly during training.

from keras.preprocessing import ImageDataGenerator

| Syntax |

ImageDataGenerator(*rotation_range,height_shift_range,*
   width_shift_range,horizontal_flip,vertcal_flip,
   brightness_range,zom_range)

| *rotation_range:* | Randomly rotate the image. Value is between 0 & 360 degrees. If pixels move out of the image, they can be filled by specifying *fill_mode*. Default is *nearest* that fills an empty area with the nearest pixel value. |
| *height_shift_range, width_shift_range: int or float,* | sometimes the object may not be centered in the image. It requires shifting of pixels horizontally or vertically. The integer value specifies constant. The float value indicates the percentage of shift. |

horizontal_flip,	
vertcal_flip:	Flips the image. It is relevant to the symmetric objects only.
brightness_range:	List of two values that change the image brightness in the given range. Value <1 darkens the image & value > 1 brightens the image.
zoom_range:	Zoom in or zoom out of the image. List of two values as lower & upper limit of the range or float value that is equivalent to [1-zoom_rage, 1+zoom_range].

ImageDataGenerator class is used as follows:

- Create an instance of ImageDataGenerator class

Syntax

img_gen = **ImageDataGenerator**(*parameters*)

The same image data generator object can be used for loading from different data directories, if the same scaling parameters are used.

- To start reading from the directory, create an iterator to progressively load images using *flow_from_directory()*.

Syntax

flow_from_directory(*directory,target_size,*
    color_mode,class_mode,batch_size,shuffle)

directory:	Directory containing images to be loaded.
target_size:	Load the images to a specific size. Default 256 × 256.
color_mode:	'rgb' for color images.
class_mode:	Type of classification task. *binary* for binary classification. *categorical* for multi-class classification.
batch_size:	Number of images to be extracted per batch.
shuffle:	Shuffle the order of images that are extracted.

- Use the iterator in the model fitting and evaluation.

(a) Now, the model can be trained using *fit_generator()*

Syntax

model.**fit_generator**(*train_iterator,steps_per_epoch,*
    Validation_data,Validation_steps, epochs,verbose)

train_iterator:	used for training.
steps_per_epoch:	Number of batches of images per epoch for train data.
validation_data:	validation iterator.
validation_steps:	Number of batches of images in an epoch of validation data.
epochs:	Number of epochs to train the model.
verbose:	Verbosity mode. 0-silent, 1-progress bar, 2-one line per Epoch

(b) Syntax

   *model.***evaluate_generator**(*test_iterator, steps*)

| *test_iterator:* | used for model evaluation. |
| *steps:* | Number of batches of images to step through for evaluation. |

(c) Syntax

   *model.***predict_generator**(*predict_iterator, steps*)

| *predict_iterator:* | for prediction. |
| *steps:* | Number of batches of images to step through for prediction. |

14.4 Text Data Loading and Preparation

Raw text data can not be directly fed to the model for processing. It needs to be cleaned and converted into numeric vectors before training the model.

Text data requires the following preprocessing steps:

- *Tokenization:* Split the text corpus into tokens and encode them into integers using the Tokenizer object and then fitting using fit_texts().
- *Sequencing:* Represent each document as a sequence of numbers using *texts_to_sequences()* method on tokenizer objects after fitting.

- *Padding:* Neural networks require inputs of the same size. But documents of the text corpus may be of varying sizes. Padding is done using *pad_sequences()* method to make the sequences to be of same size.

Keras provides the following libraries for text preprocessing:

(i) **Loading text data from the local directory:** Text files are stored in a directory with subdirectories containing files for each class. Only *.txt* files are supported.

from keras.utils import text_dataset_from_directory

Syntax

text_dataset_from_directory(*main_directory, labels, label_mode*)

main_directory:	Directory where text files are located
labels:	Directory should contain subdirectories for each class if the value is *inferred.*
label_mode:	String describing the encoding of labels.

The function **returns** dataset object. If *label_mode* is None, it returns string tensors of shape (batch_size) containing the contents. Otherwise, it yields a tuple (texts, labels).

(ii) **Convert text into a list of tokens**

text_to_word_sequence() function performs the following operations:

(a) Removes punctuation.
(b) Split the text into tokens based on split criteria.
(c) Converts the tokens into lowercase if the *lower* is set to True.

from keras.preprocessing.text import text_to_word_sequence

Syntax

text_to_word_sequence(*text, filters, lower,split*)

text:	Input text corpus
filters:	List or sequence of characters for punctuations. Default is *base_filter()*. It includes basic punctuations, tab & new line. !"#$%&()*+,-.\:;<=>?@[]^_{l}~ \t\n.
lower:	Boolean, whether to convert the text into lower case. Default is True.
split:	Criteria for splitting the text into tokens. Default is space. The function *returns* list of tokens.

Example

```
from keras.preprocessing.text import text_to_word_sequence
text = 'Deep Learning(ML): for developing smart applications?'
tokens = text_to_word_sequence(text)
print(tokens)
```

Output

```
['deep', 'learning', 'ml', 'for', 'developing', 'smart',
    'applications']
```

(iii) **Encoding tokens into integers/indices**

Syntax

one_hot(*text, n, hash_function, filter, lower, split*)

text: Input text corpus.
n: Defines hash space to encode the tokens.
hash_function: Default is *hash*. Any hash function can be specified like md5.

filter, lower, split parameters have the same meaning as in the *text_to_word_sequence()* function.

In addition to the operations provided by *text_to_word_sequence()* function, this function also maps the tokens to word indices based on the, *n*, parameter. Small hash space may generate more collisions.

Example

```
from keras.preprocessing.text import text_to_word_sequence,
    one_hot
text = 'Deep Learning(ML): for developing smart applications?'
tokens = text_to_word_sequence(text)
n = len(tokens)
one_hot = one_hot(text, round(n*1.25))
print(one_hot)
```

Output

```
[2, 6, 1, 6, 7, 7, 3]
```

(iv) **Tokenizer class** converts each document of the text corpus into vectors of integers. First, construct the tokenizer object and then fit it on the text corpus, which can then be reused by other documents. This method is useful when there are multiple documents, and the dataset is large.

> from Keras.preprocessing.text import tokenizer

| **Syntax** |

> **tokenizer**(*nb_words, filters, lower, split*)

| *nb_words:* | Consider top *nb_words* of the dataset. Each token is assigned an index. Word of rank i, gets index i. |
| *filter, lower, split* | parameters have the same meaning as in the *text_to_word_sequence()* function. |

Following are the methods of the tokenizer class that can be applied to the tokenizer object

(a) *fit_on_texts(texts)*

It creates a vocabulary of input text. This method has to be called before applying other methods. It returns an object using which more information may be derived with the following attributes.

(i)	word_counts	Dictionary of words with their counts in the input *texts.*
(ii)	word_docs	Number of documents in which the token appears.
(iii)	word_index	Unique index assigned to each token in the vocabulary. These indices help in the training.
(iv)	document_count	Number of documents in the input *texts.*

Example

```
from keras.preprocessing.text import Tokenizer
text_corp = ['Python for AI-', 'AI mimicks human brain.']
# tokenizer object
tokenizer = Tokenizer()
# fit method on the tokenizer
tokenizer.fit_on_texts(text_corp)
# attributes
print('No. of documents :',tokenizer.document_count)
```

```
print('Word indices :\n ',tokenizer.word_index)
print('Frequency of Words :\n',tokenizer.word_counts)
print('No. of documents that contain the word :\n',
    tokenizer.word_docs)
```

Output

```
No. of documents : 2
Word indices :
{'ai': 1, 'python': 2, 'for': 3, 'mimicks': 4, 'human':
    5, 'brain': 6}
Frequency of Words :
OrderedDict([('python', 1), ('for', 1), ('ai', 2), ('mimicks', 1),
    ('human', 1), ('brain', 1)])
No. of documents that contain the word :
defaultdict(<class 'int'>, {'for': 1, 'python': 1, 'ai': 2,
    'mimicks': 1, 'brain': 1, 'human': 1})
```

(b) *texts_to_sequences(texts)*

Converts tokens of text corpus into sequence of integers. Returns list of sequences, one per document

Example

```
from keras.preprocessing.text import Tokenizer
text_corp = ['Python for AI ', 'AI mimicks human brain.']
tokenizer = Tokenizer()
tokenizer.fit_on_texts(text_corp)
seq = tokenizer.texts_to_sequences(text_corp)
print('Integer sequence for tokens: ', seq)
```

Output

```
Integer sequence for tokens: [[2, 3, 1], [1, 4, 5, 6]]
```

(c) *texts_to_matrix(texts, mode)*

Converts *texts* to NumPy matrix.

Returns NumPy array

    texts: Input text corpus to vectorize.
    mode: *binary* - the presence of each token in the document
             count - Number of times the token appears in
                the document.

    tfidf— TFIDF score that indicates the relevance of word
       in the document.
    freq—Ratio of each token out of the total number of
       tokens in the document.

Example

```
from keras.preprocessing.text import Tokenizer
text_corp = ['Python for AI ', 'AI mimicks human
      brain.AI?']
tokenizer = Tokenizer()
tokenizer.fit_on_texts(text_corp)
print('Token indices : ',tokenizer.word_index)
print('Token presence in documents:\n',
   tokenizer.texts_to_matrix(text_corp, mode='binary'))
print('Token count of each word in documents:\n',
   tokenizer.texts_to_matrix(text_corp, mode='count'))
print('TFIDF value of each word in documents:\n',
   tokenizer.texts_to_matrix(text_corp, mode='tfidf'))
print('Ratio :\n', tokenizer.texts_to_matrix
   (text_corp, mode='freq'))
```

Output

```
Token indices : {'ai': 1, 'python': 2, 'for': 3, 'mimicks':
   4, 'human': 5, 'brain': 6}
Token presence in documents:
   [[0. 1. 1. 1. 0. 0. 0.]
    [0. 1. 0. 0. 1. 1. 1.]]
Token count of each word in documents:
   [[0. 1. 1. 1. 0. 0. 0.]
    [0. 2. 0. 0. 1. 1. 1.]]
TFIDF value of each word in documents:
   [[0.  0.51082562  0.69314718  0.69314718  0.
       0.  0.  ]]
   [0.  0.86490296  0.  0.  0.69314718
       0.69314718  0.69314718]]
```

Ratio :
[[0.   0.33333333 0.33333333 0.33333333 0. 0. 0.
    ]   [0.   0.4 0. 0. 0.2 0.2]

(d) *sequences_to_matrix(sequences, mode)*
Convert sequences into NumPy array

Returns numpy array

sequences:	List of sequences to vectorize.
mode:	same as in *texts_to_matrix( )* method.

Example

```
from keras.preprocessing.text import Tokenizer
text_corp = ['Python for AI ',
        'AI mimicks human brain. AI?']
tokenizer = Tokenizer()
tokenizer.fit_on_texts(text_corp)
seq = tokenizer.texts_to_sequences(text_corp)
print('Tokens into integer sequences :',seq)
print('Sequences into Numpy Matrix:\n',
    tokenizer.sequences_to_matrix(seq, mode='binary'))
```

Output

```
Tokens into integer sequences : [[2, 3, 1], [1, 4, 5, 6, 1]]
Sequences into Numpy Matrix:
 [[0. 1. 1. 1. 0. 0. 0.]
  [0. 1. 0. 0. 1. 1. 1.]]
```

(e) *texts_to_sequences_generator(texts)*
Generator version of the texts_to_sequences() method.

(v) Syntax

pad_sequences(*sequences, maxlen, padding, truncate, value* **)**

Larger sequences are truncated and shorter ones are padded with the specified value. This makes the model input equal in size.

sequences :	List of sequences to pad.
maxlen:	Length of each sequence after padding or truncating.
padding :	pre or post. Pad the shorter sequences before or after the sequence.
truncate :	pre or post—Remove larger sequences at the beginning or at the end.
value:	Value used for padding. Default is zero.

14.5 Model Building

A neural network consists of an input layer, hidden layers, and an output layer. Each layer is made up of number of computing units called neurons. Deep learning model is a neural network that is trained to learn the features from the data. It performs the learning task like classification, dimensionality reduction, data generation, etc. These models can be used for both supervised and unsupervised learning.

Keras supports two types of models—*sequential* and *functional*.

(a) *Sequential model* is a linear stack of layers where each layer has one input tensor and one output tensor. Data flows from one layer to the next until it reaches the final layer. It is a simple and easy-to-use model and most neural networks use a sequential model.

To create a sequential model

```
from keras.models import Sequential
    model = Sequential()
```

Layers are added to the model using *add( )* method.

The first layer of the model should specify the *input_dim* or *input_shape* argument. Both arguments are the same except in the representation.

input_dim is an integer indicating the number of input features.
input_shape is a tuple representing the number of features.

Example

input_dim =10 is same as input_shape=(10,)

(b) *Functional Model* is a more flexible and powerful model than the sequential model. It creates a more complex model that permits multiple inputs and outputs. This is used to create graphs of layers, sharing of layers, etc. In this model, define the layers first and then create the model, compile, fit, and evaluate.

```
from keras.models import Model
    model = Model( inputs, outputs )
```

14.5.1 Activation Functions

Each neuron computes the dot product of the input values with the weights and bias added. A non-linear activation function is then applied on the dot product that becomes the output of the neuron. Popular activation functions are *relu, leakyrelu, tanh, sigmoid, softmax*.

14.5.2 Neural Network Layers

Keras provides the following types of layers that are meant for different tasks.

(i) **Dense layer or fully connected layer:** Each neuron of this layer receives input from all neurons of the previous layer. The output of each neuron is the result of activation function applied on the dot product of all the input values with the weights and bias added. This is computationally expensive as the number of layers grows.

> from keras.layers import Dense

| Syntax |

> **Dense(** *units, activation* **)**

Important parameters are

> *units:*   Number of neurons. It represents the number of outputs of the layer.
>
> *activation*   function.

(ii) **Convolution layer** is used for detecting features in images. It uses filters to perform convolution operations. The layer summarizes the presence of features in the images. Layers close to the input layer learn low-level features and layers close to the output layer learn more abstract features like shapes and objects. It outputs feature maps. This layer is used in image processing.
Different convolution layers are Conv1D for temporal data, Conv2D for two-dimensional data.

> from keras.layers import Conv2D

| Syntax |

> **Conv2D(** *filters , kernel_size , strides, padding , activation* **)**

Important parameters include

filters:	Number of filters in the convolution.
	It represents the output dimension.
kernel_size:	Dimension of convolution window.
strides:	Amount of movement over the image.
padding:	Layers of zeros are added to the input image.
	Strategies are:
	valid - no padding.
	same - output should have the same length as input.
activation	function

Conv2Dtranspose is the transpose of the convolution operation. Conv2D applies convolution operation on the input image to detect the features in the image. Conv2DTranspose applies a deconvolution operation that creates the features of the image. It is commonly used in the decoder part of the autoencoder to reconstruct the original image.

from keras.layers import Conv2DTranspose

Syntax

Conv2DTranspose(*filters* , *kernel_size* , *strides*, *padding*)

Parameters are same as in *Conv2D()*.

UpSampling2D is scaling up of the image using the nearest neighbor or bilinear upsampling. It is used in the generative model.

from keras.layers import UpSampling2D

Syntax

UpSampling2D(*size, data_format, interpolation*)

size:	Upsampling factor for rows and columns
data_format:	String indicating *channels_last* or channels_first
interpolation	method like *nearest, area, bilinear, bicubic, Gaussian*.

(iii) **Pooling layer** reduces the dimension of feature maps produced by the convolution layer by summarizing the features present in a region of feature maps. Effectively, it replaces each patch in the input with a single output. The summarization can be in the form of maximum or averaging. Further operations are applied to these summarized features. It reduces the number of parameters to be learned by reducing the dimensions of feature maps. The pooling layer is added after the convolution layer.

Different pooling layers are MaxPooling1D, MaxPooling2D, AveragePooling1D, AveragePooling2D for one-dimensional and two-dimensional data.

from keras.layers import MaxPooling2D

Syntax

MaxPooling2D(*pool_size, strides, padding*)

pool_size: Pooling window size.
strides, padding are the same as in Conv2D.

(iv) **Recurrent layers:** Input consists of both the input data and output of previous calculations performed by that layer. Different recurrent layers are SimpleRNN, LSTM, GRU. These layers are used for natural language processing and time series data analysis.

from keras.layers import SimpleRNN

Syntax

SimpleRNN(*units,activation, use_bias, kernel_initializer,*
                recurent_initializer, bias_initializer)

units:	Dimensionality of the output space.
activation	function. Default is tanh.
use_bias:	Whether to use the bias vector.
kernel_initializer:	Initializer for the kernel matrix.
recurrent_initializer:	Initializer for recurrent kernel weights matrix.
bias_initializer:	Initializer for the bias vector.

LSTM, GRU networks solve the vanishing gradient problem faced by SimpleRNN.

from keras.layers import LSTM, GRU

Syntax

LSTM(*units, activation, use_bias, kernel_initializer,*
       recurent_initializer, bias_initializer, recurrent_activation)

Syntax

GRU(*units, activation, use_bias, kernel_initializer,*
       recurent_initializer, bias_initializer, recurrent_activation)

recurrent_activation: Activation used in the recurrent step.

All other parameters are same as in *SimpleRNN()*.

(v) **Flatten layer** converts multidimensional input tensors into a single dimension tensor. It is used when moving from a convolution layer to a fully connected layer.

from keras.layers import Flatten
Flatten()

(vi) **Dropout layer:** A fraction of neurons of the layer are randomly deactivated during training. It is a regularization technique to prevent model overfitting, especially for small datasets. This is used between the hidden layers.

from keras.layers import Dropout

Syntax

Dropout(*rate*)

rate—Fraction of input units to drop. The value is between 0 and 1.

Adding layers to the neural network

Layers are added to the model using *add()* method

Syntax

model.**add**(*layer*)

14.5.3 Methods on the Model

Keras provides the following methods on the model, to get information about the model

model.layers()	returns the list of layers of the model.
model.summary()	returns information about the layers, and the parameters
model.get_weights()	returns the list of all the weights tensors as NumPy array.
model.get_config()	returns model configuration as a dictionary object.
model.outputs()	returns list of all output tensors.
model.inputs()	returns list of input tensors of the model.
model.to_json ()	represent the model as JSON string.

14.5.4 Model Compilation

After defining the model architecture, the model has to be compiled before training. This function configures the learning process by specifying the optimizer, loss function, evaluation metrics, etc.

Syntax

model.**compile**(*loss, metrics, optimizer*)

loss:	function to calculate the errors in the learning process.
	For Regression-
	mean_squared_error
	mean_absolute_error,
	mean_squared_logarithmic_error.
	For Classification -
	binary_crossentropy for binary classification.
	categorical_crossentropy for multi-class classification.
metrics:	to evaluate the model performance. Different metrics are *accuracy, binary_accuracy, categorical_accuracy*
optimizer:	adjusts the model weights to optimize the loss function. Different optimizers are *adam, rmsprop, sgd, adagrad,* etc.

14.5.5 Model Training

> **Syntax**

model.**fit**(*xtrain,ytrain,epochs,batch_size,*
            validation_data,validation_split, callbacks,verbose)

xtrain, ytrain:	Data as NumPy array used for training
epochs:	Number of times the algorithm will go through the entire dataset.
batch_size:	Number of training samples in a batch.
validation_data:	Data on which the model loss is evaluated after each epoch
validation_split:	Proportion of data used for validation.
callbacks:	Special functions performed during training. It helps visualize training progress- checkpoints, debugging the code, generating the logs etc.
verbose:	Output of neural network during training process. 0-silent, 1-progress bar, 2-one line per epoch

14.5.6 Model Evaluation

The model is evaluated on unseen data to test how well the model is generalized. It estimates the general accuracy of the model. Keras provides *evaluate()* method

> **Syntax**

model.**evaluate**(*xtest, ytest, batch_size,steps,verbose*)

xtest, ytest:	Unseen data on which model is evaluated
steps:	Number of steps before completing the evaluation other parameters are same as in fit() method.

14.5.7 Model Prediction

Once the model is built, it can be used to predict on the given input. The input vector is passed as a parameter to the function that returns the prediction.

Syntax

model.**predict**(*xtest, batch_size, steps, callbacks, verbose*)

> *xtest:*   Samples for predictions
> other parameters are same as in **fit**() method.

14.6   Autoencoder

Autoencoder is a neural network used for unsupervised learning. It performs non-linear transformation of input data into low-dimensional representation. It consists of three parts—encoder, encoded data, and decoder. The encoder compresses the input data into an encoded representation and the decoder decompresses the encoded data to reconstruct the original input. Encoded data is the compressed representation of the input data. It is typically used for dimensionality reduction. Applications of autoencoder include

- Dimensionality reduction,
- Image denoising,
- Image generation,
- Image similarity,
- Anomaly detection,
- Missing value imputation, etc.

14.7   Case Studies

14.7.1   Regression Model on Boston Housing Dataset

It is an in-built dataset in Keras that contains 13 attributes of the houses located around Boston City. A regression model is built to predict the price of the house based on the feature values.

- Load the in-built dataset

    ```
    from keras.datasets import boston_housing
    (xtrain, ytrain), (xtest, ytest) = boston_housing.load_data()
    print(xtrain.shape, xtest.shape, ytrain.shape, ytest.shape)
    ```

Output

    Downloading data from https://storage.googleapis.com/tensorflow/
    tf-keras-datasets/boston_housing.npz

57026/57026 [==============================]
- 0s 0us/step
(404, 13) (102, 13) (404,) (102,)

- Data exploration

  (i) Find the number of features and display sample target values.

  ```
  print('Number of features : ',num_features)
  print('Sample Target values: ', ytrain[:4])
  ```

  Output

  Number of features: 13
  Sample Target values: [15.2 42.3 50. 21.1]

  (ii) Display sample train and test data

  ```
  print('Train data:\n',xtrain[0])
  print('Test data:\n',xtest[0])
  ```

  Output

  Train data:
  [1.23247 0. 8.14   0.   0.538 6.142 91.7 3.9769
      4. 307. 21. 396.9 18.72]
  Test data:
  [18.0846 0. 18.1   0.   0.679 6.434 100. 1.8347
     24. 666. 20.2 27.25 29.05]

  (iii) Feature Scaling is done using StandardScaler, as the features are in varying ranges.

  ```
  from sklearn.preprocessing import StandardScaler
  scaler = StandardScaler()
  scaler.fit(xtrain)
  xtrain_scaled = scaler.transform(xtrain)
  xtest_scaled = scaler.transform(xtest)
  print('xtrain scaled:\n',xtrain_scaled[0],'\n xtest scaled:\n',
      xtest_scaled[0])
  ```

  Output

  xtrain scaled:
  [−0.27224633 − 0.48361547 − 0.43576161 − 0.25683275
   −0.1652266 − 0.17644260.813061880.1166983
   −0.62624905 − 0.595170031.14850044
   0.448077130.8252202]

xtest scaled:
[1.55369355 − 0.483615471.0283258 − 0.25683275
1.038380670.235458151.11048828 − 0.93976936
1.675885771.56528750.78447637 − 3.48459553
2.25092074]

Note: As the in-built datasets are cleaned and vectorized, not much preprocessing is required.

- *Define the model architecture*
  A sequential model is defined with a stack of dense layers. The input layer
  includes the input dimension along with other parameters. The output layer has
  only one dense unit without activation function as the model is for the Regression
  task. The architecture includes four hidden layers.

```
num_features = len( xtrain[1] )
from keras.models import Sequential
from keras.layers import Dense
reg_model = Sequential()
reg_model.add(Dense(100, input_dim= num_features,
   activation='relu'))
reg_model.add(Dense(80, activation='relu'))
reg_model.add(Dense(50, activation='relu'))
reg_model.add(Dense(20, activation='relu'))
reg_model.add(Dense(10, activation='relu'))
reg_model.add(Dense(1))
print('Model summary:\n')
reg_model.summary()
```

Output

Model summary:

Model: "sequential"

Layer (type)	Output shape	Param #
dense (Dense)	(None, 100)	1400
dense_1 (Dense)	(None, 80)	8080
dense_2 (Dense)	(None, 50)	4050
dense_3 (Dense)	(None, 20)	1020
dense_4 (Dense)	(None, 10)	210
dense_5 (Dense)	(None, 1)	11

Total params: 14,771
Trainable params: 14,771
Non-trainable params: 0

- *Compile and fit the model.*
  Compile the model by specifying the following parameters:

  adam optimizer,
  mse for loss and metrics

  Loss function is used to optimize the model, and metrics is to assess the model performance. Other loss functions include *MeanAbsoluteError, MeanSquared-LogarithmicError*. Typically, regression uses the same function for loss and metrics. The model is trained for 50 epochs.

  ```
  reg_model.compile(loss= "mse" , optimizer="adam",
      metrics=["mean_squared_error"])
  reg_hist = reg_model.fit(xtrain_scaled, ytrain,
      epochs=50,batch_size = 64, validation_data=
      (xtest_scaled, ytest),shuffle=True, verbose=0)
  ```

- Visualize the model performance using a line graph on train and test loss.

  ```
  import matplotlib.pyplot as plt
  plt.plot(range(50),reg_hist.history['loss'],
      label='Train', marker='*')
  plt.plot(range(50),reg_hist.history['val_loss'], label='Test')
  plt.title('Regression Model Performance on Train and Test sets')
  plt.xlabel('Epochs')
  plt.ylabel('Loss')
  plt.legend()
  plt.show()
  ```

Output

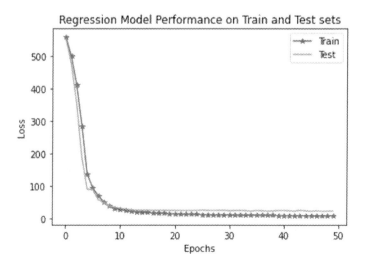

14.7.2 *Deep Neural Network for Breast Cancer Classification*

Breast cancer dataset contains 30 real-valued features that characterize the breast mass and the diagnosis indicating malignancy or not. The following code builds a standard deep neural network to classify whether tumor is malignant or benign.

- Load the dataset

```
import pandas as pd
data = pd.read_csv('/content/sample_data/Breast_cancer.csv')
print('Shape: ',data.shape)
print('Columns:\n', data.columns)
```

Output

```
Shape: (569, 33)
Columns:
  Index(['id', 'diagnosis', 'radius_mean', 'texture_mean',
    'perimeter_mean','area_mean', 'smoothness_mean',
    'compactness_mean', 'concavity_mean',
    'concave points_mean', 'symmetry_mean',
    'fractal_dimension_mean','radius_se','texture_se',
    'perimeter_se', 'area_se','smoothness_se', 'compactness_se',
    'concavity_se','concave points_se', 'symmetry_se',
    'fractal_dimension_se', 'radius_worst', 'texture_worst',
    'perimeter_worst', 'area_worst', 'smoothness_worst',
    'compactness_worst', 'concavity_worst',
    'concave points_worst', 'symmetry_worst',
    'fractal_dimension_worst', 'Unnamed: 32'], dtype='object')
```

- Remove the irrelevant attributes-*id, Unnamed: 32*

```
data.drop(['id','Unnamed: 32'], axis=1, inplace=True)
print(data.columns)
```

Output

```
Index(['diagnosis', 'radius_mean', 'texture_mean',
    'perimeter_mean',
  'area_mean', 'smoothness_mean', 'compactness_mean'
    'concavity_mean',
```

       'concave points_mean', 'symmetry_mean',
        'fractal_dimension_mean',
      'radius_se', 'texture_se', 'perimeter_se', 'area_se',
      'smoothness_se','compactness_se', 'concavity_se', 'concave
      points_se', 'symmetry_se','fractal_dimension_se',
       'radius_worst', 'texture_worst','perimeter_worst',
       'area_worst', 'smoothness_worst',
      'compactness_worst', 'concavity_worst',
       'concave points_worst',
      'symmetry_worst', 'fractal_dimension_worst'],dtype='object')

- Create the feature matrix, x, and target vector, y.

```
x = data.drop('diagnosis', axis=1)
y = data['diagnosis']
print('First row of feature matrix :\n',x[:1] )
```

Output

    First row of feature matrix :
      radius_mean texture_mean perimeter_mean area_mean
       smoothness_mean
    0 17.99 10.38 122.8   1001.0 0.1184
      compactness_mean concavity_mean concave points_mean
       symmetry_mean
    0 0.2776 0.3001 0.1471 0.2419
      fractal_dimension_mean ... radius_worst texture_worst
       perimeter_worst
    0 0.07871 ... 25.38 17.33 184.6
      area_worst smoothness_worst compactness_worst
       concavity_worst
    0 2019.0 0.1622 0.6656 0.7119
      concave points_worst symmetry_worst
       fractal_dimension_worst
    0 0.2654 0.4601 0.1189

- As the feature value ranges are varying, let us normalize feature matrix

```
from sklearn.preprocessing import StandardScaler
scaler = StandardScaler()
x_scaled = scaler.fit_transform(x)
```

- Display the sample target values

```
print('Sample target values :\n',y[:5])
```

Output

Sample target values:
0 M
1 M
2 M
3 M
4 M
Name: diagnosis, dtype: object

- As target labels are strings, convert into numeric using *LabelEncoder.*

```
from sklearn.preprocessing import LabelEncoder
le = LabelEncoder()
y = le.fit_transform(y)
print('Target values after transformation : ', y[:5])
```

Output

Target values after transformation: [1 1 1 1 1]

- Create train and test datasets to feed to the model

```
from sklearn.model_selection import train_test_split
xtrain, xtest, ytrain, ytest = train_test_split(x_scaled,
        y, test_size=0.2, random_state=40)
print(xtrain.shape, xtest.shape, ytrain.shape, ytest.shape)
```

Output

(455, 30) (114, 30) (455,) (114,)

- Define neural network architecture with dense layers.

```
from keras.models import Sequential
from keras.layers import Dense, Dropout
model = Sequential()
model.add(Dense(100, input_dim=xtrain.shape[1],
        activation= 'relu'))
model.add(Dense(80, activation= 'relu'))
model.add(Dropout(0.25))
```

```
model.add(Dense(50, activation= 'relu'))
model.add(Dense(30, activation= 'relu'))
model.add(Dropout(0.25))
model.add(Dense(10, activation= 'relu'))
model.add(Dense(1, activation= 'sigmoid'))
```

- Compile and train the model.

```
model.compile(optimizer='adam', loss='binary_crossentropy',
      metrics=['accuracy'])
hist = model.fit(xtrain,ytrain, epochs=10, batch_size=64,
      verbose=2 , shuffle=True )
```

- Draw the train accuracy curve.

```
import matplotlib.pyplot as plt
plt.plot(range(10), hist.history['accuracy'], marker='*')
plt.title('Train Accuracy ')
plt.xlabel('Epochs')
plt.ylabel(' Accuracy')
plt.show()
```

Output

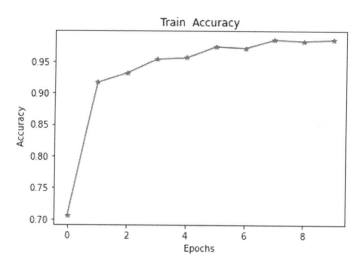

- Evaluate the model on test dataset

```
test_eval = model.evaluate(xtest, ytest, verbose=0)
print('Loss on test data :',round(test_eval[0],4),
   '\n Accuracy on test data: ', round(test_eval[1]*100,2))
```

Output

> Loss on test data : 0.1426
> Accuracy on test data: 95.61

14.7.3   Image Classification Model

A classification model is built using image dataset containing yoga poses for the popular five asanas like a goddess, plank, down-dog, tree, and warrior. The following code builds a predictive model.

```
#To deal with corrupted images, use the following code
  # before model fit
from PIL import ImageFile
ImageFile.LOAD_TRUNCATED_IMAGES = True
```

- Load the Dataset from the directory structure containing images.

```
from keras.preprocessing.image import ImageDataGenerator
data_gen = ImageDataGenerator()
train_data = data_gen.flow_from_directory
  (directory= '/content/Yoga_DATASET/TRAIN' ,
  target_size=(180,180),class_mode='categorical',
  batch_size=32, shuffle=True)
test_data = data_gen.flow_from_directory
  (directory= '/content/Yoga_DATASET/TEST' ,
  target_size=(180,180), class_mode='categorical',
  batch_size=32, shuffle=True)
```

Output

> Found 1081 images belonging to 5 classes.
> Found 470 images belonging to 5 classes.

- Data exploration and Preprocessing

  (i) Check the image size and class labels.

```
print('Image shape: ',train_data.image_shape)
print('Class Indices: ',train_data.class_indices)
```

Output

> Image shape: (180, 180, 3)
> Class Indices: {'downdog': 0, 'goddess': 1, 'plank': 2, 'tree':
>   3, 'warrior2': 4}

(ii) Display a sample image.

```
import matplotlib.pyplot as plt
print('File Names : ',train_data.filenames[:2])
print('Display Image')
plt.imshow(plt.imread(train_data.filepaths[10]))
plt.show()
```

Output

File Names : ['downdog/00000128.jpg',
              'downdog/00000129.jpg']

Display Image

- *Model building for image Classification*
  Define a convolutional neural network with two blocks consisting of convolution,
  pooling, and dropout layers followed by dense layers.

```
from keras.models import Sequential
from keras.layers import Conv2D, MaxPooling2D, Flatten,
      Dense, Dropout
model= Sequential()
model.add(Conv2D(32,5, activation ='relu', input_shape=(180,180,3)))
model.add(Conv2D(32,5, activation ='relu'))
model.add(MaxPooling2D(pool_size=(2,2)))
model.add(Dropout(0.2))
```

```
model.add(Conv2D(64,3, activation ='relu'))
model.add(Conv2D(64,3, activation ='relu'))
model.add(MaxPooling2D(pool_size=(2,2)))
model.add(Dropout(0.2))

model.add(Flatten())
model.add(Dense(256,activation ='relu'))
model.add(Dense(128,activation ='relu'))
model.add(Dense(64,activation ='relu'))
model.add(Dense(5,activation ='softmax'))
model.summary()
```

Output

Model: "sequential_11"

Layer (type)	Output shape	Param #
conv2d_44 (Conv2D)	(None, 176, 176, 32)	2432
conv2d_45 (Conv2D)	(None, 172, 172, 32)	25632
max_pooling2d_22 (MaxPooling2D)	(None, 86, 86, 32)	0
dropout_29 (Dropout)	(None, 86, 86, 32)	0
conv2d_46 (Conv2D)	(None, 84, 84, 64)	18496
conv2d_47 (Conv2D)	(None, 82, 82, 64)	36928
max_pooling2d_23 (MaxPooling2D)	(None, 41, 41, 64)	0
dropout_30 (Dropout)	(None, 41, 41, 64)	0
flatten_11 (Flatten)	(None, 107584)	0
dense_37 (Dense)	(None, 256)	27541760
dense_38 (Dense)	(None, 128)	32896
dense_39 (Dense)	(None, 64)	8256
dense_40 (Dense)	(None, 5)	325

Total params: 27,666,725
Trainable params: 27,666,725
Non-trainable params: 0

- *Compile and Fit the Model*
  rmsprop as the optimizer, *accuracy* as the performance metric. Loss function is *categorical_crossentropy* as it is multi-class classification task. The *fit( )* function returns accuracy and loss values for both train and validation datasets for each of the 20 epochs.

```
model.compile(optimizer='rmsprop', loss='categorical_
      crossentropy', metrics=['accuracy'])
hist = model.fit(train_data,
      validation_data=test_data,epochs=20, verbose=0)
```

- *Visualize the model performance*
  Visualize the accuracy for train and validation data using line graph.

```
plt.plot(range(10), hist.history['accuracy'],
      label='Accuracy', marker='*')
plt.plot(range(10), hist.history['val_accuracy'],
      label='Validation Accuracy')
plt.title('Train vs Validation accuracy')
plt.xlabel('Epochs')
plt.ylabel('Accuracy')
plt.legend()
plt.show()
```

Output

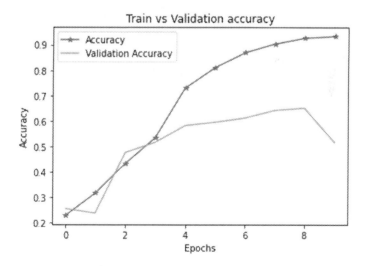

14.7.4   Text Data Classification

Quora is a platform where people can ask questions to learn from each other. The question is a text containing one or more lines. The task is to classify whether the question is sincere or not.

- *Load the Train Dataset*
  The dataset contains question Id, question text, and target.

```
import pandas as pd
raw_train_data = pd.read_csv('/content/drive/MyDrive/Python
Book/Chap 13
      ML & DL packages/Datasets/Text datasets/lstm_data/
      Quora_train.csv', encoding='latin-1')
print('Train data shape :',raw_train_data.shape)
print('Train data columns :',raw_train_data.columns)
print('Sample Train data :\n',raw_train_data
      [['question_text', 'target']].head())
```

Output

```
Train data shape : (1306122, 3)
Train data columns : Index(['qid', 'question_text', 'target'],
dtype='object')
```

Sample Train data :

question_text target

```
0   How did Quebec nationalists see their province      0
1   Do you have an adopted dog, how would you enco     0
2   Why does velocity affect time? Does velocity a      0
3   How did Otto von Guericke used the Magdeburg h      0
4   Can I convert montra helicon D to a mountain b      0
```

- *Load the Test Dataset*
  The dataset contains question ID and question text.

```
raw_test_data = pd.read_csv('/content/Text
      datasets/lstm_data/Quora_test.csv', encoding='latin-1')
print('Test data shape :',raw_test_data.shape)
print('Test data columns : ',raw_test_data.columns)
print('Sample Test data :\n', raw_test_data.head())
```

Output

Test data shape : (375806, 2)
Test data columns : Index(['qid', 'question_text'], dtype='object')

Sample Test data :

	qid	question_text
0	0000163e3ea7c7a74cd7	Why do so many women become so rude and arroga...
1	00002bd4fb5d505b9161	When should I apply for RV college of engineer...
2	00007756b4a147d2b0b3	What is it really like to be a nurse practitio...
3	000086e4b7e1c7146103	Who are entrepreneurs?
4	0000c4c3fbe8785a3090	Is education really making good people nowadays?

- Count for each label

```
import numpy as np
num_labels = np.unique(raw_train_data['target'],
    return_counts=True)
print('Target Labels and their counts : ',num_labels)
```

Target Labels and their counts: (array([0, 1]),
    array([1225312, 80810]))

- Convert text to numeric using *tokenizer()* function and fit on the text corpus.

```
# tokenization
max_words=10000
from keras.preprocessing.text import Tokenizer
tokens = Tokenizer(num_words = max_words)
tokens.fit_on_texts(raw_train_data.question_text)
print('No. of documents : ',tokens.document_count)
print('No. of word Indices : ',len(tokens.word_index))
```

Output

No. of documents: 1306122
No. of word Indices: 222186

- Display sample tokens and their word indices

```
print('First review : ',raw_train_data.question_text[0])
print('Word index of Quebec, province : ',tokens.word_index
    ['quebec'], tokens.word_index['province'])
```

Output

> First review: How did Quebec nationalists see their province
>   as a nation in the 1960s?
> Word index of Quebec, province: 6683 6107

- Convert text to sequences after applying *fit_on_texts()* method on the train data.

> xtrain = tokens.texts_to_sequences(raw_train_data.
>   question_text)
> print('After converting text to sequence vector : \n',xtrain[0],
>   '\n',xtrain[1])

Output

> After converting text to sequence vector:
>   [9, 48, 6683, 7219, 158, 55, 6107, 36, 4, 1206, 6, 1, 8333]
>   [11, 14, 24, 29, 3864, 498, 9, 35, 14, 3672, 37, 5, 3089, 10, 44, 1846]

- As sequence vectors are of varying length, make into fixed length using padding
  technique.

> max_len = 150
> from tensorflow.keras.preprocessing.sequence import
>   pad_sequences
> xtrain_pad = pad_sequences(xtrain, maxlen = max_len)
> print('Length of sequence vector before padding: ',
>   len(xtrain[0]))
> print('Length of sequence vector after padding: ',
>   len(xtrain_pad[0]))

Output

> Length of sequence vector before padding: 13
> Length of sequence vector after padding: 150

- Perform sequencing and padding on test data

> xtest = tokens.texts_to_sequences(raw_test_data.question_text)
> xtest_pad = pad_sequences(xtest, maxlen = max_len)
> print('Length of sequence vector before padding : ',len(xtest[0]))
> print('Length of sequence vector after padding :
>   ',len(xtest_pad[0]))

Output

> Length of sequence vector before padding: 21
> Length of sequence vector after padding: 150

```
print('Shapes of train & test data : ',xtrain_pad.shape,
  xtest_pad.shape)
```

Output

> Shapes of train & test data: (1306122, 150) (375806, 150)

- Create list of target labels

```
labels = list(raw_train_data.target.unique())
print('Target labels : ',labels)
```

Output

> Target labels: [0, 1]

- Model Building

1. *LSTM Model*
   Create a sequential model with Embedding, LSTM, and Dense layers. First layer
   is the Embedding layer that represents each token as a vector.

```
from keras.models import Sequential
from keras.layers import Embedding, LSTM, Dense
embedding_size=100
model = Sequential()
model.add(Embedding(input_dim = max_words,
  input_length= max_len, output_dim =embedding_size ))
model.add(LSTM(10, return_sequences=False))
model.add(Dense(1, activation='sigmoid'))
model.summary()
```

Output

> Model: "sequential"

Layer (type)	Output shape	Param #
embedding (Embedding)	(None, 150, 100)	1000000
lstm (LSTM)	(None, 10)	4440
dense (Dense)	(None, 1)	11

Total params: 1,004,451
Trainable params: 1,004,451
Non-trainable params: 0

```
print('Labels : ',raw_train_data.target.unique())
```

Output

> Labels : [0 1]

It is a binary classification task. Use *binary_crossentropy* as the loss function and *accuracy* as the metric to the *compile()* function. Then fit the model for 3 epochs.

```
ytrain = raw_train_data['target']
model.compile(optimizer='adam', loss='binary_
        crossentropy', metrics=['accuracy'])
hist = model.fit(xtrain_pad, ytrain, epochs=3,
        validation_split=0.25)
```

Model Prediction

```
pred = model.predict(xtest_pad)
pred_test_y = (pred>0.35).astype(int)
submited = pd.read_csv('/content/sample_data/
        sample_submission.csv')
submited['predicted'] = pd.DataFrame(pred_test_y)
submited.head()
```

Output

> 11744/11744 [==============================]
> - 42s 4ms/step

	qid	True Value	predicted
0	0000163e3ea7c7a74cd7	0	1
1	00002bd4fb5d505b9161	0	0
2	00007756b4a147d2b0b3	0	0
3	000086e4b7e1c7146103	0	0
4	0000c4c3fbe8785a3090	0	0

2. *GRU Model*
   Build a sequential model consisting of Embedding layer, GRU layer with 10 units, and a Dense layer. Then compile and fit the model for 3 epochs.

```
from keras.models import Sequential
from keras.layers import Embedding, GRU, Dense
embedding_size=32
model = Sequential()
model.add(Embedding(input_dim = max_words,
        input_length= max_len, output_dim =embedding_size ))
model.add(GRU(10))
model.add(Dense(1, activation='sigmoid'))
model.compile(optimizer='adam', loss='binary_crossentropy',
        metrics=['accuracy'])
hist_gru = model.fit(xtrain_pad, ytrain, epochs=3,
        validation_split=0.25)
```

3. Simple RNN Model

```
from keras.models import Sequential
from keras.layers import Embedding, SimpleRNN, Dense
embedding_size= 100
model = Sequential()
model.add(Embedding(input_dim = max_words,
    input_length= max_len, output_dim =embedding_size ))
model.add(SimpleRNN(10))
model.add(Dense(1, activation='sigmoid'))
model.compile(optimizer='adam', loss='binary_crossentropy',
        metrics=['accuracy'])
hist_rnn = model.fit(xtrain_pad, ytrain, epochs=3,
        validation_split=0.25)
```

Performance comparison using the three models

```
performance = pd.DataFrame()
performance['Train_accuracy']=[hist.history['accuracy'][-1],
        hist_gru.history['accuracy'][-1]],hist_rnn.history
        ['accuracy'][-1]]

performance['Validation_accuracy']=hist.history['val_accuracy']
        [-1],hist_gru.history['val_accuracy'][-1]],
        hist_rnn.history['val_accuracy'][-1]]

performance.index=['LSTM','GRU','RNN' ]
print(performance)
```

Output

	Train_accuracy	Validation_accuracy
LSTM	0.9602	0.9556
GRU	0.9591	0.9553
RNN	0.9540	0.9504

Chapter 15
Python for Multi-tasking

15.1 Introduction

A process is an instance of a program in execution. In a multi-tasking system, multiple processes are in execution. Each process can be in any of the following states.

- *Ready:* Just created and ready for execution.
- *Running:* Currently being executed by the processor.
- *Wait/Block:* Waiting for a resource to be assigned or for input/output.
- *Suspended:* The process is moved to secondary memory due to insufficient resources.
- *Paused* as some other process is scheduled for execution.
- *Terminated:* The process completed execution.

The operating system has to understand the states of all the processes in the system, so that system resources are effectively utilized. Information about each process is maintained in a data structure called PCB (process control block). PCB contains process ID, process state, program counter, main memory allocation, and other resources allocated to the process like input/output devices, disk, etc. In a multi-tasking system, multiple tasks or processes are in execution simultaneously. The processor has to switch between processes/threads to use the system resources effectively.

This is done by saving the current state of the process in the PCB so that the process can be resumed later. Multi-tasking can be achieved using concurrency and parallelism.

- **Concurrency:** Multiple tasks can start, execute, and complete in overlapping time periods. In the case of a single-core CPU, the system performs a context switch between tasks to make progress. The processor executes only one task at any point of time, but it looks as if multiple tasks are being executed.
- **Parallelism:** Multiple tasks are actually running at the same time. Doing so requires multiple cores in the CPU or multiple CPUs. In parallel processing, at least two tasks are executed simultaneously.

© The Author(s) 2024
A. L. Muddana and S. Vinayakam, *Python for Data Science*,
https://doi.org/10.1007/978-3-031-52473-8_15

Concurrency and parallelism mechanisms effectively utilize system resources and speed up execution. Multiple tasks can be in execution in the following ways:

- *Neither Concurrent nor Parallel:* Only one task is in execution at any time. A task is entirely executed before the next task is initiated. This means that the execution of tasks is strictly sequential.
- *Concurrent but not Parallel:* Multiple tasks are in progress, but only one is executed by the processor at any instance. The processor switches between tasks to complete execution.
- *Parallel but not Concurrent:* A task is broken into sub-tasks, which are run simultaneously by multiple CPU cores.
- *Concurrent and Parallel:* Multiple tasks are in execution simultaneously on multiple cores of a CPU or multiple CPUs. Each task can also be broken down into sub-tasks, which are also executed in parallel.

Python provides constructs to achieve concurrency and parallelism using:

1. Multi-threading.
2. Multi-processing.

15.2 Multi-threading

A process can be split into sub-tasks called threads. A thread is a sequence of instructions that can be executed independently. A process may contain multiple threads that can be activated and executed parallelly. A thread can be preempted and interrupted based on demand.

In a single-core CPU system, multi-threading is achieved by scheduling the CPU to different threads for execution. The processor executes a few lines of thread1 and then switches to thread2 and executes a few lines there, then switches to another thread, and so on. This continues until all the threads of the process are completed. Only one CPU goes back and forth between multiple threads by switching among the threads, called a context switch. During the context switch, the thread's state is saved before shifting to another thread so that it can be resumed from the same point later. The switch between threads is so fast that it appears to the user as if the CPU executes all the threads simultaneously, called virtual parallelism. Python implements concurrency using multi-threading.

Multi-threading enables the execution of many sub-tasks of one process simultaneously. Each process has a global state that is shared among its threads. This makes communication among the threads easy and efficient. In addition to the global state, each thread has its local state.

Multi-threading is a perfect choice if the process is heavy I/O-bound and spends a lot of time waiting for input/output. For example, accessing data from files, downloading from the Internet, sleeping, etc. are I/O-bound jobs. Even though multiple threads can be running concurrently in a process, the processor executes only one thread code at any point in time.

Advantages of Threads

- The use of multi-threading efficiently utilizes resources as threads share resources and memory.
- Works well for creating responsive applications.

Disadvantages

- There is overhead involved in managing multiple threads, and difficult to keep track of them.
- It increases the complexity of the program and makes debugging a bit difficult.

Python provides two modules for multi-threading: *thread* and *threading*

> *thread* module is deprecated.
> *threading* is a high-level implementation for threads.

Steps in creating threads

- Import *threading* module.
- Create a *threading* object by passing the following parameters.
  target: The function that forms the thread.
  args: Arguments to the target function.
- Activate the thread using the *start()* function on the thread object.
- Pause main thread execution until the thread completes execution using the *join()* method on the thread object.

Methods on thread object

- *start():* Starts the thread activity. It should be called only once.
  It returns an error if called multiple times.
- *run():* Denotes the activity of the thread.
- *join():* Blocks execution of other code until the thread gets terminated.

Functions on the thread object

- *activeCount():* Number of active thread objects.
- *currentThread():* Returns current thread object.
- *isDaemon():* True if the thread is a daemon.
- *isAlive():* True if the thread is active.

Every Python program is a process that has one thread called the *main* thread. Other threads can be spawned by creating an object of the *threading* class.

Example: Create a thread on a simple function and activate it.

```
import threading
import os
def fun1():
  print('\n We are in fun1')
  print('Process Id : ',os.getpid())
  print('Thread name : ',threading.current_thread().name)
  print('Thread Id : ',threading.get_ident())
  print('End of fun1')
if __name__=='__main__':
  print('We are in main function ')
  print('Thread name : ',threading.current_thread().name)
  print('Process Id of main : ',os.getpid())
  print('Thread Id : ',threading.get_ident())
  t1=threading.Thread(target=fun1)
  t1.start()
  t1.join()
  print('End of main')
```

Output

```
We are in main function
Thread name : MainThread
Process Id of main : 212
Thread Id : 140529785120640

We are in fun1
Process Id : 212
Thread name : Thread-11
Thread Id : 140529410037504
End of fun1
End of main
```

Threads speed up the execution of programs, especially when the process is I/O-bound job like accessing file data.

Example: There exist two files that contain R.No., Marks obtained in Maths and R.No., Marks obtained in Python. Define two functions that read marks from each file and find the highest marks. It is an I/O-bound job as we are accessing files.

```
import time
def read_file1(file_name):
  fd = open(file_name,'r')
  next(fd)
  high=0
  while True:
    line= fd.readline()
    if line=='':
```

```
            break
        r,m = line.split()
        m = int(m)
        if m>high:
          high=m
      print('Highest in Maths : ',high)
      fd.close()
      time.sleep(0.1)
    def read_file2(file_name):
      fd = open(file_name,'r')
      next(fd)
      high=0
      #print(type(high))
      while True:
        line= fd.readline()
        if line=='':
          break
        r,m = line.split()
        m = int(m)
        if m>high:
          high=m
      print('Highest in Python : ',high)
      fd.close()
      time.sleep(0.1)
```

Now create the main function that calls the above functions and measure the time taken to execute the process.

```
    if __name__ =="__main__":
      start=time.time()
      read_file1('/content/sample_data/maths.txt')
      read_file2('/content/sample_data/python.txt')
      end=time.time()
      print('Time Taken for execution : ',end-start)
```

Output

```
    Highest in Maths : 92
    Highest in Python : 91
    Time Taken for execution : 0.2044222354888916
```

Now execute the same program using multi-threading. Create two threads, one for each function, and measure the time taken.

```
    import threading
    if __name__ =="__main__":
      start=time.time()
```

```
t1=threading.Thread(target=read_file1,args=
   ('/content/sample_data/maths.txt',))
t2=threading.Thread(target=read_file2,args=
   ('/content/sample_data/python.txt',))
t1.start()
t2.start()
t1.join()
t2.join()
end=time.time()
print('Time Taken for execution : ',end-start)
```

Output

Highest in Maths : 92
Highest in Python : 91
Time Taken for execution : 0.10691332817077637

Note: The time to execute the process using multi-threading (two threads) is almost half the time taken without multi-threading.

Threads of a process share data of the main thread. When multiple threads access the shared data simultaneously, the operations by different threads may be interleaved, and the result may not be as expected. A *critical section* is a fragment of the process code that accesses or modifies shared data. The operations in the critical section must be performed as atomic operations. Otherwise, the result of the operations may not be correct.

Multi-threading applications may face the following problems:

(i) *Race conditions* occur when two or more processes simultaneously access or modify the data in the critical section.
(ii) *Deadlocks* occur when different threads or processes try to acquire a resource. Each thread is holding a resource and waiting for the resource held by the other thread/process. No one gets a chance as it waits for a resource held by the other process.

15.2.1 Threads Synchronization

The threading module provides a Lock object for thread synchronization to deal with race conditions, deadlocks, and other multi-thread-based issues. The thread that wants to access the shared data has to acquire a lock on the resource before accessing and releasing the lock once the operations are completed on the shared data. When the resource's state is locked, no other process can access that resource and has to wait until the lock is released.

Lock is to be imported from the *threading* class.

```
from threading import Lock
```

Example: x is a global list object that the threads of a process can access. Two threads are created. The first thread appends the values from 0 to 50 with a step of 10, and the second appends the values from 500 to 550 with a step of 10. Execution of these two threads may be interleaved, and the threads may append the values in any sequence.

```
import threading
import time
x=[]
def fun1():
  global x
  for i in range(0,50,10):
    print('fun1 is updating ', end=' ')
    x.append(i)
    print(x)
    time.sleep(0.01)
def fun2():
  global x
  for i in range(500,550,10):
    print('fun2 is updating ', end=' ')
    x.append(i)
    print(x)
    time.sleep(0.01)
if __name__ =="__main__":
    t1 = threading.Thread(target=fun1)
    t2 = threading.Thread(target=fun2)
    t1.start()
    t2.start()
    t1.join()
    t2.join()
    print('Final list : ',x)
```

Output

```
fun1 is updating  [0]
fun2 is updating  [0, 500]
fun1 is updating  [0, 500, 10]
fun2 is updating  [0, 500, 10, 510]
fun1 is updating  [0, 500, 10, 510, 20]
fun2 is updating  [0, 500, 10, 510, 20, 520]
fun1 is updating  [0, 500, 10, 510, 20, 520, 30]
fun2 is updating  [0, 500, 10, 510, 20, 520, 30, 530]
fun1 is updating  [0, 500, 10, 510, 20, 520, 30, 530, 40]
fun2 is updating  [0, 500, 10, 510, 20, 520, 30, 530, 40, 540]
Final list :   [0, 500, 10, 510, 20, 520, 30, 530, 40, 540]
```

If *Lock* is used by a thread while accessing the shared object x, the other thread waits until the lock is released.

This ensures that the values in the list object are in sequence, as shown below.

Example

```
import threading
import time
x=[]
lock = threading.Lock()
def fun1():
  global x
  lock.acquire()
  for i in range(0,50,10):
    print('fun1 is updating ', end=' ')
    x.append(i)
    print(x)
    time.sleep(0.01)
  lock.release()
def fun2():
  global x
  lock.acquire()
  for i in range(500,550,10):
    print('fun2 is updating ', end=' ')
    x.append(i)
    print(x)
    time.sleep(0.01)
  lock.release()
if __name__ =="__main__":
    t1 = threading.Thread(target=fun1)
    t2 = threading.Thread(target=fun2)
    t1.start()
    t2.start()
    t1.join()
    t2.join()
    print('Final list : ',x)
```

Output

```
fun1 is updating  [0]
fun1 is updating  [0, 10]
fun1 is updating  [0, 10, 20]
fun1 is updating  [0, 10, 20, 30]
fun1 is updating  [0, 10, 20, 30, 40]
fun2 is updating  [0, 10, 20, 30, 40, 500]
fun2 is updating  [0, 10, 20, 30, 40, 500, 510]
```

fun2 is updating   [0, 10, 20, 30, 40, 500, 510, 520]
fun2 is updating   [0, 10, 20, 30, 40, 500, 510, 520, 530]
fun2 is updating   [0, 10, 20, 30, 40, 500, 510, 520, 530, 540]
Final list :   [0, 10, 20, 30, 40, 500, 510, 520, 530, 540]

15.3 Multi-processing

Computer systems with multiple-core CPUs are becoming common. Hence writing parallel code improves the system's performance. Python provides a *multi-processing* module to write parallel code. Multiple unrelated processes can run simultaneously by different cores of the CPU or different CPUs. The operating system schedules each process separately so that the program gets a larger share of system resources. As these processes are independent, they do not share resources. Every process gets its own instance of Python interpreter, processor, memory, and other resources for completing the task. Different processes cannot share the same global variable, but each process makes a copy of the global variable if required. Multi-processing is best if the task is CPU bound and the machine has multi-cores or processors. Multi-processing is more efficient as processes are run concurrently. Python implements parallelism using a *multi-processing* module.

Multi-threading Versus Multi-processing

- In multi-threading, multiple threads belonging to a single process can run simultaneously. In contrast, multi-processing runs multiple processes across different CPU cores or multiple CPUs simultaneously.
- Multi-threading is used to implement concurrency. Whereas multi-processing is used to implement parallelism.
- In multi-processing, each process gets a new instance of Python interpreter and hence a different GIL (Global Interpreter Lock). In contrast, GIL can execute only one thread at any movement. Hence there may not be much performance improvement in multi-threading.

Python provides a *multi-processing* module with libraries for implementing multi-processing, interprocess communication, and data sharing. The multi-processing module has a *Process* class for creating new process objects. Following are the steps in creating processes:

- Create a *Process* object by passing the following arguments:
  target—function to be executed by the process.
  args—arguments to the function.
- Start the process using *start()* method on the process object.
- Wait for the process to be completed using *join()* method on the process object.

Example: A program has functions to calculate the area of a triangle and the area of a circle. Let us execute it with a single process and multiple processes and see the reduction in the time taken for execution.

```
def triangle(b,h):
  print('Triangle Process Id : ', os.getpid(), end=' ')
  print(' Area : ',0.5*b*h)
  time.sleep(0.1)
def circle(r):
  time.sleep(0.1)
  print('Circle Process Id : ', os.getpid(), end=' ')
  print(' Area : ',3.14*r*r)
```

a. Execute the Program Using a Single Process

```
import time
import os
if __name__ == '__main__':
  print('Main Process Id : ', os.getpid())
  start= time.time()
  triangle(5,6)
  circle(5)
  end = time.time()
  print('Time taken with single process : ', end-start)
```

Output

```
Main Process Id : 473
Triangle Process Id : 473 Area : 15.0
Circle Process Id : 473 Area : 78.5
Time taken with single process : 0.20311737060546875
```

b. Execute the Program with Two Processes

```
import multiprocessing
import time
import os
if __name__ == '__main__':
  print('Main Process Id : ', os.getpid())
  p1 = multiprocessing.Process(target=triangle, args=(5,6))
  p2 = multiprocessing.Process(target=circle, args=(5,))
  start= time.time()
  p1.start()
  p2.start()
  p1.join()
  p2.join()
  end = time.time()
  print('Time taken with two processes : ', end-start)
```

Output

> Main Process Id : 473
> Triangle Process Id : 2665 Area: 15.0
> Circle Process Id : 2666 Area: 78.5
> Time taken with two processes : 0.16042232513427734

There is a significant reduction in execution time. As spawning a process takes little time, the reduction in time is not half.

15.3.1 Interprocess Communication

Processes are independent units, each has its system resources, and multiple processes are executed in parallel. But still, processes can communicate with one another. In Python, interprocess communication is achieved using the following classes of *multi-processing* module:

- Queue
- Pipe
- Manager
- Shared memory

(i) **Queue Class**

Queue is a high-level mechanism for sharing data among multiple processes. Each process can put the data and also access the data from the queue. The queue is designed to be used with multiple producers (put the data into a queue) and multiple consumers (take data from the queue). It is a bi-directional data flow method. This is similar to *queue*. *Queue* class which is a FIFO data structure. Different processes can use **get()** and **put()** methods to add or consume the data in the queue. This data structure includes a lock mechanism to avoid race conditions, and users need not worry about synchronization.

Example: A program containing two producers and one consumer process. These processes communicate using queue objects.

```
from multiprocessing import Process, Queue
import time
def producer1(lst,q):
    for ele in lst:
        area=0.5*ele[0]*ele[1]
        print('put by Producer1 ', area)
        q.put(('Producer1 ',area))
        time.sleep(0.01)
def producer2(lst,q):
```

```
    for ele in lst:
      area= ele[0]*ele[1]
      print('Put by Producer2 ', area)
      q.put(('Producer2 ',area))
      time.sleep(0.01)
  def consumer(q):
    time.sleep(0.2)
    while not q.empty():
      print('Consumed ',q.get())
      time.sleep(0.01)

  if __name__ == "__main__":
    lst=[(2,3),(5,6),(7,8)]
    q=Queue()
    p1 = Process(target=producer1, args=(lst,q))
    p2 = Process(target=producer2, args=(lst,q))
    p3 = Process(target=consumer, args=(q,))
    p1.start()
    p2.start()
    p3.start()
    p1.join()
    p2.join()
    p3.join()
```

Output

```
    put by Producer1 3.0
    Put by Producer2 6
    put by Producer1 15.0
    Put by Producer2 30
    put by Producer1 28.0
    Put by Producer2 56
    Consumed ('Producer1 ', 3.0)
    Consumed ('Producer2 ', 6)
    Consumed ('Producer1 ', 15.0)
    Consumed ('Producer2 ', 30)
    Consumed ('Producer1 ', 28.0)
    Consumed ('Producer2 ', 56)
```

(ii) **Pipe Class**

Pipe is a connection between two processes. It is a low-level mechanism, and usually, one process sends data into the pipe, and the other process consumes the data from the pipe. Creating a pipe generates two connection objects representing two endpoints. **send()** and **recv()** methods are used for sending and receiving data from the pipe. Pipe is a simpler and more efficient mechanism to share the data faster between two processes.

Example: One producer and one consumer communicating using **_Pipe_** object.

```
from multiprocessing import Process, Pipe
import time
def producer(lst,end):
  for ele in lst:
    area=round(3.14*ele*ele,2)
    print('Sending ', area)
    end.send(area)
    time.sleep(0.01)
def consumer(lst,end):
  while True:
    data = end.recv()
    if data==0:
      break
    print('Received ',data)
    time.sleep(0.1)

if __name__ == "__main__":
  lst=[6,8,10,0]
  end1, end2 =Pipe()
  p1 = Process(target=producer, args=(lst,end1))
  p2 = Process(target=consumer, args=(lst,end2))
  p1.start()
  p2.start()
  p1.join()
  p2.join()
```

Output

```
Sending 113.04
Received 113.04
Sending 200.96
Sending 314.0
Sending 0.0
Received 200.96
Received 314.0
```

(iii) **Manager Class**

When a program starts, the server process is started. A new process is created by sending a request to the server process. Server process controls the shared data and allows other processes to manipulate it. The *Manager* class of the multi-processing module controls the server process. The manager object creates shared data and updates it when processes manipulate it. Shared data may contain objects like dictionaries, lists, Array, Value, Queue, etc.

Example: Three processes communicating using *Manager* object.

```
from multiprocessing import Process, Manager
import time
def add_process(pandavas, names):
  for name in names:
    print('Adding ', name)
    pandavas.append(name)
def del_process(pandavas):
  time.sleep(0.2)
  print('deleting last element ', pandavas.pop())
def display_process(pandavas):
  time.sleep(0.3)
  print('Displaying shared memory data :')
  for element in pandavas:
    print(element)
if __name__ == '__main__':
  manager = Manager()
  pandavas = manager.list(['Duryodhan', 'Bheem'])
  names=['Arjun', 'Nakul', 'Sahadev']
  p1 = Process(target= add_process, args=(pandavas,names))
  p2 = Process(target=del_process, args=(pandavas,))
  p3 = Process(target=display_process, args=(pandavas,))
  p1.start()
  p2.start()
  p3.start()
  p1.join()
  p2.join()
  p3.join()
```

Output

```
Adding Arjun
Adding Nakul
Adding Sahadev
deleting last element Sahadev
Displaying shared memory data :
Duryodhan
Bheem
Arjun
Nakul
```

(iv) **Array and Value Objects**

Ctypes is a mechanism for sharing data among processes in a multi-processing environment. The *multi-processing* module provides *Array* and *Value* classes that are of ctypes for sharing array and value among the processes.

Example

```
from multiprocessing import Process, Array, Value
def power_2(a,v):
  for i in range(len(a)):
    a[i] = 2 ** i
def sum_arr(a,v):
  v.value = sum(a)/len(a)
if __name__ == '__main__':
  val = Value('d',0.0)
  arr = Array('i', range(5))
  p1 = Process(target= power_2, args=(arr,val))
  p2 = Process(target= sum_arr, args=(arr,val))
  p1.start()
  p2.start()
  p1.join()
  p2.join()
  print('Array elements : ',arr[:])
  print('Average of array elements : ',val.value)
```

Output

```
Array elements : [1, 2, 4, 8, 16]
Average of array elements : 6.2
```

15.3.2 Process Pool

Creating a new process using the *Process* class increases computational costs if we are creating and destroying many processes. Instead, we can create and keep processes ready for use with the help of a process/thread pool.

Process pool is a pool of generic worker processes that are ready to run a task. This is a more efficient way than creating a thread/process on demand, especially when a large number of processes/threads are required. Unused processes in the pool can be made to wait without consuming computational resources.

Python 3.2 has *concurrent.futures* module that has constructs for creating both pool of threads and pool of processes. This is an abstraction layer on top of *threading* and *multi-processing* modules. It uses *ThreadPoolExecutor* and *ProcessPoolExecutor* to manage process pools and thread pools. Life cycle of process pool

1. Creating an object of *ProcessPoolExecutor*

   Pool = ProcessPoolExecutor(*max_workers*)

   max_workers—the maximum number of processes in the pool. Default is the total number of CPU cores

2. Submit the task using map() or submit()

map()

> Apply the function for each element in the iterable
> One process per loop iteration
> Returns an iterable that can be used to access the result

submit()

> Submits one task per process
> Returns *future* object. Use *result()* on future object to access the result.

3. Wait for the results using *wait()*, as_completed().
4. Close the process pool using *shutdown()* method.

The below example creates a pool of 10 processes for finding the prime numbers between 2 and 20.

Example

```
from concurrent.futures import ProcessPoolExecutor
import time
def is_prime(n):
  for i in range(2,n):
    if n%i==0:
      return n,'Not prime'
  else:
    return n,'Prime'
if __name__ == '__main__':
  start=time.time()
  pool = ProcessPoolExecutor(max_workers=10)
  result = pool.map(is_prime, range(2,20))
  end=time.time()
  print('Time taken using process pool : ', end-start)
  for r in result:
    if r[1]=='Prime':
      print(r,end=' ')
  pool.shutdown()
```

Output

> Time taken using process pool : 0.08892011642456055
> (2, 'Prime') (3, 'Prime') (5, 'Prime') (7, 'Prime') (11, 'Prime')
>   (13, 'Prime') (17, 'Prime') (19, 'Prime')

Exercises

1. Given a list of decimal numbers, write functions to find binary, octal equivalents. Write the number, corresponding binary, and octal equivalents into a file. Use multi-threading, multi-processing, and measure the time.
2. Write a program to find the divisors of elements of a set using a process pool.
3. Write a program to find the number of words and English language articles in a file using multi-processing.
4. Write a producer function to generate perfect numbers between 1 and 200 and a consumer function to display them. Use pipe for interprocess communication.
5. Take a global list object. Write two threads, one for inserting odd numbers and the other for inserting even numbers between 0 and 25. Use thread synchronization.

Review Questions

(1) The module that supports multi-threading in Python

  (a) Multi-threading
  (b) Threading
  (c) Thread
  (d) Threads

(2) Which of the following method forces one thread to wait until another thread completes?

  (a) start()
  (b) pause()
  (c) join()
  (d) close()

(3) Which of the following method is used for interprocess communication using Pipe?

  (a) insert()
  (b) send()
  (c) append()
  (d) put()

(4) Which of the following method is used for interprocess communication using Queue?

  (a) insert()
  (b) send()
  (c) append()
  (d) put()

(5) Which of the following object is used for thread synchronization?

    (a) Sync
    (b) Lock
    (c) Hold
    (d) Pause

(6) .... is used to execute multiple activities in a single processor.

    (a) Multi-processing
    (b) Multi-threading
    (c) Both multi-processing and multi-threading
    (d) None of the above

(7) The method used to pause a thread for certain amount of time.

    (a) sleep()
    (b) pause()
    (c) time()
    (d) thread_sleep()

(8) Threading module of Python provides functions to achieve parallelism.
True/False

(9) Which of the following method is not a supported method on *Thread* object?

    (a) start()
    (b) run()
    (c) join()
    (d) getpid()

(10) Each process in the process pool is allocated system resources.
True/False

Appendix A
Solutions to Review Questions

Chapter 1

1. (c) Welcome Python
2. (a) NameError: name 'Pi' is not defined
3. (c) False
4. (c) 200
5. (d) 25
6. (b) 10
7. (b) 2
8. (a) True
9. (c) 2
10. (d) –2
11. (a) 0
12. (d) 20
13. (a) 5
14. (b) Bye
15. (d) Any of the above
16. (c) Indentation
17. (d) do while
18. (a) Yes
19. (a) True
20. (b) 15+5j

Chapter 2

1. (c) 31
2. (d) error is generated

© The Author(s) 2024
A. L. Muddana and S. Vinayakam, *Python for Data Science*,
https://doi.org/10.1007/978-3-031-52473-8

3. (a) 1
4. (b) 10 314.0 None
5. (a) None
6. (a) Function body should have at least one return statement
7. (b) (1, 2, 3, 4, 5, 6, 7)
8. (a) –15
9. (c) 2
10. (c) tuple

Chapter 3

1. (a) Python is an object-oriented language
2. (c) Python is high-level language and object-oriented language
3. (c) 20 % 7 = 6
4. (d) LanGuaGe
5. (b) 0
6. (c) 16
7. (b) Sclicing
8. (a) split()
9. (c) +
10. (a) String objects are mutable.

Chapter 4

1. (d) elements cannot be accessed using the index
2. (a) add( )
3. (d) [6,5]
4. (b) Red
5. (c) [1,2]
6. (a) [1, 3, 7, 10, 20]
7. (a) data[–1]
8. (a) [6, 25, 0, –5, 7, 1]
9. (d) 4
10. (b) [3, 2, 8, 5, 6]

Chapter 5

1. (d) 3.14
2. (a) (6, 7)

3. (b) 4
4. (b) n
5. (b) ['H', 'e', 'l', 'l', 'o']
6. (a) 2
7. (d) ['h', 'n', 'o', 'p', 't', 'y']
8. (a) (5, 10, 5, 10)
9. (d) error is generated
10. (b) 9.14

Chapter 6

1. (b) { ('White', 'Black'), 'Red', 'Blue', 'Green', 'Black'}
2. (d) Error is generated
3. (c) {('White', 'Black')}
4. (b) { 'Red','Green', 'Blue', ('White','Black') }
5. (b) set()
6. (a) ('Red', 'Blue', 'Black', 'Green')
7. (a) Sets elements are Mutable objects
8. (c) update()
9. (b) Relational
10. (c) {   }

Chapter 7

1. (d) error is generated
2. (a) False
3. (b) {'Name': 'Karna', 'Phone': 9999}
4. (b) {'Dec': 31, 'Jan': 31, 'Jun': 30}
5. (d) set
6. (b) Delhi
7. (d) {'Banana': 50, 'Apple': 80, 'Orange': 65, 'Grapes': 90}
8. (d) Error is generated
9. (b) 3
10. (a) {'Banana', 'Apple', 'Orange'}

Chapter 8

1. (c) w+ and a+
2. (a) seek(0)

3. (a) Beginning of the file
4. (a) c:\usr\sample.txt
5. (b) seek(0) ; read(5)
6. (d) both a and c options
7. (c) aw
8. (a) .exe
9. (c) open('sample.txt','w')
10. (b) tell()

Chapter 9

1. (c) 10
2. (b) 2
3. (a) Tablet
4. (a) (5,2)
5. (b) 2
6. (d) Row labels of dataframe can be only integers
7. (c) pop( )
8. (d) Both a & b
9. (c) df.to_csv()
10. (b) len()

Chapter 10

1. (a) File
2. (b) Connect()
3. (a) import sqlite3
4. (b) cursor
5. (a) fetchall()
6. (c) ALTER
7. (c) sqlite3.connect('database')
8. (d) ALTER
9. (c) SELECT
10. (b) UPDATE

Chapter 11

1. (a) ('W*lc*m* t* Pyth*n', 5)
2. (c) Is*it*ver*3*7*

3. (b) ['Python', 'is', 'an interpreted language']
4. (d) ['Python version ', '.7']
5. (c) '–' Means one or more Occurrences
6. (a) ^
7. (d) [' total ']
8. (a) <re.Match object; span=(36, 42), match='python'>
9. (c) search()
10. (b) [ ]

Chapter 12

1. (d) best
2. (c) scatter()
3. (a) bins()
4. (b) Quartile 2
5. (b) annot
6. (b) Scatter
7. (c) Distance of Wedge from the center
8. (a) Line
9. (a) Seaborn has built-in piechart()
10. (c) Boolean

Chapter 15

1. (b) threading
2. (c) join()
3. (b) send()
4. (d) put()
5. (b) Lock
6. (b) Multithreading
7. (a) sleep()
8. False
9. (d) getpid()
10. False

Appendix B
Python Installation

I. Python in Google Colaboratory

1. Go to your Google drive and click '**+new**' button at the left side
2. Click on '**More**' and check if '**Google Colaboratory**' is present in the list
3. If not

    a. Go to '**Connect more apps**' in '**More**'
    b. Type **colab** in the search box of **Google Workspace Marketplace**
    c. Click on '**Colaboratory**' to add to the apps list

    Now Google Colaboratory is added to the apps list in '**More**'
4. Now click on '**+new**' of your google drive then go to '**More**' and select '**Google Colaboratory**'
5. Click on the '**CREATE AND SHARE**' button.

Now the notebook opens.

Notebook contains two types of cells: (i) **Code cell** (ii) **Text cell**

You can write the Python code in code cells. Execute the code cell by pressing **Shift + Enter** or click on **Run button** of the cell.

Text cells are for documentation purpose.

Code/Text cells can be inserted by choosing '**+Code**' , '**+Text**' buttons available below the notebook menu.

Note: Google Colaboratory requires a **gmail** account and internet connection.

© The Author(s) 2024
A. L. Muddana and S. Vinayakam, *Python for Data Science*,
https://doi.org/10.1007/978-3-031-52473-8

II. Python for Windows

1. Go to official website of Python: https://www.python.org
2. Goto **downloads** and select **Windows**
3. Choose the **installer** for your OS and download
4. Run the installer and select the check boxes and click **Next, Install**

To Verify if Python is installed

1. Open command prompt
2. Type **python** and press enter
3. If Python is successfully installed, you get the display similar to the following

```
Command Prompt - python                                                  —  □  ×
Microsoft Windows [Version 10.0.22000.795]
(c) Microsoft Corporation. All rights reserved.

C:\Users\laksh>python
Python 3.10.4 (tags/v3.10.4:9d38120, Mar 23 2022, 23:13:41) [MSC v.1929 64 bit (AMD64)] on wi
n32
Type "help", "copyright", "credits" or "license" for more information.
>>> _
```

>>> is the Python prompt. Now you can type the Python statements and press enter for execution.

To run the Python script

1. Write a Python script using any text editor like **Notepad** and save it in a file with **.py** extension.
2. Go to the command prompt.
3. Type **python** *file_name.py* and press Enter

III. Python for Ubuntu

Ubuntu comes with Python preinstalled.

To check if Python is installed, type the following in the terminal window

   python

You will get the display similar to the following

```
gitam@gitam-Vostro-3268: ~                                    ↑↓ En    ◂ᴺ  3:16 PM  ⚙
gitam@gitam-Vostro-3268:~$ python
Python 2.7.12 (default, Mar  1 2021, 11:38:31)
[GCC 5.4.0 20160609] on linux2
Type "help", "copyright", "credits" or "license" for more information.
>>> █
```

>>> is the Python prompt. Now you can type the Python statements and press enter for execution.

To run the Python script

1. Write a Python script using any text editor like **vi / gedit** and save it in a file with **.py** extension.
2. Open a terminal window (press Ctrl + Alt + T)
3. Go to the directory where Python script file is present
4. Type **python** *file_name.py* at $ prompt and press Enter.

Index

© The Author(s) 2024
A. L. Muddana and S. Vinayakam, *Python for Data Science*,
https://doi.org/10.1007/978-3-031-52473-8

Printed in the United States
by Baker & Taylor Publisher Services